Alpha
Teach Yourself

Management
Skills

ALPHA

A Pearson Education Company

in 24
hours

Alpha Teach Yourself Management Skills in 24 Hours

Copyright © 2001 by BookEnds, LLC

International Standard Book Number: 0-02-864143-4
Library of Congress Catalog Card Number: 2001089689

Printed in the United States of America

First printing: 2001

03   02   01   4   3   2   1

Note: This publication contains the opinions and ideas of its author. It is intended to provide helpful and informative material on the subject matter covered. It is sold with the understanding that the author and publisher are not engaged in rendering professional services in the book. If the reader requires personal assistance or advice, a competent professional should be consulted.

The author and publisher specifically disclaim any responsibility for any liability, loss or risk, personal or otherwise, which is incurred as a consequence, directly or indirectly, of the use and application of any of the contents of this book.

Produced by BookEnds, LLC.

Trademarks

All terms mentioned in this book that are known to be or are suspected of being trademarks or service marks have been appropriately capitalized. Alpha Books and Pearson Education cannot attest to the accuracy of this information. Use of a term in this book should not be regarded as affecting the validity of any trademark or service mark.

SENIOR ACQUISITIONS EDITOR
Renee Wilmeth

DEVELOPMENT EDITOR
Nancy D. Warner

SENIOR PRODUCTION EDITOR
Christy Wagner

COPY EDITOR
Catherine Schwenk

INDEXER
Tonya Heard

PRODUCTION
John Etchison
Mary Hunt
Heather Hiatt Miller

COVER DESIGNER
Alan Clements

BOOK DESIGNER
Gary Adair

PUBLISHER
Marie Butler-Knight

PRODUCT MANAGER
Phil Kitchel

MANAGING EDITOR
Jennifer Chisholm

Overview

Contents

About the Author

Patricia Buhler is an adjunct professor at Goldey-Beacom College and a consultant with Buhler Business Consultants specializing in management issues. She is a contributing editor for *Supervision* magazine, writing a bi-monthly column titled "Managing in the New Millennium."

She has been working in or with business for over 25 years. Author of over 100 published articles, she has also delivered numerous seminars across a wide variety of management topics.

She holds a doctorate in business administration and an MBA in management. Dr. Buhler received the Excellence in Teaching Award, twice received the Goldey-Beacom College Marketing-Management Role Model Award, was acknowledged for her outstanding contribution to consulting in the International Who's Who of Professional and Business Women 2000, and was named to Who's Who Among America's Teachers in 1999.

Dr. Buhler has also been active in her community. She works with her local Chamber of Commerce and has served on the boards of local colleges, assisting in the development of business curriculum offerings.

Dr. Buhler resides with her husband, daughter, and son in Newark, Delaware.

Dedication

This book is dedicated to my husband, Jim, and to my children, Jennifer and Matthew—my three biggest supporters who help my dreams come true.

Acknowledgments

I wish to thank Jessica Faust of BookEnds, LLC, who patiently stood beside me, taught me the ropes, and most important, made this book a reality.

I also wish to thank Nancy D. Warner, Christy Wagner, and Catherine Schwenk for their diligent efforts to edit this project.

Introduction

Because management is all about people, the skills you learn in this book are organized as basic building blocks. Each of these blocks is important in improving your ability to be effective in any position in today's workforce.

Part I, "An Introduction to Management," provides an understanding of the context within which managers operate today. Starting with a fundamental discussion of management and its changing role today, it concludes with a discussion of managerial decision-making.

Part II, "Getting Started on the Basics of Management," addresses the basics of management. A review of financial statements, budgets, project management, developing processes, managing relationships, and negotiation skills is included.

Part III, "Managing People Effectively," focuses on specific skills necessary to manage people effectively. A discussion of the diverse workplace sets the stage for understanding the management of people. Motivating people, managing their performance and their careers is followed by a review of groups and teamwork in today's workplace.

Part IV, "Business as an Organization," emphasizes the need to understand how your business is impacted by organizational issues. The structure of organizations, culture, power, politics, leadership, and communication are discussed as organization-wide issues.

Part V, "Special Management Challenges," addresses the special challenges that come with the territory, so to speak, of a manager. Stress, meeting facilitation, and interviewing are discussed. A review of the importance of business etiquette completes your lesson on management.

Last but not least, this book has a lot of miscellaneous cross-references, tips, shortcuts, and warning sidebar boxes. Here's how they stack up:

JUST A MINUTE

 This sidebar offers advice or teaches an easier way to do something.

STRICTLY DEFINED

Strictly Defined boxes offer definitions of words you may not know.

PROCEED WITH CAUTION

 Proceed with Caution boxes are warnings. They warn you about potential problems and help you steer clear of trouble.

 FYI boxes provide extra information that isn't immediately relevant to the task at hand.

GO TO ▷

This sidebar gives you a cross-reference to another chapter or section in the book to learn more about a particular topic.

PART I

An Introduction to Management

HOUR 1
What Is Management?

- Understanding the dual track of effective management.
- Doing the right job vs. doing the job right.
- Performing management functions.
- Using the contingency approach to management.
- Understanding the three basic management skills necessary for success.
- Making the transition to management.

As you've assumed the title of manager (or perhaps supervisor, leader, or coordinator) you wonder how to fulfill this new role. Or perhaps you aspire to a management position. You may even fill a staff position and possess a desire to acquire a broader working knowledge of management. Whether you are a new manager, a seasoned manager, or no manager at all, this book will provide you with the tools for navigating the changing territory of business today. It provides an understanding of what is occurring in the ranks of management across all organizations today.

Nearly everyone (regardless of job title) is engaged in management. Everyone today must get things done through others. You don't have to have a manager's title to benefit from management skills. Each person will be more successful in performing their job if management skills are acquired.

In this information age of knowledge workers, effectiveness in the vast majority of jobs involves the use of management skills—that is, working effectively with other knowledge workers. While this book refers to management skills, you can benefit professionally from the acquisition of these skills and knowledge, even if you are not currently holding a management position.

There has been continued emphasis on the soft skills in the American workplace. Employers nationwide have responded in survey after survey that soft skills are in demand—and there is a shortage in the supply. Most employers have confidence in their ability to teach the technical skills to new employees. They are more concerned, however, with the soft skills. Employers prefer that employees come to them already proficient in these areas. These are many of the general management skills taught in this book. So you are well on your way to increasing your employability by picking up this book.

The challenges to be faced by managers in the twenty-first century require a new skill set. Playing by the "old rules" does not provide the opportunities for success needed in today's rapidly changing world. As a manager, you must be multitalented with a broader array of skills than ever before.

LEARNING THE NEW RULES OF THE GAME

The key to effective management is to recognize that the rules of the game have indeed changed. Today's business environment is changing, and the rate of change is certainly without precedent.

The manager's job has changed. It is no longer straightforward. The old paradigm suggested that power over people was critical with the command-and-control manager as dictator. There was a clear distinction between management and workers.

Today's environment is drastically different. The paradigm today suggests there is a partnership between management and employees. Management today is about taking responsibility and making decisions. It's about listening to your instincts and realizing that you don't have to be perfect. It's about setting priorities and being proactive.

There are those who would tell you that effective management is nothing more than mere common sense. Having worked with numerous organizations and the managers within their ranks, I can tell you that a good dose of common sense is an essential element of effective management, but many concrete skills are also required for success.

PROCEED WITH CAUTION

Effective management is a moving bull's-eye. Changes are constantly impacting management. The journey is never truly finished. Management should be thought of as an ongoing process.

Successful management requires that you be well-informed about your organization (its products and services), the people within that organization, your industry (the competition and the trends impacting it), general management processes, and human resource management. Management almost requires that you become a jack of many trades. You must be a skilled human resource manager, project manager, marketing manager, process manager, and accounting manager all rolled up in one. Most important, effective management means keeping your eyes and ears open to continuously learn.

This book is intended to offer you an opportunity to acquire new skills, refine some skills that may have been forgotten or become rusty from lack of use, and update other skills to better meet the challenges of today's changing business environment.

To accomplish this goal, then, you begin with a clear vision of your end goal; that is, you must know what it is that you are striving toward. You begin your journey to effective management by gaining a clear understanding of what effective management means in today's business environment.

DEFINING EFFECTIVE MANAGEMENT

Management is all about getting things done. If you accomplished very little, you would no doubt lose your job in a relatively short period of time. In today's highly competitive environment, organizations have little time, resources, or patience for those who cannot deliver.

And, you must deliver continuously. Your company cares little about what you accomplished last year. They want to know what you are doing for them today. Effective management helps you to contribute continuously to your organization.

Effective management is tied to your organization's overall performance. This can be envisioned as a pyramid of building blocks. The failure of any one of these blocks to hold its weight results in the destruction of the whole pyramid. Your ability to effectively manage plays a critical role in the success (or failure) of your organization.

Effective management is really twofold. That is, the effective manager is operating concurrently on two tracks. It involves task accomplishment and employee satisfaction. You may first envision this as an either-or choice. But it is not. The effective manager accomplishes both simultaneously. In fact, both task accomplishment and employee satisfaction must be achieved in order for you to be an effective manager.

Because managers get things done through other people, you must address both issues. Your task accomplishment depends on getting others to do their work. Many times a large part of the nature of your work is overseeing the work of these other employees. And dissatisfied employees are not as likely to get that job done.

JUST A MINUTE

Management means getting things done through others. This does not mean doing everything yourself.

Task accomplishment means that you are able to complete the job(s) at hand. For managers in today's world, this often means multiple projects with overlapping time schedules. The key is to understand the job to be done and be able to effectively delegate to the appropriate people.

Employee satisfaction has become critical in management. While research has provided a link between productivity and satisfaction, you have probably intuitively recognized this connection for years. The key, then, is for you to provide a good quality-of-work life for your employees that will contribute to a higher level of job satisfaction. This pays off for you with improved work performance in your business unit.

The importance of employee satisfaction is emphasized in tight labor markets. As employees become less satisfied with their jobs, turnover increases. You cannot possibly be as productive in your position if you are constantly working shorthanded and recruiting new employees. The learning curve for new hires can also be very steep in some jobs. During training, new employees are not as efficient in their jobs, thereby impacting your ability to be effective as a manager.

UNDERSTANDING EFFECTIVE VS. EFFICIENT

The terms *effective* and *efficient* may sometimes be confused and even used interchangeably. They are, however, very different.

A shorthand way of defining these terms often helps. Effective means doing the right job. Efficient means doing the job right. While you may think this insight even more confusing, consider the following example.

You're hired to present a guest lecture on effective management in one hour or less. You arrive and present an excellent, well-organized 55-minute lecture on the advantages and disadvantages of buying versus leasing a new automobile. You have certainly been efficient—you did the job right. But you certainly weren't effective. That is, you did not do the right job. You failed to present a lecture on effective management.

Effective management involves doing the right job. This means accomplishing the task at hand and simultaneously generating higher levels of employee satisfaction. The two are tightly integrated into the management role.

THE CHANGING ROLE OF MANAGEMENT

Management has undergone numerous changes in the last few decades. You've witnessed the slow demise of the command-and-control manager. No longer does the manager's power rest on legitimate authority inherent in the position occupied within the organizational hierarchy.

Management is the stabilizing factor that enables the work of the organization to be completed. Managers get their work done through others. You can accomplish very little on your own in today's organizations. You need other people and must know how to effectively interact with others to get your own work done.

GO TO ▶
Refer to Hour 18, "Organizational Politics and Power," for a discussion of the sources of personal power that are more effective in today's workplace.

Through the downsizing decades, organizations have flattened their structures. This has resulted in fewer people in most organizations. So now fewer people are performing the same amount of work. This means that most of you are wearing more than one hat. You are being asked to take on additional responsibilities with virtually no increase in manpower. This further heightens the critical nature of effective management to get that work done.

Today the key lies in personal power and strong interpersonal skills. With the exception of the top management positions within the organization, as a manager you walk a tight rope. You are sandwiched between your employees and a higher management level. Only strong interpersonal skills and a sound understanding of your organization and how it works will enable you to be successful.

JUST A MINUTE

Management is not for everyone. A manager needs to be comfortable supervising others and exercising power.

STUDYING THE FUNCTIONS OF MANAGEMENT

According to Fayol, a French engineer who developed his theories based upon his experiences at a French mining and metallurgical company, the four functions performed by management are as follows:

- Planning
- Organizing
- Controlling
- Leading

Each of these functions will be discussed in the sections that follow.

PLANNING

As a manager, you are responsible for planning. You must decide on the courses of action to be taken at some future point. You must gather information and generate a list of possible alternatives. Then you must select an alternative as your decision. Once an alternative is selected, the means by which that choice will be achieved (i.e., the implementation) must be planned.

GO TO ▶
Refer to Hour 4, "Managerial Decision-Making," for a discussion of the processes of generating and selecting alternatives.

As you move up the organizational hierarchy, the time horizon for planning broadens. At the lower management levels, you are generally planning out to one year at most. The focus tends to be on daily operations and keeping things running smoothly. Middle managers usually plan in the 1- to 5-year range while top managers focus the bulk of their planning efforts in the 5- to 20-year range.

In this high-speed society, planning is critical—though compressed. With the competitive advantage of organizations getting shorter, the time frames are getting faster. Everyone moves and works more rapidly than ever before.

The key to planning today is to recognize that this is a continual process. This is no longer a once a year exercise that you engage in. You must be planning and revising on a regular basis. And planning is for every management level. It requires that you think. Critical input comes from reading and keeping your eyes and ears open.

PROCEED WITH CAUTION

Strategic management has played an increasingly important role in organizations. Centered on seeing the big picture and making decisions today to position the company for the future, the responsibilities for strategic planning are no longer exclusively held by top managers. Now the responsibility to strategically plan is delegated throughout the organization as every managers' responsibility.

While informal planning is fine for a start, you need to formalize your planning efforts. Write down your plans and don't put them in a drawer where they only see the light of day once a year. These plans should be living documents that are routinely revisited and revised. As new information becomes available, take out your monthly plan and adjust it accordingly.

Plans are not meant to be etched in stone. The call today is for flexible planning. Although this may seem like an oxymoron, it is exactly what you need to be responsive. To play your part in ensuring that your organization remains flexible and agile, flexible planning ensures that you are ready to respond to the changes that may occur.

Never think of your plans as final documents or directives to be followed to the letter. Think of them as works in progress—always in need of modification.

ORGANIZING

Organizing is a critical function for every manager. This involves decisions about how you divide up the work that is to be completed.

In top management positions, the organizing function becomes broader. That is, more decisions are made concerning the overall structure of the organization. At lower management level, the organizing function focuses more on how to package tasks into jobs and how to group jobs into work units. Rapid technological changes have significantly impacted how organizing is performed. With new technologies available, jobs are redesigned and regrouped on a regular basis. These technological changes have even changed the structure of most organizations—moving more to fluid structures with strategic partners to achieve greater flexibility, agility, and responsiveness to markets.

In actuality, your efforts to organize pertain to how you use all the resources at your disposal. As you recruit and train your employees, you are fulfilling the organizing function. This involves getting the right people in the right positions.

GO TO ▶
Refer to Hour 16, "Organizational and Structural Design," for a discussion about the organizational design options and departmentalization alternatives.

CONTROLLING

Controlling is often misunderstood. New managers are most prone to this misunderstanding. Controlling pertains to performance and has nothing to do with the overbearing supervision of people or micromanaging.

The controlling function is often overlooked. The heart of controlling is the comparison process. You fulfill the controlling function by comparing the actual performance with the desired performance. The key is to then take the necessary corrective actions when deviations exist between the two.

Controlling begins with a clear understanding, by all employees, of what the desired performance is. Most importantly, they must all have a clear idea of how they can specifically contribute to this desired performance level.

While all management levels are responsible for controlling, the scope of activities monitored broadens as you move up the organizational hierarchy. Top management tends to focus more of their controlling efforts on organization-wide processes (such as the achievement of the corporate strategy or whether to move the company into a new consumer market niche). At lower management levels, the tactical or day-to-day operations are being monitored (such as how many widgets a specific department produced in a given week or how many defects were found during that week).

Included in effective controlling is the recognition that not everything can be monitored. The 80-20 rule is especially important here. Eighty percent of your success is determined by 20 percent of what you do. Because you don't have the time or resources to control everything, you select the 20 percent of your responsibilities that account for 80 percent of your success. That is what you measure and control.

JUST A MINUTE

The 80-20 rule can be used to explain much of what you do. Eighty percent of a company's profits come from 20 percent of its activities.

You must also establish acceptable levels of deviation in fulfilling the controlling function. Management by exception suggests that you don't want to hear about everything. However, it's better to be informed about those things that are going wrong; then you can take the necessary corrective action. But do you want to know about small deviations? In most cases, the answer is "No." You establish deviation ranges so that only those activities performing outside that range are brought to your attention.

For example, if you have budgetary responsibility for 50 line items with an annual budget of $50,000 each, you certainly do not want to waste your time hearing about the printing budget that ran over by 22¢ last month. With a $50,000 budget, you might decide that anything within a 2 percent deviation is more than acceptable on a monthly basis. Therefore, you would evaluate only those items that were $1,000 or more over budget.

Be careful, however, to watch for trends. You want to ensure that you have a mechanism in place to catch trends that are developing over time so that you are not blindsided at the end of your budget year. You may want to establish deviations for year-to-date figures as well. That way, if your printing budget ran 1.5 percent over budget every month for four months in a row, you would want to examine the causes and take action before you ended the year with a large amount in excess of the budget.

JUST A MINUTE

The boiled frog syndrome warns of waiting for environmental jolts. The key is to monitor trends as they develop. The frog learned this the hard way. When placed in boiling water, the frog jumps out—recognizing the danger. When placed in room temperature water that is gradually brought to a boil, the frog will boil to death—never recognizing the slowly evolving danger presented.

LEADING

The leading function is said to be the essence of the management function. This involves the actual supervision of employees. While some of the literature may refer to the leading function as directing, this is almost a misnomer. Directing implies the old management style of telling. This is no longer appropriate in most situations in today's workforce.

Leading is actually the preferred terminology now in many management circles. Some of the more progressive organizations have replaced the "manager" title with that of "leader" to reflect this new mind-set.

Leading is performed in much the same way at all management levels. There is, perhaps, more responsibilities in top management positions to set the tone for the entire organization. Though this is not to say that every manager does not have to set a good example. Top management's examples, however, provide the cue for the rest of the organization. Leading in higher management levels also involves more mentoring today. The shift to more team-oriented work environments has changed the nature of leading at all management levels. It is no longer appropriate to use the command-and-control technique. Leading today means more of a coaching role.

GO TO ▶
Refer to Hour 19, "The New Leadership," for a more detailed discussion of the role of leadership and the new leadership in today's organizations.

The motivation of employees is the heart of the leading function. As a manager, you want to encourage your employees to go that extra mile and contribute to the organization. Your ability to perform the leading function will determine in part what level of contributions your employees make.

Those managers that perform the leading function poorly often have units that deliver marginal performance and employees that only do what is minimally acceptable. Those managers that perform the leading function well usually have top performing units with star employees who have bought into the vision and know how to contribute to enable the organization to meet its objectives.

This also involves the communication process. Leading requires that you be able to clearly articulate what it is that you expect of your employees. This means selecting the most appropriate channel of communication and ensuring that the message is clearly understood.

JUST A MINUTE

Management is geared toward maintaining stability and ensuring that day-to-day operations are carried out. Leadership focuses more on making changes within the organization in order to affect transformations.

All four functions are performed at every management level. The emphasis, however, may change from one function to another as you move up the organizational hierarchy or from one management position to another. You must be skilled in the performance of each function of management to be effective.

PUTTING IT TOGETHER

There is no one best way to manage. As a manager, you will find that the key to your effectiveness is in the contingency approach. That is, it depends. Management comes with no universal truths; the *right* course of action will depend on the situation at hand.

Your success will depend on the size of your management tool bag. The more tools and techniques you have mastered, the more successful you will be in selecting the best tool to use in a given situation. No one management style is effective in every situation. Success depends on knowing when to utilize each of the different tools and techniques that you have mastered.

Effective management also comes with the mind-set (one which you can develop) that people really do matter. The past CEO of a Fortune 100 company once said that with all companies having access to virtually all the same information and technology at just about the same time, the real difference in organizations' performance lies with the people.

Your job as a manager centers on people. Believing that people are a valuable asset of the organization should drive your actions. Your ability to successfully motivate and focus these individuals is critical to effective management.

NEW MANAGEMENT FUNCTIONS MEETING THE CHALLENGES OF TODAY'S WORKPLACE

Some new management functions have been added to the traditional functions. These include the ability to inspire others—specifically by example. When you "walk the talk," it provides the necessary spark to excite others. Another of the new functions is empowering others. This doesn't mean giving up managing, it just means sharing the responsibility and autonomy. You are still ultimately responsible, you just provide employees with the opportunity to excel at what they do best.

The new management functions also include the need to create a supportive environment. Employees must feel comfortable taking risks. This environment should be characterized by trust, openness, and honesty. Employees should be encouraged to be problem solvers. And finally, a new function is the management of information. You must effectively communicate information and share it with others.

ANALYZING YOUR SKILLS

Robert Katz, author of the 1974 *Harvard Business Review* classic article, "Skills of an Effective Administrator," suggests that all managers need three basic skills to be successful. These are as follows:

- Conceptual
- Technical
- Human relations

All managers need to develop all three of these skills. As you move up the organizational pyramid, these skills change in the mix. All are important, but their contribution to the whole may shift. That is, at lower management levels, more technical skills are needed; while at higher levels, more conceptual skills are critical to success.

CONCEPTUAL SKILLS

Conceptual skills reflect the ability to see the big picture. As an effective manager, you must be able to understand the interrelated nature of your organization. Each action in one unit of the business has a reaction in another. That is, each action you take will have consequences that are felt throughout the organization.

You must overcome the functional silo mentality to develop strong conceptual skills. You cannot think of your unit as an island unto itself. You are part of a larger organization with parts that are all interdependent. The success of one part depends upon the success of another part. Likewise, the failure of one part can threaten the very survival of the entire organization.

An external perspective is also important in developing conceptual skills. This requires that you be able to identify changes that are occurring in the external environment and understand how they impact your business.

JUST A MINUTE

No organization operates in a vacuum. The impact of the external environment continuously grows.

Conceptual skills become critical to the success of managers at the higher organizational levels. While strategic management responsibilities are being delegated throughout the organization, conceptual skills are required at all levels. But the primary responsibility for seeing the big picture continues to lie with the top management levels.

TECHNICAL SKILLS

Technical skills encompass the ability to understand the technology available to perform the job. It is sometimes necessary in lower management levels for you to demonstrate skills to employees—thereby placing more emphasis on the need for technical skills at lower management levels.

The closer you are to the actual work being performed, the more important the technical skills. As you move up the organizational hierarchy, the need for technical skills decreases. In first-line supervisory positions where operations personnel are directly supervised, heavier technical skills are required.

Technical decisions are also more an integral part of lower levels of management. The design of socio-technical systems (in organizations in which managers are able to better utilize both the technology and the people available) is performed more at lower management levels today.

HUMAN RELATIONS SKILLS

Human relations skills are required at all management levels in equal amounts. This means that throughout your management career, you need to focus on strong people skills. You must be able to get along with others. First-line managers are said to spend just under half of their time at work utilizing these interpersonal skills.

A recurring theme of this hour has been the focus on the importance of people in effective management. As a manager, you must work with people. If you want to avoid working with others, management is not the job for you. And you must value people and the contributions that they make to your organization.

JUST A MINUTE

To gain greater insight into your managerial potential, you might ask yourself how much you like people.

People provide the intellectual capital of the organization, and, as a manager, you have been entrusted with this precious resource. Human relations skills are critical to management at all levels. This is not a skill that you can grow out of. And with the trends in the business environment today, human relations skills are only likely to become more important.

MAKING THE TRANSITION TO MANAGEMENT

Moving into a management position is not as easy as it may have looked from your old desk. It's the same as the proverbial Monday morning quarterback—but in reverse. From your old desk, you knew just what to do and say. You knew all the mistakes that your manager made. You maybe even said, "If I'm ever a manager, I'll never …." Now you are the manager and all of a sudden, you're not sure.

If you are having trouble shedding the old image, try to make changes in your personal appearance. You might consider an update to your wardrobe or a change in hairstyle to help convey the change in a subtle way.

The tools and techniques presented in this book are designed to provide you with the necessary information to make better decisions about your courses of action as a manager. In the meantime, think of these tips while in transition:

- Remember that your subordinates are not your friends. You can be friendly, but you must assume a new role.

- Take the time to get to know your staff. And ask them what they think!

- Don't change everything overnight. When contemplating a change, include the employees who will be impacted in early discussions.

- Set quiet time aside to reflect. Without this, you could find yourself in the mode of ready-fire-aim.

- Recognize the importance of your peers and cultivate those relationships.

- Ask for help. You are not expected to know everything and you don't have to go it alone. The choice is yours.

- Remember what it was like for you as an employee. History can easily repeat itself if you don't guard against it.

- If promoted internally to a management position from the ranks, remember that you will have to overcome the prior image that company people had of you.

- Take the necessary time to develop a comfort level with the new position.

- Develop the ability to recognize the cultivation of both superiors and subordinates; this is critical to success.

PROCEED WITH CAUTION

 While many may warn you of the pitfalls of management, remember that the rewards are also great.

Be aware that you become more effective as you practice your management techniques. Learn what works (and what doesn't work) for you.

HOUR'S UP!

Management is harder than it may look. It is a combination of both art and science. Take a moment to answer these questions to see what you picked up in this hour.

1. Effective management …

    a. Is really just common sense.

    b. Involves both task accomplishment and employee satisfaction.

    c. Means getting the job done.

    d. Means having happy employees.

2. Management is all about …

    a. Getting things done through other people.

    b. Making lots of money.

    c. Telling others what to do.

    d. Doing everything yourself.

3. If you are effective …

    a. You get more money.

    b. You're not well-liked.

    c. You're doing the job right.

    d. You're doing the right job.

4. Management …

    a. Is not for everyone.

    b. Requires strong interpersonal skills.

    c. Has undergone massive changes in the last few decades.

    d. All of the above.

QUIZ

5. The planning function of management ...

    a. Involves selecting future courses of action.

    b. Involves putting everything in writing.

    c. Only applies to the top tier of management.

    d. Involves comparing actual and desired performance.

6. The contingency approach to management ...

    a. Basically says it depends on the situation.

    b. Suggests there is no one best way to manage.

    c. Means you have to have a big "management tool bag."

    d. All of the above.

7. Leading and managing ...

    a. Are rarely seen in organizations.

    b. Perform separate valuable functions in the organization.

    c. Are the same basic function.

    d. Are mutually exclusive.

8. Conceptual skills ...

    a. Reflect the ability to see the big picture.

    b. Are unnecessary at lower management levels.

    c. Help us get along with others.

    d. Emphasize the use of technology.

9. Human relations skills ...

    a. Are required at all management levels.

    b. Become less important as you move up the organization.

    c. Are becoming less important in today's environment.

    d. Deal with union negotiations.

10. When making the transition to management ...

    a. Prior images must be overcome.

    b. New relationships must be cultivated.

    c. You must be patient with yourself.

    d. All of the above.

QUIZ

HOUR 2

Management in the New Workplace

LESSON PLAN:

In this hour you will learn about …

- Understanding the management environment.
- Recognizing management trends.
- Working with technology.
- Identifying employee expectations.
- Loyalty and the organization.
- Working with customers expectations.
- Downsizing and its impact.
- Understanding management's role in the learning organization.
- Becoming a lifelong learner yourself.

After completing Hour 1, "What Is Management?" you know where your journey to effective management will ultimately take you. Now it is important to understand the context within which you are managing today. That is, you must gain greater insight into the environment that is shaping your job and the role you play within your organization.

The workplace today is drastically different from the workplace of only a generation ago. The changes have greatly impacted the nature of managerial work. Managing today is not the same job it was 20 years ago. The soft skills have become a more critical component of success in today's marketplace. Leadership, teamwork, and change management—just to name a few—have become essential.

While the basic functions of management as discussed in Hour 1 have remained the same, the way in which they are performed and the "tools of the trade" have significantly changed. For example, the tools that you utilize for planning today very likely include a computer. A weekly computer report (that you can access at will) can inform you at a glance of your forecast for the month-end sales. Your projections can be updated daily as each actual daily sales number is added—instantaneously generating a new projection. This also impacts the controlling function you perform.

Today, the feedback for monitoring and comparing performance is faster, thereby giving you an opportunity to take corrective action much sooner than in the past. Of course, there are also pressures that come with this instantaneous information—because you are usually expected to act on it immediately.

Organizations do not operate in a vacuum. To truly grasp the role of management, it is essential that you understand the bigger context within which organizations operate.

MANAGEMENT'S ENVIRONMENT

The analogies of the white water rapids versus calm waters are often used to help clarify the importance of change. See which of the following descriptions more closely matches a description of your organization:

- **The calm waters analogy:** The organization is like an ocean liner that is traveling the same route taken many times across a calm ocean. Even when a storm brews, the captain simply makes small corrections to keep the ocean liner on track. The crew remains together trip after trip.
- **The white water rapids analogy:** The organization is more like a raft that is traveling a river never before seen or traveled. This river is filled with white water rapids. At irregular intervals, the raft pulls to the shore and takes on new members while letting others disembark.

Most of you will select the second analogy. And this perspective of your organization highlights the change that permeates your job. The job itself that you perform is constantly changing. Seldom do you perform exactly the same tasks routinely in exactly the same way. And you certainly are not performing them with the same people consistently. Most organizations are like revolving doors with employees coming and going. This attrition further complicates your work. Further complicating your work is the fact that you are dealing with simultaneous changes of many varieties.

TRENDS IMPACTING MANAGEMENT

Today's environment is dynamic. To be an effective manager, you must be adept at reading the trends in the external environment. And most important, you must be able to understand how these trends are impacting the work you perform and the workforce that you manage.

Organizations have been bombarded with changes from various directions—all reshaping the workplace:

- Global competition has forced you to look at the practices of other countries.

- Technology has lead to shorter product life cycles and a need for decentralized organizations to make faster decisions.

- Boundaries have disappeared between companies while regulatory changes have reshaped industries.

- Mergers and acquisitions, downsizing, and reorganizations have streamlined operations and created leaner companies.

- More educated consumers have demanded higher quality products and services—emphasizing the need to be market-driven and continuously improve.

Few stable environments exist today because change has become the overwhelming characteristic of environments. The nature of change, then, must be understood to effectively manage in today's world.

THE NATURE OF CHANGE

Complexity and change characterize managerial challenges today. The single most important trend that permeates management in general is change. Simultaneous changes of varying degrees are the norm. Managers are needed to drive the change process and implement the changes.

JUST A MINUTE

It is no longer sufficient for you to manage change. In today's environment, you must become skilled at creating some of this change.

Your job has become more difficult as the pace of change has increased and you are expected to respond to this change instantly. As our organizations strive to be more agile and market-driven, it is your responsibility as a manager to read these changes and to be flexible enough to respond appropriately to them—usually on a moment's notice.

Above all else, you must be comfortable with change. If you yearn for stability, management is not the right place for you. (Though in today's world, this stability is found in very few jobs.) Your greatest challenge is dealing with change. This means recognizing what these changes are, how they are impacting your industry, your organization, the work of your employees, and your job.

THE SHIFT TO THE GLOBAL ECONOMY

GO TO ▶
Refer to Hour 7, "The Basics of Process Development," for a detailed discussion of the change process and how to manage change.

The move to the global economy has emphasized how closely integrated all countries have become. What happens halfway around the world often has an impact in the United States. This has been clearly seen with the performance of the world's stock markets. A sharp decline on one exchange has certain ramifications immediately on others around the globe.

With increased globalization, production can be moved anywhere around the globe. Labor can also be recruited from anywhere. Opportunities are plentiful in the global arena, but trends must also be monitored worldwide.

WORKFORCE CONSEQUENCES OF THE GLOBAL ECONOMY

GO TO ▶
Refer to Hour 12, "Managing Performance," for a discussion of different rewards that can be offered to help increase the retention of employees.

Most organizations today no longer expect you to stay in the same job for a lifetime. This means that your employees are also expected to be short-timers. Of course, there are steps you can take to increase the retention of your employees.

Today's employees are only expected to remain with an organization for two to three years. This is a drastic shift from the prior generation where many people stayed a lifetime with one company. Many employees today view a job as a notch on their resumé belt. That is, each job is evaluated in terms of what it can contribute to the job that is ultimately desired. Each job, then, is a rung on the ladder carrying employees closer to their goal.

Projections for today's workforce also indicate that you and your employees are likely to have three separate careers. Not only will employees change employers; they will also make major career changes.

A dual trend is putting additional pressure on managers when designing jobs and hiring. There are two growing portions of the workforce population— the very well educated and the functionally illiterate. This is referred to as the *bimodal workforce*.

More employees are getting college degrees. And many of those are advanced degrees. The workforce is taking the call for additional skills and updating of skills very seriously. But this represents only one part of today's workforce.

JUST A MINUTE

The growing number of nontraditional students in colleges and universities has prompted changes in the format in which courses are delivered. Accelerated evening programs and distance learning are two of the growing options.

At the opposite end of this continuum are the ranks of the functionally illiterate. More people than ever before are entering the workforce without basic reading, writing, and math skills. These are people who cannot complete an employment application and cannot tell if they have received the correct amount of change from a small purchase.

Employers have had to step up to the plate to address this challenge. In a tight labor market, this large group cannot be ignored. So many of the bigger companies have developed remedial reading, writing, and math classes that are delivered at company facilities for their employees.

The additional challenge for you lies in utilizing both of these groups. You need to design challenging jobs for the well-educated employees. They want to use technology and have autonomy built into their jobs. They want to utilize the skills, knowledge, and abilities that they have acquired. The types of jobs for the functionally illiterate must be simplified and adjustments must be made—while addressing their training needs and attempting to provide them with appropriate workplace skills.

Understanding Technology's Role Today

Technology is rapidly changing and this technology is integral in redesigning jobs and reshaping the very way you work. The Internet has created myriad opportunities. The computer has revolutionized the way work is performed. Few jobs have escaped the impact of the computer.

GO TO ▶
Refer to Hour 7 for a discussion of the role of job enrichment in creating more challenging jobs and job simplification in creating more routine tasks.

Organizations must "stay ahead of the curve." That is, as a manager you must be aware of current technological advances and how they can be used effectively to improve your business. And you must adopt this technology before your competitors do so (or at least at the same time).

The virtual office has created a new component of the workforce—the telecommuting population. Millions of employees now work from home. Projections suggest that in just a few short years, telecommuters could comprise as much as 25 percent of the workforce. Taking advantage of the technological advancements now available, they electronically link to their company from off-site locations.

This has created new challenges for you, however. Just as myriad changes have altered the way in which you must manage, now a new component has been added—employees who you don't even see each day.

STRICTLY DEFINED

> To better meet the changing staffing needs of organizations, temporary and contract workers are used to supplement the full-time company workforce. Known as the **contingent workforce,** they reduce the need for layoffs in economic downturns and provide a source of skilled employees during busy cycles. The contingent workforce now numbers 34 million people. This is approximately one third of the American workforce.

Some tips to better manage this growing segment of telecommuters in the workforce include the following:

- Recognize that managing a telecommuter is different from managing an onsite employee.
- Understand that direct control over the telecommuter is not possible.
- Establish early (and then regular) discussions with the telecommuter to outline objectives to be met and the specific role that you can play in supporting their work.
- Set milestones (or interim goals) with specific timetables.
- Maintain contact with the telecommuter. Because random meetings in the hall are not likely with the teleworker, you must make an effort to keep the channels of communication open.
- Most important, you must trust your telecommuters. Carefully selecting those who are appropriate for telecommuting work will go a long way in making you comfortable and secure with the work arrangement.
- Be prepared to deal differently with the development of the telecommuter's career. "Out of sight, out of mind" is often the mind-set in business. When promotions are available, visibility plays an important role. It is your responsibility to help ensure that your telecommuters maintain the necessary level of visibility and do not get forgotten.

JUST A MINUTE

> Telecommuters (also known as teleworkers) may not necessarily work from their homes. Some work out of satellite offices established in suburban areas. These are sometimes referred to as "electronic cottages."

Technology is shaping the workplace in other ways as well. Ergonomics has become important for managers. Special care must be taken when fitting people and machines together. The key is to fit the machine to the person. The importance of ergonomics is readily seen with the redesign of computer workstations to ensure that workers experience fewer injuries as they spend more time on their computers.

Technology has resulted in an increase in the use of robotics. Now robots can perform some of those jobs that present dangers to humans. Computer Integrated Manufacturing (CIM) and Flexible Manufacturing Systems (FMS) have helped streamline manufacturing operations with the use of advanced technology.

Technology has also increased the monitoring of employees on the job. Your every key stroke on the computer and your every movement on the company grounds can be monitored—thanks to modern technology. Someone may very well review your e-mails even after you have deleted them!

The tools of your trade have been greatly influenced by technology. Voice mail, e-mail and teleconferencing are some of the technological advances that you may now consider routine. Management Information Systems (MIS) generate instantaneous information for your review.

Expert systems help your employees in performing tasks that they may not have been qualified for in the past. Expert systems are programs that store specialized expertise on a given topic. They enable others less skilled to act like an expert and benefit from this knowledge as they are guided through the decision-making process. Financial planning and credit approvals are two of the numerous growing areas in which expert systems are enabling lower-level employees to make higher-level decisions.

The move to e-commerce is a direct result of the advanced technology that is now available. Many companies now use the Internet to conduct some of their business. A few even use the Internet exclusively in conducting their business. It is important that you understand the role that technology can play in your own company's business. Keeping abreast of the competition is helpful.

GO TO ▶
Refer to Hour 4, "Managerial Decision-Making," for a discussion of the role of technology in managerial decision-making.

DIVERSITY MANAGEMENT

One of the biggest trends impacting the face of the workforce is diversity. Diversity is reflected in the broad mix of workers. Gender, race, age, ethnicity, and religion are just some of the differences that comprise this diversity.

Diversity management is all about appreciating these differences. It is the development of an organization-wide mind-set that celebrates the differences of the workforce.

Projections have estimated that by the year 2005, Hispanics will comprise 27 percent of the U.S. workforce making this population the largest minority group.

Diversity has moved up on the list of important business issues. Once considered a "soft" issue, diversity is now known to impact your organization's bottom line. It is said to play a key role in helping your organization achieve a competitive advantage in the marketplace. Diversity truly is good for business. It brings creativity and innovation through a heterogeneous workforce.

GO TO ▶
Refer to Hour 10, "Managing People," for a more in-depth discussion of diversity in general as well as tips on managing diversity.

Different people want different things from their employers. As a manager, you must become more skilled in interacting with and managing people from different cultures.

Part of the change in today's diverse workforce is seen with increasing numbers of women. Gender differences do indeed impact the way that people interact in the workplace and the benefits to be offered. With more women with small children in the workforce, day care issues have become more important. In addition, the increase in the number of working women has resulted in dual career couples. These are families where both the husband and wife are working.

GO TO ▶
Refer to Hour 3, "The Global Environment," for a basic discussion of culture and the different dimensions of it to help you better understand how to learn about cultural differences.

Dual career couples have really become the norm in today's world. Married workers are sometimes less likely to take relocation opportunities since the spouse's job is also at stake. As a result, you might consider assisting the spouse in finding work at the new location. Outplacement firms can also be utilized whereby they help the trailing spouse find a job. Some companies are relaxing their policies about employing spouses and actually place the trailing spouse in another part of the firm.

As the workforce ages, there are also ramifications on promotions. With older workers staying on the job longer, there are fewer openings for upward mobility for younger workers. This means that you must be more creative in growth opportunities offered to your employees.

You might consider more lateral moves to offer good employees a challenge. The lateral movement serves two purposes. First, lateral moves present the opportunity for the organization to develop a well-rounded employee with a broad-based skill set. Each move enables the employee to potentially develop more skills that become valuable to the organization in eventually moving this individual into higher positions.

JUST A MINUTE

With the move away from specialists and to generalists, the acquisition of broad-based skills becomes even more critical.

Second, lateral moves offer a creative solution to presenting challenges for good employees. Keeping good people challenged often means giving them something new to do. Many employees are happy to be learning new skills. Since this fits the need for building a resumé, the employee may be enticed to remain with the company for a little longer.

Diversity brings additional responsibilities for you. Diversity management includes being accountable for this diverse workforce—beyond simply hiring. It also means you must develop this diverse workforce. This could involve developing networks or support groups for some protected groups in your organization. In some cases, you may want to address special mentors for minorities to ensure that they are being appropriately prepared for advancement in the organization.

The workforce today is comprised of more than just full-time, permanent employees. Many options are open to you in filling vacancies. You can consider contract employees, temporary employees, or part-time employees. More companies are also choosing to lease employees. The traditional workforce no longer exists.

GO TO ▶
Refer to Hour 13, "Career Development: Your Responsibility," for a discussion of developing careers.

DOWNSIZING

Corporate America has had a love affair with the downsizing strategy. Even though it has often been ineffective in achieving the desired cost reductions, Wall Street has sent positive messages to companies implementing downsizing strategies. As a result, many organizations have simply "copied" their competitors' downsizing strategies.

This strategy has resulted in fewer management levels and has left survivors in its wake. Managing a recently downsized unit takes extra care. These employees tend to be a bit gun-shy and are overworked as they take on the job responsibilities of their colleagues who were laid off. You must carefully rebuild their trust—in you and your organization. You need to communicate that the layoffs are over (only if they really are).

GROWING LEGISLATION

In recent years, everything from plant closings to the use of polygraphs in the interviewing process has been addressed. The government has periodically closely regulated American business. While major pieces of legislation have been passed since 1890 (with the Sherman Act), it is the management of people within the organization that has been the target of heavy legislation.

GO TO ▶

Refer to Hour 23, "Interviewing," for a discussion of questions that are considered illegal in the interviewing process.

Since the Fair Labor Standards Act in 1938, legislation has continued to protect the rights of workers. Equal pay for men and women was the topic in the Equal Pay Act of 1965. Discrimination has been addressed in the Civil Rights Act of 1964, the Equal Employment Opportunities Act in 1972, and the Age Discrimination Act of 1967. The safety of the work environment was addressed in the Occupational Safety and Health Act of 1970 and pension plans were the issue in the Employee Retirements Income Security Act of 1974. The Americans with Disabilities Act (ADA) addressed discrimination of those people with disabilities and required reasonable accommodations be made by employers. A more detailed discussion of the ADA is found in Hour 10.

GO TO ▶

Refer to Hour 10 for a more detailed description of sexual harassment and the steps you can take to protect yourself and your organization.

Sexual harassment has been an especially visible topic in the popular business press. There are specific guidelines as to what you can and cannot do in the workplace. While the courts are still grappling with the letter of the law in clarifying the interpretation, the spirit of the law is clear. You cannot engage in behavior that creates an uncomfortable work environment for others. As a manager, it is critical that you observe your employees to ensure that they do not create an uncomfortable environment. You can be held responsible for what one of your employees does.

ALTERNATIVE WORK ARRANGEMENTS

Today's workforce requires flexibility. As employers are trying to help their employees balance work and nonwork (or family) issues, it is imperative that you think creatively. The way in which work is performed today can be more flexible.

Flextime is being used more extensively today. As organizations have tried to provide a measure of flexibility to their employees, a policy providing an opportunity for flexible working hours has been very effective.

Flextime is the policy of allowing employees to work a more flexible schedule. Many organizations have realized that it is not necessary to have standard working hours for every one of the employees in their workforce. Instead, some have identified a window within which they prefer to have their employees work. This ensures that they can meet their customers' needs.

You might want to examine the hours that your employees work. If you know that most of your customer contact occurs between 10 A.M. and 2 P.M., you might offer your employees the opportunity for flexible hours. You could denote 10 to 2 as the required core working hours and then let employees choose any eight-hour day that fits that schedule. The key is that the employees are selecting the hours that best fit their needs. And you are still getting the coverage that you need during your peak hours.

You also have the option of scheduling flexible work hours. You know best when you are needed on the job. With good hiring practices, you need not be present every hour that one of your subordinates is on the job.

The compressed workweek is another alternative that you can explore. This is any combination of the traditional hours (usually 40) worked in less than five days. The most popular compressed workweek is referred to as the 4-40. This is working 40 hours in 4 days—usually 10-hour days.

Job sharing has grown in popularity in the last decade. With job sharing, two part-time employees share one full-time position. This is especially beneficial if a working mother decides to leave a full-time position. Rather than losing a good employee, offering her the flexibility of sharing a full-time position with another part-time employee could provide the perfect win-win situation. You could retain an employee who already knows the job and is trained (instead of going to the expense of hiring and then training a new employee).

Using temporary employees is on the rise. Sometimes referred to as a contingent workforce, this provides you and your organization with considerable flexibility. As there are peaks and valleys experienced in your organization you can utilize the contingent workforce. These workers can be called in to work when the need for additional workers arises. Because they are not permanent employees, any decrease in productivity will not create layoffs. This technique can be especially helpful in retail and manufacturing organizations with known cyclical demand.

Part-time positions are also used more extensively today. These part-time positions may be permanent or temporary. Contract employees and consultants can also be used to better meet the dynamic needs of the workplace. Once again, they provide the company with a measure of flexibility to better meet the changing needs of the organization.

CHANGING EXPECTATIONS

Organizations today have rather clear cut and reasonable expectations. Above all else, they expect to employ a workforce that is loyal, ethical, and that contributes. It is your responsibility to ensure that you fit the bill and your employees deliver on their end of the employment "contract."

GO TO ▷
Refer to Hour 23 for a discussion of your role in the staffing function to hire the right people for the job.

The paternalistic relationship between employer and employee is gone. Your employer is no longer expected to take care of you for life.

Just as your organization expects loyalty, you, too, should expect loyalty from your employees. While this loyalty may be shorter than in the past (due to shorter times of employment), it is, nonetheless, expected. You should encourage your employees to refrain from open negative discussions of the company and the people employed by the company. It is always bad politics to bad-mouth someone in the company anyway.

GO TO ▷
Refer to Hour 18, "Organizational Politics and Power," for a discussion of organizational politics and the importance of loyalty.

Loyalty does not mean blindly following and obeying, however. It is possible to be loyal yet still disagree with something that the company is doing or disagree with someone in the company. The key is to disagree tactfully and to ensure that you and your employees are really putting the company's best interests first.

Companies also expect an ethical workforce. With the public outcry for socially responsible companies, this places increasing pressure on you to review your ethics and those of your employees. You must remember to fulfill not just the letter of the laws governing your conduct as a manager, but the spirit of the law as well.

JUST A MINUTE

As more companies place a premium on ethics, college recruiters are checking the transcripts of many applicants to ensure that they have taken business ethics courses.

ORGANIZATIONAL LEARNING

The need to be a learning organization has been emphasized in today's highly competitive and dynamic environment. The learning organization acquires knowledge and then uses that information to make the necessary adaptations to improve organizational performance.

You cannot yearn for the past. To manage the uncertainty characterizing today's world, your organization must be continually learning. You must assist your organization by proactively scanning the external environment for knowledge that is critical to the health of your company.

The learning organization transforms itself while working to ensure all its employees become lifelong learners themselves. You can constantly upgrade your skills and ensure that your employees are doing the same. It is this constant learning that helps ensure that your organization is continuously improving.

JUST A MINUTE

The rate at which people are changing careers and acquiring new skills is evident in institutions of higher education. Students with degrees in one area are returning to college in record numbers to peruse degrees in unrelated fields. For example, many MBA programs are seeing increasing numbers of engineering students.

COMPETENCIES FOR MANAGEMENT TODAY

Now that you've examined the trends impacting the workplace today, it may seem that your environment is even more complex than you had imagined. A list of skills may be helpful. You might use this as a simple self-assessment to inventory your skills. To help you better manage in this environment of change and complexity, the following skills have become critical:

- Flexibility helps you better respond to the uncertainty characterizing today's environment.

- Change management is a core competency of management today. You must successfully manage change (and sometimes create change) by tactfully challenging the status quo.

- Creativity is essential to ensure that you do not cling to the old ways of doing things, but rather continuously improve and search for that proverbial "better mouse trap."

- An ability to work in teams and build teams is critical as organizations create more self-directed work teams.

- Interpersonal skills help you get things done through people. With tighter labor markets, retention becomes even more important. You must be able to get along with others.

- Strategic thinking is essential. Managers must think in terms of the big picture and the long-term.

- Conceptual skills become even more critical in a constantly changing environment. You must continually monitor trends in the external environment and use this information to ensure that your organization appropriately adapts.

- Technical skills must continually be upgraded. Just as your computer quickly becomes obsolete, your technical skills can likewise become obsolete if you are not careful.

- An ethical perspective is required for the lens through which you make your decisions.

- A commitment to continuous improvement is necessary. This includes the processes you use and the knowledge, skills, and abilities that you utilize. You are instrumental in leading the way toward the learning organization.

- A commitment to be a lifelong learner is also key. Your learning never stops. Nor should the learning of your employees.

Hour's Up!

Check what you've learned about the new workplace and the context within which you manage. Try reviewing these questions to jog your memory.

1. Speed in responding to the market requires that you should …
   a. Be flexible and agile.
   b. Be slow and methodical.
   c. Spend less time monitoring the environment.
   d. Control what customers should get.

2. The basic functions of management …
   a. Change with each decade.
   b. Change only in the tools that are used to perform them.
   c. Are obsolete.
   d. Now number in the hundreds.

3. Change is …
   a. One of the greatest challenges for you.
   b. The single most important trend.
   c. Happening faster than ever before.
   d. All of the above.

4. Today's employees …
   a. Want a job for life.
   b. Expect to change jobs every two to three years.
   c. Only want part-time positions.
   d. Look just like the employees of 20 years ago.

5. The virtual office …
   a. Has created a new component of the workforce—telecommuters.
   b. Has created new challenges for you.
   c. Electronically links offices with homes.
   d. All of the above.

6. Diversity …
   a. Is a temporary phenomenon.
   b. Is of no concern to you.
   c. Is reflected in the broad mix of workers.
   d. Is just a soft issue.

7. Downsizing …

    a. Has left many survivors in its wake.

    b. Has increased workloads for many.

    c. Has decreased management layers.

    d. All of the above.

8. Organizations today expect employees …

    a. To stay for lifetime employment.

    b. To contribute regularly to the organization.

    c. To blindly obey their directives.

    d. To leave their ethics at home when they come to work.

9. The learning organization …

    a. Sounds good on paper, but doesn't really work.

    b. Is found only in educational institutions.

    c. Gathers information and uses it internally to make adaptations.

    d. Maintains the status quo.

10. You need to be flexible today …

    a. To better respond to uncertainty in your environment.

    b. To better respond to change in your environment.

    c. To be more creative.

    d. All of the above.

QUIZ

HOUR 3

The Global Environment

CHAPTER SUMMARY

LESSON PLAN:

In this hour you will learn about …

- Working in a global economy.
- Dimensions of culture.
- Differences among cultures.
- Multicultural workforces.
- Roles of expatriate managers.
- Learning in a global environment.

Today's environment for organizations is the world. No longer can American businesses think only in terms of what happens within the confines of the American borders. The world in which you operate is a global economy where countries are interconnected.

American companies are not as globally competitive as they once were. The competition from around the world has increased and the rules of the game have changed. The importance of tapping into profits overseas has, however, become even more critical to the success of firms. Increasing numbers of firms are expanding beyond domestic markets. Some companies have even been pushed into the global arena for their very survival.

The world today has been called "borderless" and "boundaryless." National boundaries are no longer important when conducting business. It is no longer easy to tell what products are made in the United States.

It is hard to determine the country where goods are manufactured with Hondas manufactured in the United States and Chevrolets manufactured in South America. Even those companies with American sounding names are foreign owned. Falling trade barriers and the creation of trade alliances make it easier to move goods across borders now.

Even consumer tastes are converging. More people across the globe want to eat the same fast food, drink the same soda, drive the same cars, and wear the same jeans.

The rise in global product standards also reflects this interconnectedness. Global quality standards (such as ISO 9000 set by the Geneva-based International Standards Organization) continue to be created to assist in the smooth operation of international business.

 FYI When Mexico, Canada, and the United States signed the North American Free Trade Agreement (known as NAFTA), a $6 trillion consumer market was united.

International trade has increased as the cost of transporting goods across borders has decreased. Improvements in communication have improved chances to trade globally. Trade barriers and restrictions have been reduced across the globe. And developing countries have sought partnerships and opportunities with companies from more developed nations.

Competing in the international arena has really become more of a necessity for most organizations. The stakes are now higher with international business comprising approximately one third of the profits in American corporations. The real growth potential for companies going forward is represented in the global arena. Some business writers have suggested that the choice for companies today is to "globalize or perish."

Technological advances have played a major role in shaping this global village. Events that occur today really are "heard around the world." And today they are heard almost instantaneously thanks to electronic communication.

WORKING IN A GLOBAL ECONOMY

Globalization isn't just an issue for larger companies in corporate America. Every business (including the "Mom and Pop" operations) must compete in the international arena. The level of involvement and the intensity in the global arena may vary. For smaller organizations, it may mean the need to stave off global competitors. Even if you work for a small, domestic firm, you must be prepared to compete with a foreign firm operating just across the street.

Being a part of this global economy means thinking with a broader perspective. This global mind-set recognizes the interdependence of the world's countries.

Working in a global economy means increasing your awareness of differences among cultures. Harmony is critical in the Japanese culture. Vague discussions often are the result, in order to save face. Americans have difficulty dealing with this vagueness. For example, a Japanese counterpart often will refrain from directly voicing disagreement with you while your American counterpart may have few reservations about open disagreement.

Globalization usually begins with exporting. Companies maintain operations in their home country while sending goods across borders. Then a move is made to more extensive global operations.

MNC is the acronym used for multinational corporations. These are companies that conduct business outside of their home borders. They operate in several countries and have a truly global mindset—especially when designing strategy. A general rule of thumb is that at least 20 percent of their sales are generated from operations outside the home country.

Today there are over 35,000 multinational corporations around the globe. This number continues to grow. As the number of foreign affiliates of these multinational corporations grows, the need for managers to take foreign assignments will similarly grow.

The impact of international trade is critical, accounting for about 20 percent of the jobs in America.

Companies are also using licensing agreements to build a global presence. A licensing agreement occurs when the company collects money for allowing another company to manufacture its goods (or in the case of a service firm, to market its service) or use its name. More international strategic alliances are also being created. Companies partner with other firms to the benefit of each. Firms can especially improve the learning curve in a new country by partnering with a local firm.

IDENTIFYING THE IMPACT ON MANAGEMENT

Beginning in the 1980s, there has been more interest in global management as America's global competitiveness began to diminish. The loss of global competitiveness can be seen especially in the world banking community. The world's top 10 largest banks include fewer U.S. banks now than ever before.

More firms have recognized the importance of global leadership. Companies don't just need financial resources to expand; they also must have human resources as well.

Whether your company is a MNC or a company operating exclusively in the domestic arena you are still impacted by this global environment. You are likely to find yourself accepting an international assignment—responsible for a workforce from another culture. Or at the very least, you will be working with people from other cultures. These people can be superiors, subordinates, or peers.

As a manager, you must view this globalization as an opportunity to be taken advantage of—not as a threat to be avoided. You can expect to be offered more overseas assignments yourself and expect to offer more to your employees in this global economy. Almost one half of American firms surveyed are expected to increase the number of managers they are placing in expatriate assignments.

This globalization requires new ways of thinking. As a manager, you need expanded competencies. You need to understand that differences exist. You may, therefore, need to be flexible, re-think some of your practices, and accommodate others' cultures.

While nearly all the resources of American businesses flow across national borders, people (the human resources of organizations) are one of the critical components that you must manage from a number of perspectives. You are also responsible for developing an international workforce. This is at the heart of the success of global competitiveness.

The name "cosmopolitan" manager has been used as the preferred terminology over global manager in some circles. *Cosmopolitan* is strictly defined as "belonging to the world." Whichever term is used, the impact is the same. To increase your marketability today, you must know about the world and the people in it.

The manager who exhibits cultural sensitivity and strong intercultural communication skills is in demand today—both in and outside America.

FYI MNCs based in the United States employ over 100 million workers in other countries.

Monitoring trends in the external environment no longer means just keeping tabs on what is happening in the United States. Now you must monitor global trends as well. This means being familiar with the political and legal environments of various countries, socio-cultural trends, economic conditions, and technological environments. This also includes watching for changing preferences of consumers across the world because new consumers are being developed each day.

THE MULTICULTURAL WORKFORCE

People are moving across borders more extensively and freely now. Some of this movement is to take advantage of employment opportunities. People are more accessible the world over now.

Highly skilled people have left some of the developing countries to accept employment in some of the more developed countries. This has created concern for "brain drain" in those countries.

The people of a country share a set of values. But this doesn't mean that only one culture is found in a country. The United States is a good example of this. The United States is multicultural; there is no one culture, but rather many cultures represented. The multicultural aspect is often referred to today as a mosaic to better reflect the nature of the issue.

THE EXPATRIATE MANAGER

A global presence is required for success in many organizations today. And, this requires managers who can effectively operate overseas and are comfortable working in cultures other than their own. Cultural competencies have become critical.

U.S. multinationals are estimated to send 100,000 Americans abroad each year at a corporate investment of $1 million over four years. These managers who are sent overseas to a foreign facility are known as *expatriate managers*. It is increasingly likely that you will take an overseas assignment at some point in your career—whether with your current employer or a future employer.

Multinationals have three choices when filling an overseas assignment. They can select parent country nationals (known as expatriates), host country nationals (referred to as locals), or third country nationals. Transferring a German employee to a position in Australia in a Brazilian firm is an example of a third country national. An expatriate is more likely to be used when a foreign operation is newly established or when operations are established in undeveloped countries.

While you may think that the use of expatriate managers is a relatively new concept, it is not. Even before multinational corporations existed, the leaders of large empires used expatriate managers to oversee regions long distances away.

The use of expatriate management positions helps businesses become more successful. Organizations need to learn more about other cultures and their values to operate more effectively in the global arena. Foreign assignments provide you with the international expertise that has become vital. The global world demands cross-cultural leaders in business.

 FYI The cost of failed assignments by expatriate managers has been estimated to exceed $2 billion annually to American businesses.

A recent survey conducted by the National Industrial Conference Board revealed that staffing overseas positions was the second most serious consideration for top executives of multinational corporations. It has become even more important as there have been more profits at stake overseas.

UNDERSTANDING CULTURE

Culture is defined as a society's shared beliefs and ways of doing things. Your own culture determines how you manage as well as how you view others. You look at others through your own cultural lens. It is important to understand just what that lens is. Before you begin learning about other cultures, you must first understand your own.

Learning about other cultures requires that you be able to overcome ethnocentrism and parochialism. *Ethnocentrism* is the belief that your culture's ways are the only ways. *Parochialism* is the belief that your culture's ways are the best ways. You can't be cosmopolitan with either of these beliefs. These are the attitudes that have led to the term "the ugly American" abroad. Even more importantly, these views can cost your company profits.

As technology brings the world closer together, you are forced to deal with cultural differences on a magnified scale. An understanding of cross-cultural differences is critical today.

JUST A MINUTE

 The culture in Saudi Arabia tends to value the spoken word. People make their point in conversation very slowly so they can enjoy the spoken word. This is in contrast to American businesspeople who tend to prefer getting to the point quickly.

HOFSTEDE'S DIMENSIONS OF CULTURE

Geert Hofstede was a Dutch researcher who created a framework for understanding cultural differences based on his study in 1980 of a multinational corporation that was doing business in 40 different countries. Hofstede's dimensions of culture help you gain insight into the differences among cultures. Based on averages in these cultures, he identified five cultural dimensions:

- Individualism-collectivism
- Power distance
- Uncertainty avoidance
- Masculinity-femininity
- Short- or long-term orientation

 FYI Originally, Hofstede proposed individualism-collectivism, power differences, uncertainty avoidance, and masculinity-femininity as the four dimensions of culture. Short or long-term orientation was added later as a result of Michael Bond's work on Confuscian dynamism. Bond conducted cross-cultural psychology research.

Hofstede's dimensions of culture reflect the basic values of the culture. Knowing where cultures fall on these dimensions can help you gain better insights into the adaptations you must take to be more successful.

Individualism-collectivism refers to a continuum. On one end of the scale is individuaism—where the individual is the focus. Individuals work primarily for their own personal interests. Collectivism is a group effort. The group's interests are considered to be the most important.

The American culture is more individualistic, where people work more for their individual, personal success. The Japanese culture is a good example of collectivism. The collective interest is generally the focus. Collectivism buys almost absolute group loyalty.

There is an old Japanese proverb that suggests that the nail that sticks up will be hammered down. In the Japanese culture, individualism is not valued.

This is a basic issue in the move toward teamwork in the United States—which conflicts with the team approach.

 FYI Hofstede recognized America as among the most individualistic of all the cultures he studied.

Power distance reflects the degree to which the people of a culture are comfortable with differences in power or status. That is, people accept uneven power distributions whereby everyone is not on equal footing. A culture is defined as having a high power distance if people accept that there are broad differences in the distribution of power. People in this culture tend to respect authority and status.

For example, workers in Mexico respect one's social status. They don't want to call their manager by a first name. It would be considered uncultured if you told a Mexican subordinate to call you by your first name.

The dimension referred to as uncertainty avoidance reflects the level of comfort with ambiguity. That is, uncertainty avoidance is the comfort level the culture has for risk. A culture that is low in uncertainty avoidance tends to be comfortable dealing with uncertainty and risk.

An employee from a high uncertainty-avoidance culture may not want much movement into other jobs. They are simply not as comfortable with the uncertainty or risk associated with a new position.

PROCEED WITH CAUTION

 Learning about different cultures should not replace learning about individuals within these cultures. Cultural stereotypes can be detrimental. Remember that each individual is unique.

Masculinity-femininity is the fourth dimension Hofstede identified. This dimension's components represent the values traditionally associated with each of the genders. Masculinity reflects more competitive behavior while femininity reflects more of a concern for others. Femininity comprises more of the "softer" issues in management today. The Japanese culture tends toward the high end of masculinity.

The long-term orientation of the final dimension reflects persistence. The short-term orientation focuses more on immediate results. America has been identified as a short-term culture.

Understanding these dimensions of culture may make it easier when implementing management practices across cultures or with a multicultural workforce. You can gain insight into how to better approach people—especially people from different cultures.

OTHER CULTURAL DIFFERENCES

One of the most apparent cultural differences is that of language. You can readily identify language differences between two cultures. While other cultural differences may be less subtle, it is equally critical to understanding these differences.

Space orientation refers to the way cultures use space and the identification of personal space varies. Americans tend to carefully guard their personal space. The area one to three feet surrounding you is your personal space. Others are not supposed to violate that space. Your reaction to those who invade that area is probably to immediately back away. Standing nose to nose is not usually comfortable in the American culture.

Middle Eastern cultures are comfortable with closer distances while some other cultures tend to extend that personal space. When you are talking to someone from another culture, then, it is important to be aware of this space orientation and to adapt to make him or her comfortable.

You can easily offend people if you are unaware of these cultural differences. Middle Eastern cultures may think you too distant if you don't get close enough while cultures may think you rude and obnoxious if you are standing too close.

Time is an interesting dimension of culture. The American culture is extremely time conscious. You probably carefully account for your time, plan it, and recognize it as a precious resource. Even the language you use reflects this value the American culture places on time. In the English language clocks "run." Many other languages are literally translated to say clocks "walk" instead.

JUST A MINUTE

The Japanese routinely entertain business colleagues late into the evening. This is an expected method of doing business.

This time orientation is very evident as meetings are scheduled across cultures or with people attending representing different cultures. Americans schedule an 11 A.M. meeting and expect everyone to arrive a few minutes early and be prepared to start at 11 sharp. Germans likewise value time and abhor tardiness. An 11 A.M. meeting in a South American culture means "around" 11 A.M. This could be 12 P.M. One is not right while the other is wrong. It is simply a difference in the way these cultures view time.

AVOIDING CULTURAL BLUNDERS

History is ripe with stories of cultural mistakes by companies. Key aspects of culture have been misunderstood, overlooked, or in many cases, even ignored. And surprisingly enough, others have repeated these mistakes. It seems as though business is destined to repeat history until the underlying lesson is finally learned.

Going international for a company does not mean simply extending to other countries what is done at home. Instead, cultural adaptations must be made. You can readily see this with the Walt Disney Company.

After decades of overwhelming success in the theme park industry, they began operating internationally. When they opened EuroDisney outside Paris, France, they failed to understand the impact of cultural differences. The French culture did not lend itself to the Disney formula for operating theme parks. Even Disney's informality in greetings and use of name badges with first names was counter to the formality of the French culture. Dogs are prohibited in Disney parks. Disney failed to recognize that the French are used to taking their beloved dogs everywhere with them—including restaurants.

Some companies have encountered problems in the international arena with language. As companies market their products overseas, the language should be considered. Chevrolet marketed their Nova in South America. After a poor launch, the company discovered that there was a problem with the name. A literal translation of Nova meant "no go." Not many people were willing to run out and buy a car named "no go."

The maiden flight of an Asian route for an airline created quite a panic. As passengers from the new Asian departure point boarded the plane they were presented with white flowers. Unfortunately, these white flowers were associated with funerals in that culture.

These examples are just a few of the thousands of international blunders committed. It is essential that you consider culture and make the necessary adjustments as you operate in other countries or markets.

JUST A MINUTE

Marketers are even using segmentation to identify different cultural groups in America. The Hispanic community is recognized as one of the fastest growing segments in the United States. The awareness of cultural differences has been important in these marketing efforts.

Learning in a Global Environment

Part of the new thinking that is required for organizational success today is to become a learning organization. Changing customer expectations requires that companies respond. With the pace of change, this learning has become more crucial.

In a global economy, it is absolutely critical that the information gathered have a global approach. You must learn from the best practices around the globe.

Being a global learning organization requires that everyone be included. It is an organization-wide commitment. This does not just involve management. And, you are responsible for ensuring that all your employees become committed to learning. This learning must be more self-directed now. Perpetual learning is the goal.

It also means that each member of the firm transfer the learning. That is, as you learn from the best practices around the globe, you must apply it to the workplace. The application of this knowledge is the key to improved performance. A global learning organization also builds a better, more knowledgeable worker.

Continuous learners consider the impact of change in an international perspective. As a manager, you must reward learning and publicize those who are meeting the challenge.

JUST A MINUTE

The official Web site of many countries provides information on the customs and ways of conducting business in their country. The State Department also provides insight, including political risk concerning doing business. Some of the larger accounting firms also have booklets available to help people understand, doing business in different countries.

DOING BUSINESS INTERNATIONALLY: SOME MANAGEMENT TIPS

The following are management tips for doing business internationally:

- Always err on the conservative side. Therefore, dress conservatively and remain formal—especially in your introductions and communications.

- Be sure to take your business cards to Japan with you. They are relied upon in introductions and enable the Japanese businessperson to identify your place in your organization.

- Use last names and titles (for example, Dr. Smith or Professor Higgins). Do not use first names until directed to do so. Otherwise you may offend those who do not appreciate informality.

- International travel on and off the job is important. While it doesn't guarantee that you will become cosmopolitan, it certainly helps.

- Who attends a meeting is often a reflection of the culture. Carefully explore the cultural norms prior to issuing invitations. For example, those from Arab cultures invite only high-ranking people.

- Remember that cultural values are changing across the globe.

- Nonverbal communication varies form one culture to another—often meaning different things in different cultures. You must be especially guarded in your hand motions and your facial expressions. For example, Americans and Arabs use smiles to communicate hospitality. Smiles in the Japanese culture hide embarrassment.

- Arabs and Japanese value harmony and therefore avoid direct confrontation.
- Indonesians prefer an informal atmosphere at meetings. They also expect breaks during longer meetings.
- Periods of silence are common in telephone conversations with people from the Japanese culture. Americans may feel uncomfortable with this silence and try to fill it. The Japanese are using this as a time for reflection. You should let the Japanese be the one to break the silence.

HOUR'S UP!

All companies operate in a global village. Try answering the following questions to get a handle on what this means to you.

1. The world today has been called …
    a. Borderless.
    b. Boundaryless.
    c. Interconnected.
    d. All of the above.

2. Being a part of this global economy means thinking …
    a. With a narrower mind-set.
    b. With a global mind-set.
    c. Only about American business.
    d. About exchange rates.

3. Culture …
    a. Is irrelevant in the international arena.
    b. Is a society's shared way of doing things.
    c. Interests only anthropologists today.
    d. Is country-specific—one to a country.

4. An individualistic culture …
    a. Focuses on the collective good.
    b. Is found in the United States.
    c. Is compatible with teamwork.
    d. Is rarely found.

5. Learning about different cultures …

    a. Should replace learning about individuals.

    b. Isn't really relevant in a multicultural workforce.

    c. Helps you understand others in a multicultural workforce.

    d. Means just learning the language and religion of the culture.

6. Going international …

    a. Means your company is doing more of what you do at home.

    b. Is a strategy that's being adopted by more organizations.

    c. Involves more risk than gains today.

    d. All of the above.

7. Competing internationally …

    a. Is becoming more of a necessity.

    b. Can mean just staving off competition at home.

    c. Provides greater opportunities for growth and profits.

    d. All of the above.

8. Expatriate managers …

    a. Are expected to decrease in numbers.

    b. Are sent overseas to a foreign facility.

    c. Are a new concept.

    d. Provide little real value to the company.

9. Space orientation …

    a. Varies from culture to culture.

    b. Reflects the way cultures use space.

    c. Suggests that personal space varies among cultures.

    d. All of the above.

10. Learning in a global environment …

    a. Means benchmarking across the world—not just domestically.

    b. Is really not necessary if you are operating domestically.

    c. Means checking out just your own industry in a few countries.

    d. All of the above.

QUIZ

HOUR 4
Managerial Decision-Making

LESSON PLAN:

In this hour you will learn about ...

- Steps in rational decision-making.
- Programmed and nonprogrammed decisions.
- Escalation in the decision-making process.
- Creative problem-solving.
- How to recognize the blocks to creativity.
- How to encourage creativity.
- Behaviors of successful decision-makers.

Decision-making is defined as the choosing among alternative courses of action. Decision-making is central to management. Effective managers make literally hundreds of decisions each day—many without even really thinking about them.

Every level of management makes decisions; it is not exclusive to the topmost ranks. The types of decision, however, will vary from one level to the next. The degree of centralization (that is, whether the organization is centralized or decentralized) will determine in large part who makes the decisions within the firm.

As a manager, you must often diagnose the situation to determine who the best decision-maker is. An individual or a group can make a decision. The actual problem and the situation will help to determine who should make the decision. Individuals generally are better with more structured problems. Groups tend to do better with less-structured problems and those decisions that require commitment (perhaps to effectively implement the decision).

THE RATIONAL DECISION-MAKING MODEL

The rational decision-making model suggests that the process is comprised of specific steps. While at first glance the model may appear to be very orderly, the actual implementation of the decision-making process is anything but orderly.

GO TO ▶
Refer to Hour 16, "Organizational and Structural Design," for a more detailed discussion of centralization as a design choice for organizations.

The steps in rational decision-making are as follows:

1. Identification of the problem
2. Development of alternatives
3. Evaluation of the alternatives
4. Selection of an alternative
5. Implementation of the alternative
6. Evaluation of the choice

The rational decision-making process is not necessarily linear. That is, the process is not always in this predictable order. In some cases, the process can be carried out in fits and starts reverting to prior steps.

GO TO ▶
Refer to Hour 14, "Groups," for a detailed discussion of group decision-making, including when a group is the best choice to make the decision.

IDENTIFICATION OF THE PROBLEM

Getting started may be one of the hardest steps to actually carry out. The quality of the decision-making process will be impacted by your ability to actually identify what the problem is. Without a clear understanding of the issue at hand, the process cannot be effectively implemented.

Problems are often identified when there is a gap between the expected performance and the actual performance. A reason for the discrepancy is then sought, which is identified as the problem.

Part of identifying the problem is to move beyond the symptoms to clarify the root causes. You must also know when to maintain the status quo and when to change—for example, when the "old" way is no longer working. In addition you must be able to face up to the problem—even when it is unpleasant—and take the responsibility. Too often it is easier to ignore a problem that threatens your reputation or job performance.

PROCEED WITH CAUTION

Problem analysis is biased by the avoidance of negative information. There is a tendency to eliminate the evaluation of information that may reflect poorly on you.

To be more effective in identifying problems, you should be aware of conditions that increase the probability that problems and opportunities will not be correctly identified. Some of those conditions include …

- When you are "handed" a problem already identified, you tend to accept the problem as identified and formulated rather than perform your own identification.

- When a solution is needed quickly, you tend to spend the little time that you do have on the rest of the decision-making process (not on identifying the problem or the opportunity).

- When the issue is emotional, you move quickly to a solution without spending sufficient time on problem identification.

- When you don't have experience identifying or defining problems, you tend to be ineffective. (Try to get more practice.)

- When there is a complex problem, it is harder to define just what the problem is due to the variety of variables.

JUST A MINUTE

American business culture tends to deny identifying problems while Japanese business culture focuses more attention on identifying problems. In American business you are thought to be more successful if you don't have problems.

Criteria (objectives to be met) guide the decision-making process and outline what you want to accomplish. They can include such factors as cost, risk, or quality to name just a few. This is a key component of the problem identification stage.

The criteria are used to "measure" the effectiveness of solutions. This measurement is conducted in the final stage of evaluation. This analysis, then, indicates whether the solution met the criteria outlined for the problem.

DEVELOPMENT OF ALTERNATIVES

To make good decisions, it is critical to generate good alternative courses of action from which to make the selection. Unfortunately, the tendency is to begin the search with what is already known—and sometimes even already tried. Many organizations examine what their competition has done if they faced a similar problem. It is an easy choice to then just copy what they have done.

You need to generate as many ideas as possible. This provides you with a list of good alternatives to select from. It also helps to solicit input from others. They will have more ideas and different perspectives to share with you. This doesn't mean you have to let them make the decision—just provide you with input. And you should be clear on this point to avoid misunderstandings.

According to the rational decision-making approach, if a good choice is identified, the search for more alternatives is halted. Ironically, this short-changes the process. Stopping before all the alternative courses of action are listed cheats the rational decision-making approach, and then creative alternatives are not always explored.

EVALUATION OF ALTERNATIVES

Evaluating the alternatives involves assessing the value of each alternative. Assessing alternatives includes examining the consequences (both positive and negative) of the alternatives that have been deemed acceptable. Using advantages and disadvantages, it is possible to rank the alternatives.

You must consider whether or not those who are responsible for implementing it or those who will be affected by it will accept the alternative. This evaluation should also include an assessment of the risk and cost of each alternative course of action.

When evaluating the alternative courses of action, you must identify the environment within which you are making your decision. The environments are certainty, risk, and uncertainty. These will impact your decision.

Certainty is the decision-making environment in which you know everything you need to know. You have basically perfect information. You are also knowledgeable about each of the possible outcomes.

JUST A MINUTE

Information is critical to the decision-making process. Information must be reliable and timely. As a decision-maker, you are responsible for the quality of the information you use.

Risk is the environment characterized by an ability to assign a level of risk to each alternative's outcome. In a decision-making environment of risk, you can use probabilities. For example, you could use past experience to assign a probability for the number of quality rejects likely to be produced in a specified period of time under specific conditions in a manufacturing firm. This tends to be the environment within which most decisions are made.

Uncertainty is the decision-making environment in which you are not really sure about each alternative's outcome. High levels of ambiguity where little is known characterize this environment.

SELECTION OF AN ALTERNATIVE: THE SOLUTION

Selecting the solution is rarely a straightforward process. This stage of actually making the choice is what is traditionally thought of as decision-making. In actuality, the whole process is really decision-making.

There are a number of problems encountered when selecting the alternative. Two of the more common problems are as follows:

- A problem arises when there is no single alternative that meets all the criteria. The next decision is then whether to start over or to settle for an alternative that does not meet the criteria.
- A dilemma occurs when choosing among many alternatives that are thought to be acceptable. This may signal the need to fine-tune the criteria to get a clearer idea of a good alternative.

IMPLEMENTATION OF THE ALTERNATIVE

Once the decision has been made, it must be implemented. That is, the choice must be carried out. Implementation is everything, yet it is not easy. Resistance often occurs at this stage. For effective implementation, you must be sensitive to those employees impacted by the decision and plan out the implementation strategy.

If the implementation is poor, the prior steps in the decision-making process can become irrelevant. To effectively implement the decision, resistance to change must be overcome.

GO TO ▶
Refer to Hour 7, "The Basics of Process Development," for a detailed discussion of the change process, resistance to change, and tactics to minimize the resistance to change.

You must ensure that people understand how and why the decision was made. It is critical to involve those impacted because a lack of commitment will result in poor implementation.

Planning for implementation requires you to do the following:

- Clearly envision what the implementation looks like. If this vision is clear to you, then you will be more effective in articulating this to others.
- Outline the specific tasks that must be completed to successfully implement the chosen course of action.

- Identify the resources that are required for each of the tasks that are to be completed.
- Identify how much time it will take to complete each of these tasks.
- Make sure someone has been assigned the responsibility for each of these tasks.

EVALUATION OF THE CHOICE

Evaluation is required to ensure that the desired results are attained. This is the assessment of the consequences of the decision. The results of the implementation are observed. It is important to know both the positive and the negative consequences. The criteria from the first stage of problem identification are used in this final stage to assess the effectiveness of the solution.

If an evaluation is not conducted, then there is no clear indication of whether the objectives were actually met. If the criteria are not met, corrective action must be taken. This evaluation stage may lead back to the problem identification stage—thereby making the process circular in nature.

HOW TO MAKE HIGH-QUALITY DECISIONS

Making high-quality decisions is critical to effective management. You need to pay particular attention to the decision-making procedure itself. Consider the following tips when using the rational decision-making model:

- Carefully select the criteria against which your alternatives will be tested and your final solution will be measured. Inappropriate criteria will lead to faulty decision-making and poor decisions.
- Generate several ideas. The more ideas that are generated, the better your chance of selecting the "best" solution.
- Weigh the pros and cons of each alternative. Don't dismiss any alternatives too soon. Objectively evaluate each of them.
- Keep searching for new information. You especially want to include information that contradicts what you think you know.
- Ensure that you are well aware of the consequences of the implementation of each of the alternatives.
- Plan meticulously for the implementation. This is a critical part of the decision-making stage that requires time and attention—as do the other steps. Develop contingency plans as well.

THE BOUNDED RATIONALITY MODEL OF DECISION-MAKING

The basic assumption underlying Herbert Simon's bounded rationality model of decision-making is that there are limitations in decision-making. The primary limitations are …

- Lack of perfect information.
- Constraints (both time and money).
- Complexity of problems.

As a result of these limitations, you don't usually select the optimal alternative. Instead, you "satisfice." That is, you select satisfactory alternatives that meet your criteria, but are not optimal. You select the first alternative arising that provides a satisfactory solution to the problem at hand—even though the optimal solution may later present itself.

To differentiate between optimizing and satisficing, a classic example is often used:

Optimizing is searching in a haystack for the sharpest needle.

Satisficing is searching for any good needle in the haystack.

TYPES OF DECISIONS

The types of decisions you make will impact the decision-making method you use. Most problems encountered are either programmed or nonprogrammed.

Programmed decisions are of a routine nature. These are problems that are familiar to you. They are recurring—that is, the problem frequently arises and tends to be predictable.

Standard Operating Procedures (SOPs) are used to address programmed decisions. This ensures consistency throughout the organization. With simple problems, you generally have a procedure or canned response. You use existing procedures rather than reinventing the wheel. Simple problems don't warrant a great deal of your time and attention. Computers have even helped to simplify more complex problems to make them into programmed decisions that can be more easily solved.

Nonprogrammed decisions are new, nonroutine decisions. These problems tend to be unpredictable. There are generally no procedures because they are new. Creative problem solving is needed due to the unusual events leading to the problem.

More programmed decisions are handled at the lower levels of the organization and more nonprogrammed decisions are made at the higher levels. There are significant complications when top managers spend more time on routine decisions. This results in ineffective management.

TOOLS FOR DECISION-MAKERS

Strategic decisions are generally made at the higher levels of the organization. You should, however, recognize that more of the strategic management responsibilities are being delegated throughout the organization. Strategic decision-makers may consider the following tools to assist in the decision-making process:

- The strategic decision-making matrix is used to select a strategy for the organization.
- The BCG (Boston Consulting Group) Growth Share Matrix provides a portfolio approach for strategy formulation.
- The GE (General Electric) Matrix (also known as the GE Business Screen) is a portfolio approach to determine the strategic position of a business based on attractiveness of the industry and strength of the business unit.

JUST A MINUTE

Computer-based methods are available to assist you in making decisions. Management information systems (known as MIS) have become critical in supporting daily operations and decision-making.

Operational decisions are usually made at the lower levels. The following tools can be helpful in the decision-making process at these levels:

- Payoff tables provide a conditional value matrix of the elements of the situation.
- Decision trees are "tree" diagrams depicting alternatives and pay offs.
- Break-even analysis performs an analysis of the relationship between the output generated and the associated revenue and costs to determine the level of output where the company breaks even financially.

- Linear programming is an aid in allocating resources.
- PERT (Performance Evaluation and Review Technology) is a network approach to project scheduling.

A number of tools are available for decision-makers. The tools presented in this section come with a brief description of what decisions they can assist with. A thorough discussion of each of these can be found in an "Operations and Production Management" book (such as *Operations Management* by Jay Heizer and Barry Render) or a "Strategy" book.

ESCALATION: A SPECIAL PROBLEM IN DECISION-MAKING

Escalation is a major issue in decision-making. People's egos cause them to stick to their decision, even if it is not working. People continue to invest resources to make it work. They don't want to lose, so they commit more to make it work.

Decision-makers also think about the sunk costs—which is a mistake. Managers must justify their financial expenditures. Because money was initially invested at the beginning stages, failure means that money will not return a profit. To minimize escalation, don't think in terms of what has already been spent. Instead, think in terms of future costs—as if the decision to continue is a new decision.

In strategy, this is often referred to as the losing hand. Companies (just like individuals) must know when to cut their losses and move on. If a strategy is not working, don't throw good money after bad.

A need to justify a previous decision (even though it may appear to be failing) may drive the escalation. The feeling is that if the decision is abandoned, then it will signal to others that it was a mistake.

To be effective in making decisions, then, you must also know when to call it quits. Gamblers refer to this as knowing when to fold their cards. The key is to recognize when to move to another choice.

JUST A MINUTE

Interestingly enough, escalation is driven by ego concerns. It has been found that those people who are more self-confident believe in their decision and engage in escalation more so than those who are not as confident in their decisions and with themselves.

CREATIVITY AND INNOVATION

All problems cannot be effectively solved with rational decision-making; many require a different approach. Organizations cannot stay the same. Business cannot be conducted exactly the same way it was just a decade ago. Every business must make changes just to stay competitive and responsive to environmental changes. Creativity and innovation are required. Creative problem-solving will provide you with new alternatives.

FYI While innovation has always been linked more to smaller organizations, a research study concluded just the opposite. Larger organizations have been found to be more innovative in general.

Creativity and innovation are necessary to the health of your organization. Creativity is the generation of unique ideas. Innovation is using these unique ideas.

The four phases of creativity are as follows:

1. Preparation
2. Incubation
3. Insight
4. Verification

Preparation involves preliminary hard work. It is more than just flashes of insight. The key is to combine two bodies of unrelated knowledge. This is what occurred when penicillin (a medicine) was discovered by finding a mold growing in a laboratory dish. Another classic example was the connection made between glue and marking pages in a church hymnal. This is how the Post-it note was created.

The phase of incubation requires that you step back for reflection and relaxation. This phase is all about thinking—not doing.

Insight involves identifying new relationships. A solution becomes clear at this phase. While observers may think that this insight is an overnight revelation, in reality it is gradual and the product of the former phases.

The fourth phase of creativity is that of verification. The testing of the idea is performed in this final phase. There is verification that the idea works and can be used.

The four phases of creativity are not necessarily linear. That is, there can be an overlap and a regression through the phases. Some of the phases may even occur simultaneously. Since this is a creative process, it is not rigid.

BLOCKS TO CREATIVE PROBLEM-SOLVING

There are a number of blocks that hinder the creative problem-solving process. Being aware of these blocks is the first step toward overcoming them.

Creativity will be inhibited with supervisors that punish or demonstrate a low tolerance for mistakes. Rigid structures (especially high degrees of centralization) leave no room for creativity.

One of the biggest blocks to creativity is a lack of time. When there is no time for reflection, there is no time for creativity.

 As you age, you become less creative. A three-year-old child is more creative (on average) than a grown adult. This is readily seen when that three-year-old plays with a straw for over 30 minutes. You probably would not even be able to think of that many things to do with a straw given twice that time. Adults tend to thrive more on routine.

Looking for the one right answer will block creativity. In most cases, there is more than one right answer, and focusing on a single idea will not encourage creativity. The search for solutions cannot always be logical, and the focus cannot be on following the traditional rules if creativity is the goal. Being practical hinders the creative process.

Part of your job as a manager is to manage uncertainty. In creative problem-solving, you cannot avoid these uncertainties or you may miss opportunities. Ironically enough, you also don't want to avoid problems outside your area of expertise. Most people stick to what they know. Outside of your area of expertise, though, you can make connections that others more expert in the field may not be able to make. They tend to be shackled by what they already know.

Bottom line: Creativity is blocked when you think that you cannot be creative. Everyone can be creative. Instead of worrying about looking silly and trying to avoid mistakes, you need to make playfulness a part of your job and you will find that creativity becomes easier. Two books that could serve as good references in getting started are *Think Out of the Box* (by Mike Vance and Diane Deacon) and *Test Your Lateral Thinking IQ* (by Paul Sloane).

How to Encourage Creativity

Creativity is essential in a turbulent environment. You must not only be creative yourself, you must also be able to encourage creativity in others.

To encourage creativity in those around you, consider the following tips:

- **Hire creative people.** Your organization needs infusions of creativity. In addition, these creative types will also serve as role models to current employees.

- **Train employees to be more creative.** Everyone can learn to be more creative. Commit resources for this training to develop your employees' creativity. You can find help in several good online resources. The official Web site of Edward De Bono (who coined the term "lateral thinking") provides resources addressing creative thinking. There is also a Centre for the Development of Creative Thinking that contains current resources in the field. Resources for creativity and innovation along with techniques for creative thinking can be found at www.oze. mail.com.

- **Create a climate that encourages creativity.** Ensure that the organizational processes and structures encourage creativity. Ensure that there are both intrinsic and extrinsic rewards available for creative endeavors.

- **Build in flexibility.** Provide people with free time on the job to develop their own ideas and projects. If you schedule every minute for them, there is little time left for creativity.

- **Value new ideas.** Don't avoid trying new things. Let your employees know that there is no risk to trying new ideas.

- **Provide opportunities for employees to interact.** Encourage employees to cooperate with one another. Creativity often requires that people share ideas.

- **Celebrate successes.** When creative ideas are adopted, be very public about the success. Others will be motivated to be more creative.

JUST A MINUTE

More creativity occurs in organizations when there are more difficult goals and specific deadlines. While intuitively it may seem to inhibit creative types, the difficult goals propel creative types to higher levels of performance. They also perform better with tight deadlines.

The Characteristics of Creative Organizations

Creative organizations can be distinguished from other companies. These creative organizations generally exhibit the following characteristics:

- **Communication is open with a free flow of ideas.** Employees interact freely with one another and exchange ideas with anyone—not just those in the formal chain of command.

- **There are no limits on how to perform work.** Employees are given latitude in making decisions on how their work should be done. This opens the door for creative ideas.

- **The workforce is heterogeneous.** And there are large numbers of generalists rather than specialists.

JUST A MINUTE

People in a good mood tend to be more creative. Bad moods shut the door on creativity.

- **Evaluation of ideas is objectively based on merit.** The person who presented the idea is not as important as the idea itself.

- **Creative organizations encourage risk-taking.** Creative ideas are not generated with each try. These organizations are willing to accept mistakes.

- **A decentralized structure is critical.** There is some level of flexibility in the structure. The highly centralized structure makes decisions at the top and leaves little room for creativity. To let creativity flourish, these companies create an environment of autonomy and participative decision-making that is only possible in decentralized structures.

- **Personal freedom is found in the creative organization.** There is no close monitoring of employees, and they are free to try new ideas.

JUST A MINUTE

A person's tolerance for ambiguity is related to their creativity. Those who have a high tolerance for ambiguous situations tend to be more creative. There are a variety of tests that determine this. One is known as the "Tolerance for Ambiguity" adapted from Paul Nutt.

SUCCESSFUL DECISION-MAKERS

Successful decision-makers share some behaviors. Consider what successful decision-makers do and think about how many of these behaviors you engage in:

- **Always be prepared.** Decision-making requires that homework is done and information is gathered.
- **Know the culture of the organization.** Decision-making is grounded in organizational culture. The decisions are guided by the core values of the culture.
- **Really use the decision-making process.** Base decisions on data, not emotions.
- **Include employees in the decision-making process.** Listen to those who are actually performing the work.
- **Support group decision-making where appropriate.** You don't have to make every decision yourself. You do, however, need to know who should make the decision.
- **Ensure that reliable information is used.** The quality of the information used impacts the quality of the decision. (Remember GIGO— garbage in, garbage out.)
- **Use creative problem-solving when appropriate.** All problems cannot be solved with rational problem-solving.
- **Create an open climate to encourage feedback.**

PROCEED WITH CAUTION

The approach to decision-making is impacted by culture. American decision-makers attempt to solve problems that arise. Decision-makers from the Indonesian culture tend to accept the situation and make adjustments while relying on fate to correct the situation.

HOUR'S UP!

Recognizing that decision-making is critical to effective management, review these questions to determine how much you have learned about the decision-making process.

1. Decision-making …
   a. Is an uncommon occurrence for managers.
   b. Is choosing among alternative courses of action.
   c. Is the concern of primarily top management.
   d. Is irrelevant in decentralized organizations.

2. According to the rational decision-making model …
   a. Decision-making proceeds in an orderly, linear fashion from one stage to the next.
   b. Problem and opportunity identification is the beginning.
   c. Evaluation is unnecessary if implementation was done properly.
   d. All of the above.

3. In developing alternatives …
   a. The tendency is to begin the search with what is already known.
   b. If a good choice is identified, sometimes the search for more alternatives is halted.
   c. The quantity is important.
   d. All of the above.

4. In the rational decision-making model …
   a. Selecting the solution is really the decision-making process.
   b. Evaluation is unnecessary if the right decision is made.
   c. Implementation is critical because poor implementation can in essence negate the whole process.
   d. Once the decision is made, the process is complete.

5. The bounded rationality model of decision-making suggests that as a result of certain limitations …
   a. You usually select the optimal decision.
   b. You satisfice—selecting the satisfactory alternatives that meet the criteria.
   c. You search for the needle in the haystack.
   d. You always have perfect information when making decisions.

6. Programmed decisions …
   a. Are routine in nature.
   b. Generally have a canned response.

c. Tend to be handled at lower organizational levels.

d. All of the above.

7. Creativity …

    a. Is seldom needed.

    b. Is just seen in smaller organizations.

    c. Is generating unique ideas.

    d. Is actually using unique ideas.

8. Creative organizations …

    a. Have more centralized structures.

    b. Punish risk taking.

    c. Have open communication with a free flow of ideas.

    d. Have homogeneous workforces with a large number of specialists.

9. To encourage creativity …

    a. Build in flexibility.

    b. Value new ideas.

    c. Provide opportunities for employees to interact.

    d. All of the above.

10. Successful decision-makers …

    a. Don't have to prepare because the necessary information will come to them.

    b. Don't have to include input from others if the decision is their responsibility to make.

    c. Don't have to make every decision themselves; they can delegate the decision.

    d. Don't have to know the culture of the organization; it is irrelevant to the decision-making process.

QUIZ

PART II
Getting Started on the Basics of Management

HOUR 5

Financials

CHAPTER SUMMARY

LESSON PLAN:

In this hour you will learn about ...

- Using numbers to make decisions.
- Understanding financial statements.
- Working with basic organizational forms.
- Reviewing financial ratios and their meaning.
- Controlling the business with budgeting.
- Learning when to use open-book management.

While the appearance of financials may be cloaked in mystery, this is not the reality—if you know some of the basic information. You just need to understand the terminology and the tools of financial analysis.

Financial statements give an indication of how financially healthy a business may be at one given moment in time.

The key to analyzing financial statements is to identify trends and find reasons behind the numbers. The secret to determining whether a business is healthy is to analyze several periods (years, if possible) to determine trends.

Trends tell the true financial picture behind every business entity. Companies that are particularly well run will possess an upward sloping trend line that rises with the economic health of the country. Businesses that are facing financial problems will have a downward sloping trend line that shows a performance that is less than the current economic condition would indicate.

Because every business can be faced with an adverse situation at any particular time, it is important to get as much historical information as possible on an entity. In order to do this, every manager needs to possess a basic understanding of financial statements and the direction these statements show that the business is headed.

Financial record-keeping in business is in response to the Sixteenth Amendment to the Constitution of the United States, which allows for the collection of taxes. As more companies became publicly owned, shareholders demanded financial disclosure—thereby formalizing the need for financial information.

The Securities and Exchange Commission (SEC) sets the standards and requirements for financial reporting in publicly held corporations. All public companies are required by law to submit financial information to the Securities and Exchange Commission. The information consists of three quarterly financial statements presented in a 10-Q report and a yearly financial statement presented as a 10-K report.

JUST A MINUTE

The 10-Q reports are due at the SEC no later than 45 days after the quarter ends. The 10-K report is due to be filed with the SEC no later than 90 days after a company's year-end financial cycle has been completed.

FINANCIAL STATEMENTS

Financial statements simply help you monitor your financial resources—to ensure that you are making more money than you are spending. They are a critical component in your decision-making process.

Financial statements use a system called double-entry bookkeeping. This system requires the use of accounts called debits and credits. A debit is an item that is placed on the left-hand side of an account. A credit is placed on the right-hand side of an account. Every time a debit is recorded on a set of financial statements, a corresponding credit must be recorded for the same amount on the financial statement. By following this procedure, the corporate books are said to be in balance because debits must always equal credits.

There are four primary financial statements:

- The balance sheet
- The income statement
- The cash flow statement
- The statement of changes in stockholders' equity

THE BALANCE SHEET

The balance sheet provides information concerning your company's assets, liabilities, and owner's equity. A typical balance sheet will have assets on the left-hand side and liabilities and owner's equity on the right. Assets are accounts that list what is owned by the business. These accounts are broken down into short-term assets and long-term assets. Short-term assets are assets that can be converted to cash in less than one year's time. Long-term assets are assets that have an expected life greater than one year. An example of a long-term asset would be a building. Buildings are constructed to last for many years, and, therefore, the benefit of the building will continue for years into the future.

JUST A MINUTE

The common-size balance sheet is a valuable tool for financial analysis. The total assets are set equal to 100 percent with all assets listed as a percentage of these total assets. On the right side of the balance sheet, the account labeled "total liabilities and equity" is set equal to 100 percent. All liability and equity accounts are then represented as the appropriate percent of the total liabilities and equity. This statement helps analyze the distribution of various accounts on the balance sheet. Of particular interest on the asset side are the percentages of total assets comprised by cash, inventory, and accounts receivable.

Liabilities are obligations to creditors that the company has acquired throughout the normal course of business. Like assets, they can be broken down into short- and long-term obligations. Typical short-term obligations would be acquiring goods or services on credit. Businesses are generally extended credit terms that provide 30 days or more to pay for current obligations. This type of credit is normally listed on the balance sheet as an account payable.

Companies are also granted credit for more than one year if the credit is being used to finance an item that may last for more than one year. If a company takes out a mortgage to finance a building, this loan would normally be granted for a number of years because the underlying asset being financed has a life expectancy of more than one year (similar to an individual purchasing a home).

Owner's equity is the final group of accounts on the balance sheet. As the title indicates, these are accounts that deal with the net worth of a business. This net worth is the difference between the assets and liabilities of a company and shows how much of the assets are being financed by the owners as opposed to how much is financed by the creditors (liabilities).

The balance sheet is a snapshot in time. This provides a picture of the company's financial position on the date stated. Balance sheets contain all the company's permanent accounts. Unlike income statements these account balances are carried from period to period and year to year. The balance sheet is generated by a business at least once a month. Many of the accounts on the balance sheet are reviewed and analyzed more than once a month because of their vital importance to running a business.

Current assets include the following:

- Cash
- Accounts receivable
- Inventory
- Prepaid expenses

JUST A MINUTE

Remember that you can read the footnotes in financial statements to get clarification of the firm's numbers.

Long-term assets include the following:

- Plant and equipment
- Land and buildings
- Accumulated depreciation

Cash is the first asset listed on the balance sheet. It is the most vital component on the company's balance sheet because it is the means by which a company can pay for supplies, meet its payroll, and invest in assets that can help the company generate income.

The designers of financial statements constructed all statements to list and group accounts by order of liquidity. Cash is the most liquid asset because it is already in a medium of exchange that is widely accepted. After a company's cash accounts are listed on its balance sheet, the next item in order of liquidity would be accounts receivables. These are obligations owed to the firm by individuals or companies that have been extended credit on account.

All assets are listed on a balance sheet at historic or purchase price value unless the asset has been *impaired*. Inventory is an example of an asset that can be impaired. Because inventory is acquired and then stored until consumed or sold, you run the risk that it may become damaged or obsolete.

Under current accounting rules when this happens the asset must be recorded at the lower of cost or market price. In other words, if the cost for an inventory item is $10 and subsequent to use or sale it has been determined that it is only worth $5, then this item must be reduced to the lower value on the balance sheet.

Short-term liabilities include the following:

- Accounts payable
- Accrued expenses
- Short-term debt
- Income tax payable

Long-term liabilities include the following:

- Mortgage payable
- Long-term debt

Short-term liabilities are obligations that the company must repay in less than one year's time. Often times these liabilities are due in 30 days or less. Accrued expenses are expenses the business has incurred but has not yet been presented with an invoice to pay. A company wants to make sure all its known liabilities have been recorded as quickly as possible. By doing this, it is able to show a clearer picture of its financial health sooner to internal management, creditors, and owners of the business.

Stockholders' equity includes the following:

- Capital stock
- Additional paid in capital
- Retained earnings

Capital stock is the face value of the number of shares of company stock the company has outstanding multiplied times the par or stated value of the stock. Normally, when you review a financial statement this shows up as a very small number because the stock may have a value of one dollar per share or one cent per share. However, one of the most common ways stock is shown on a financial statement is at no par value. By doing this, the company is saying they have not assigned any monetary value to their stock. When they receive money for their outstanding stock they list only a small portion of this money being paid for the stock and the remainder of this money is recorded as *additional paid-in capital*. Additional paid-in capital is the difference between the face value of a share of stock and the price a buyer actually pays for the stock from the company.

Retained earnings are prior earnings the company has generated that they have decided to retain in the business in order to help it grow. Often a portion of a company's earnings is returned to the stockholders in the form of a dividend. Companies that pay a dividend generally distribute these dividends quarterly.

In order to completely understand the balance sheet, you must understand the basic formula. This formula is as follows:

Assets = Liabilities + Net Worth

THE INCOME STATEMENT

The income statement provides a picture of the company's financial performance over a specified period of time. This statement depicts the income generated and the expenses incurred by the firm during this period—painting a picture of how the company got to the point of the balance sheet. This cycle, which is one year in length, can follow a calendar year or use another yearly time period (which is referred to as a *fiscal* year). An example of a fiscal period would be February 1 to January 31 of each year.

Bottom line: The income statement tells you if there is a profit or loss as a result of the year's operations. Net income (commonly referred to as a profit) occurs when revenue exceeds expenses. There is a net loss when the expenses exceed the revenue.

The cash accounting method does not recognize items that are prepaid or accrued. Revenues are reported in the period in which they are paid. For example, sales made in March but paid for in May would be reported as revenue in May in the cash accounting method.

The same is true of expenses. They are reported in the accounting period in which they are actually paid. For example, if you bought a copy machine for your department in October, but it was not paid for until December, the expense would not be booked until December under the cash accounting method.

Accrual accounting records income and expenses when they occur. The accounting principle this follows is called the matching principle. The matching principle requires expenses to be matched or recorded against the revenue the expenses helped to generate. By recording these accruals at that time, a clearer picture of the profitability can be shown to internal and external users of the financial statements.

Most larger companies use the accrual method. Small businesses generally opt for the cash accounting method since they usually do not have many significant deferred or accrued items to materially impact their financial statements.

The three choices when accounting for inventory include:

- **LIFO.** The principal behind LIFO is that the last items going into inventory will be the first items sold out of inventory. This method came about when inflation was running at very high levels. By matching the last items into inventory against the selling price, less profit was recorded during inflation; therefore, less tax was being paid. LIFO will also better reflect replacement cost for inventory.

- **FIFO.** This method states that the first items into inventory will be the first items out of inventory. This method is more widely accepted than the LIFO method.

- **Weighted average.** This method does not look at the time the inventory was received. It looks at the total value of the inventory and determines an average price based upon all the items in the current inventory.

During periods of rising prices, LIFO offers a tax advantage to its users. LIFO assigns the most recently purchased items to cost of goods sold (which impacts profit and loss). The weighted average inventory method would be used when price levels are stable and you are trying to use a more uniform price for your cost of goods sold.

Improved efficiency in managing inventory can positively impact the company's cash position. Lower inventory levels mean less cash is invested in inventory. Yet care must be taken to ensure that sufficient inventory levels are on hand to meet customer needs. Just-in-time (JIT) inventory methods have helped to better manage inventory levels by ensuring that appropriate amounts are on hand when needed. A JIT supplier is responsible for delivering goods just when they are needed and in the amounts in which they are needed. This reduces inventory-carrying costs for the firm, because they are getting the goods exactly when they want to use them and do not have to store the goods.

THE CASH FLOW STATEMENT

The cash flow statement reflects the cash position of the firm. It starts by listing cash at the beginning of the fiscal period, and then shows how cash was generated and used by a business. That is, this statement details the sources and uses of cash.

The general formula utilized in the cash flow statement is …

Cash Inflows – Cash Outflows = Net Change in Cash

The terminology *cash sources* (inflows) and *cash uses* (outflows) may be used in this statement. Sources of cash would include noncash expenses such as *depreciation* and *amortization*. Depreciation and amortization are expenses booked against current operations that have been paid for in a prior period. Other sources of cash would be net profits, positive changes in assets and liabilities, and company borrowings. Uses of cash would include purchases of long-term assets, net losses, loan paybacks, and dividends paid to stockholders.

FYI The cash flow statement was not standard accounting practice until the 1980s. As companies began to realize the importance of cash, the cash flow statement kept growing to greater value by people reading financial statements. Financial statement users quickly realized that a company that could not internally generate enough cash to fund operations would have to look to outside sources in order to keep itself running. Realizing that capital markets and lenders can be fickle caused the truly wise investor to focus in on the cash-generating operations of the business.

THE STATEMENT OF CHANGES IN STOCKHOLDERS' EQUITY

The statement of changes in stockholders' equity reconciles the net worth of the business and provides an analysis of the change in that net worth. This statement tracks the net worth of the owners of the business beginning with their initial investments and adjusting for changes to these investments.

Items that are recorded on this statement would be net profit or net loss; the company selling additional shares of its stock to investors; and repurchases by the company of its own stock. (These transactions are called treasury stock transactions.) Dividends would also be recorded on this statement.

JUST A MINUTE

If you were a potential investor, the statement of changes in stockholders' equity would be a good place to look. It would provide an insight into the changes to your investment over time.

BASIC ORGANIZATIONAL FORMS

The three basic organizational forms are *sole proprietorships*, *partnerships*, and *corporations*. The sole proprietorship has one owner (as the name implies). This is known as the simplest of the organizational forms. A major drawback of this form of ownership is that the owner is personally liable for all the business's obligations.

Partnerships have two or more owners. As with sole proprietorships, in a simple partnership, the owners have unlimited liability. Many large accounting firms are organized as partnerships.

JUST A MINUTE

The choice of organizational form impacts the management of the firm, the personal liability of organizational members (and owners), and the tax treatment. The more common forms are selected to meet the individual needs of each organization.

Unlike the proprietorship and the partnership, the corporation is a legal entity separate from its owners. In a corporation, owners hold stock and are known as shareholders. The advantage to this organizational form is limited liability. This is possible because a corporation is treated as a separate legal entity.

A corporation also has some drawbacks. Profits from a corporation are taxed twice. First they are taxed to the corporation, and then they are taxed when the corporation distributes them to the shareholders. Another disadvantage of a corporation is the higher costs associated with operating a corporation.

A number of hybrid forms of corporations have sprung up to avoid the double taxation of corporations. One of these hybrids is the Subchapter S corporation. In a Subchapter S corporation, the owners must declare the income or loss from the corporation on their tax returns in proportion to their ownership of the corporation. It was designed by Congress for a small company to take advantage of the corporate organizational form.

The limited liability company (known as the LLC) is a more recent organization form. It limits the liability of managers in the company. Generally, a manager in an LLC cannot be held personally liable for the company's obligations. This is in contrast to the sole proprietor, who is personally liable for all debts and obligations.

Companies may be either *privately held* or *publicly held*. The privately held company has no publicly traded stock. The owners retain control of the business and are not required to file information that is available for public inspection. There are fewer financial reporting demands, with more reporting options being left up to the manager. These privately held companies do, however, still have to meet the requirements of the tax authorities.

The publicly held company is governed by securities regulations. These include financial reporting requirements and the need for independent auditors to oversee annual financial statements.

FINANCIAL RATIOS

Financial ratios are used to provide insight into how effectively the company is being managed. Financial ratios measure the relationship of one item to another in a mathematical expression. In order for the ratio to have any significance, there must be a relationship between the two figures you are measuring. Even after you have determined that a relationship exists, you must still do further analysis to determine the full impact of this relationship and how it hurts or helps your company.

A number of different types of ratios are utilized to examine different components of the financial statements.

PROCEED WITH CAUTION

Using any one financial ratio as an indicator is insufficient in painting a picture of the company's financial position. One ratio tells you very little. You need to use these ratios in combination with others.

Liquidity ratios provide an indication of the company's ability to pay its short-term debts. They examine the relationship of current assets to current liabilities.

The *current ratio* is one of the most popular ratios that companies use. This is the ratio of current assets to current liabilities. If the current ratio is 1:1, there is $1 in assets existing to pay $1 in debt.

This ratio should be at least 2:1 for a comfortable level. When the current ratio is less than one, the business cannot generate enough cash flow to meet its current obligations. This is obviously a dangerous position for the company to be in.

This ratio does have a major disadvantage to be considered. This number is generated with no regard to the timing of current assets. It may, therefore, distort the financial position of the firm.

The *quick ratio* uses "quick assets" as opposed to all current assets in the current ratio. The ratio specifically excludes inventories. The quick ratio is generated as …

Cash + Accounts Receivables = Current Liabilities

JUST A MINUTE

Inventories are excluded from the quick assets because turning over inventory quickly would mean making significant price concessions that would negatively impact the financial position of the firm.

This ratio provides an indication of the company's ability to quickly pay their bills. A 1:1 ratio is considered good for most firms.

Receivables turn is the speed at which receivables are collected; the ratio is generated by dividing sales by accounts receivables. This provides the number of times that accounts receivables are turned in a specified period of time. Ideally, you want a faster turn to make cash available more quickly.

Payables turn is the speed at which the business is paying its bills; it's generated by dividing the cost of goods sold by the accounts payables.

Debt to equity is simply the ratio of the firm's debt to equity. That is, the ratio of the company funds from owners to those from lenders. The range considered good is between 1:1 and 4:1. The larger ratios indicate greater risk to those lending money to the business. Greater risk to a lender will lead to a firm paying more for the credit it is extended.

BUDGETING

Budgeting is a tool used to control the business. This involves measuring the firm's actual performance against the expected performance. Generally, the current period's actual performance is compared against last year's actual performance and the current period's budget.

JUST A MINUTE

Zero-based budgeting (ZBB) begins the budgeting process at zero and builds each line item from this point. In ZBB, it is not acceptable to use last year's figures and add a predetermined amount.

The budgeting process is important for every size organization—no matter how small or large. Budgeting runs the gamut from simple to complicated. The budget is a powerful tool (if used appropriately) in the planning function. Budgeting makes sure that you are moving toward your plan. It is a check, if you will, that you are moving in the right direction.

The same accounting systems that provide the information to generate financial statements provide the information for the budgeting process. The budgets determine what financial resources you have at your disposal.

The budgeting process is identified as a "game" in American business. Just as in the game of chess, there are some standard "moves." The most common tactic is to pad expenses (with more than you really need) to ensure coming in under budget. This can be varied to ask for more line items than you really want (so you can "sacrifice" some and be seen as a good guy).

Historical data is usually the starting point for your projections. You must take the past into consideration when making decisions about the future. To smooth the way for the budgeting process, consider these tips:

- Solicit input from your employees.
- Review past budgets and actual performance trends.

- Use your discretion to fine-tune the numbers.
- Review a draft to ensure it makes sense and is complete.

PROCEED WITH CAUTION

It is important to consider GIGO when developing budgets. That is, garbage in, garbage out. The quality of information you use for input will impact the quality of your budget.

Monitoring your budget enables you to identify variances and then take corrective action. This can make the difference between having a good reputation (and recognition) and a bad reputation. When there are early signs that your budget is getting out of line, you should consider the following tips:

- Watch your discretionary expenses.
- Don't hire any new employees.
- Delay any noncritical projects.

If your budget is in serious danger, you may need to consider delaying pay increases for your employees. At the most critical level, you may need to lay off employees. Monitoring budget performance in the early stages should avoid these measures.

OPEN-BOOK MANAGEMENT

Open-book management has become more popular in the last decade. This is the process of opening up the operating numbers to the employees of the company. While some companies tend to shroud the financial performance of the firm in secrecy, those using open book management keep their employees informed. They try to expand the stake of the employees in the business.

This ownership culture is an attempt to assist the employees in understanding the performance of the firm.

 Open-book management became highly publicized in American businesses with the turnaround of Springfield Remanufacturing. Under Jack Stack's leadership, open-book management was used to effect a culture change that was instrumental in the turnaround.

The basic foundation of the effective use of open-book management is to ensure that employees and managers see themselves as playing on the same team in a cooperative relationship—versus an adversarial relationship.

Only by understanding the financial position of the company can employees make better decisions concerning their contributions to the company's profitability. Secrecy concerning financial performance makes it more difficult for employees to make this connection to better contribute.

But just providing information is not enough. Employees must be taught how to read and use this information. The tools for understanding the information they are being provided are essential. An internal training program is a key component of effective open-book management.

All bonus systems should be tied directly to the financials. This is even more of an incentive for employees to learn what the numbers mean and how they are read.

You have a big role in open-book management. You must let go and empower employees to act—giving them opportunities to improve their area's financial performance. But accountability must accompany this empowerment. Employees are accountable for their performance and should also be included, then, in the development of forecasts (or projections).

Part of open-book management is displaying results and openly sharing this information. As good performance is widely publicized and celebrated; poor performance should be addressed jointly (by management and employees) to develop a plan for corrective action.

JUST A MINUTE

Many companies are using scoreboards to monitor the progress of units toward their goals. Specific measures are selected and then posted to keep employees aware of progress.

Open-book management doesn't necessarily mean that all financial data must be disclosed to employees. There are degrees of disclosure that can still be successful in getting employees onboard. The key is to begin to divulge some financial information and then educate employees as to what this information means.

HOUR'S UP!

Now that you have read about the terminology and tools of financial analysis, review these questions to decide how much you have learned about the management of financials.

1. The key to analyzing financial statements is …

    a. To have big numbers.

    b. To identify trends and find reasons behind the numbers.

    c. To have a profit.

    d. To just know the trends—whether they are good or bad.

2. All public companies are required by law to submit financial information to what?

    a. SEC

    b. FASB

    c. GAAP

    d. DOD

3. The balance sheet lists …

    a. Assets on the right.

    b. Liabilities and owner's equity on the left.

    c. Assets on the left and liabilities and owner's equity on the right.

    d. Only current assets.

4. Short-term liabilities …

    a. Are obligations that the company must repay in less than 10 years' time.

    b. Are obligations that the company must repay in less than one year's time.

    c. Include the mortgage payable.

    d. Include long-term debt.

5. The income statement …

    a. Depicts the income generated.

    b. Depicts the expenses incurred.

    c. Provides a picture of the company's financial performance over a specified period of time.

    d. All of the above.

6. The inventory method that best reflects the replacement cost for inventory is …

    a. LIFO.

    b. FIFO.

    c. Weighted average.

    d. FIDO.

7. The cash flow statement …

    a. Reflects the firm's position with regard to long-term assets.

    b. Disregards how cash is used in the operation of the business.

    c. Reflects the cash position of the firm.

    d. Disregards how cash is generated in the operation of the business.

8. The current ratio is …

    a. A liquidity ratio.

    b. Is one of the most popular ratios.

    c. An examination of the relationship between current assets and current liabilities.

    d. All of the above.

9. The budgeting process …

    a. Is only appropriate in large organizations.

    b. Must be complicated to be effective.

    c. Involves measuring the firm's actual performance against the expected performance.

    d. All of the above.

10. Open-book management …

    a. Opens up the financial books of the firm to expand the stake of the employees in the business.

    b. Creates an adversarial relationship between management and employees.

    c. Requires only that information be provided, but educating employees on how to use this information is not necessary.

    d. Cannot improve decision-making.

QUIZ

Hour 6
Project Management

LESSON PLAN:

In this hour you will learn about ...

- Defining a project.
- Understanding the three phases of project management.
- Planning the project.
- Identifying the resource requirements for projects.
- Setting project objectives.
- Scheduling the activities of the project.
- Learning techniques for controlling the project.
- Introducing the project team.

Everyone is being asked to do more with less. You are also being asked to make regular contributions to your organizations. Many of these contributions require projects. As organizations become networks of simultaneous projects, you will be responsible for project management on an increasingly frequent basis.

With shorter project life cycles, the strategic importance of project management has grown. Projects are ripe with uncertainties—especially with regard to time. You can increase your managerial effectiveness through improved project management, which enables you to plan and execute your projects more effectively.

The field of project management is only 50 years old. It is said to be the management of change in today's organizations. Project management provides a methodical approach to the effective management of projects. This has become increasingly important as organizations are now characterized as portfolios of projects. Effective project management ensures that the project meets the requirements of the customer, is completed on time, and is completed under budget.

FYI Twenty years ago, 50 percent of all information technology projects failed. Today, 90 percent of these projects fail in terms of time, budget, or needs. Forty percent of these projects don't even make it to completion.

With a large number of failed projects, it pays to know why projects are failing. Many fail due to a lack of ownership or accountability. (Lame excuses are used to avoid accountability.)

The barriers to effective project management focus on a few key issues:

- Good communication is a must in order for a project to escape failure.
- There must be a plan that is clearly communicated to all the team members.
- Everyone involved must agree on what needs to be done.
- Effective management is critical to avoid project failure.

Using sound project management principles can help avoid these failures.

A project is a series of tasks completed to achieve a major outcome. It is not the same as your daily responsibilities. Your daily responsibilities are on-going. A project has a definite beginning and a definite end. Projects can range from a week to several years, and they require special management. Even older, repetitive projects must be managed in a constantly changing environment.

Many projects (whether introducing a product or service, building a high-way, merging two companies, or launching a space shuttle) are complex, large-scale, and may be one-time events for an organization. Delays in these projects often come with significant price tags.

JUST A MINUTE

 Cost overruns on large projects can run into the millions. Delays can be the result of poor scheduling and poor project management.

PHASES FOR PROJECTS

Projects occur at all organizational levels—strategic, tactical, and operational. To ensure more success, a systematic approach to project management should be taken.

Projects may be thought of as occurring in three phases.

Phase I: Planning
        Work Breakdown Structure
        Resource Requirements
        Why Plans Fail
Phase II: Scheduling
Phase III: Controlling

Phase I: Planning

Planning helps to ensure that the project will be completed at the desired quality level, within the prescribed time frame, and within the budget constraints. Planning also means that the people on the project team have the resources they need to get the work done. The time you take to plan is an investment in the effectiveness and success of the project.

STRICTLY DEFINED

Enterprise project management views a business as a portfolio of projects to be managed. This reflects the large number of projects that are not repetitive operations in today's organizations. It also stresses the importance of simultaneous projects that are conducted to reach corporate goals.

Planning is the process by which you identify who, what, where, and how much with respect to the project. That is, who is going to be involved, what the project is, where it affects the organization, and how much it is going to cost. This involves three main issues:

- Developing a vision
- Setting objectives
- Identifying boundaries and constraints

Developing a Vision

The vision of the project is a clear statement about exactly what this project entails. This vision communicates the scope of the project—stipulating what is included and what is not included. It specifically articulates the changes to be made in the organization and where these changes will be made (for example, who will be affected). These changes must be valuable contributions to the firm. This clear definition of the project is the foundation to success.

Setting goals is critical to planning. Goals keep everyone on the same page so everyone moves in the same direction. This requires that everyone agree on these goals. Agreement garners support and commitment of the team members.

SETTING OBJECTIVES

GO TO ▶
Refer to Hour 11, "Motivation," for a discussion of the role of goal setting in groups and joint goal setting to gain commitment.

Everyone must agree on the objectives being set. These objectives include the variables to be managed, who will be responsible for its accomplishment, and the needs to be met. Objectives should indicate who will be served and what the project will do.

The key is to create measurable objectives. These are then used to monitor progress (in the final stage of project management), and then determine the ultimate success of the project at completion—by measuring actual performance against the objectives. The usual performance criteria include time, cost, and quality.

JUST A MINUTE

The Project Management Institute provides a wonderful resource for information and aids to better manage your projects. Visit www.projectmanagementinstitute.com.

You must carefully identify the constraints within which you are working. The time and financial constraints are generally some of the greatest that you will encounter. Each organization has finite resources. You have only a certain amount at your disposal.

IDENTIFYING BOUNDARIES/CONSTRAINTS

GO TO ▶
Refer to Hour 15, "Teamwork," for a detailed discussion of the increase in the use of teams and the more effective management of teams in the workforce.

A key component of planning is identifying problems. This is time well spent because it will speed up the implementation of the project. You can minimize the effects of things going wrong by using a contingency plan.

Part of the planning stage must be the consideration of timing and feasibility. You must consider whether it is the appropriate time for the project to be undertaken. The political climate of every organization is such that there are better times than others for specific projects. This means taking into consideration the impact of the project on the business and constraints involved. These constraints include whether the right people are available, whether the needed resources are available, and even whether there are sufficient financial resources to fund the project through to completion.

Force-field analysis is a helpful tool in analyzing the feasibility of projects. The driving forces and the resisting forces are identified. If the driving forces outweigh the resisting forces, there is a good likelihood that the project will be successful.

WORK BREAKDOWN STRUCTURE (WBS)

The crux of planning is taking the large project and breaking it down into smaller parts that can be more easily managed. This process is a continuous one. Known as Work Breakdown Structure (WBS), you keep breaking down jobs into smaller and smaller tasks. For each of these smaller tasks, you must then decide on the people, resources, and equipment needed.

PROCEED WITH CAUTION

You must be prepared to change. The plan does not mean that your project is etched in stone. You must be flexible enough in your planning to make adjustments as you proceed. As the implementation is monitored, revisions to the plan may be in order.

Once activities are identified, they must also be grouped together. This grouping makes them easier to manage, and you are able to see how the activities are related to each other. Your team can be instrumental with this task.

The project team and the stakeholders can help you identify these activities. You want an exhaustive list that is comprehensive. Then you can think of a logical order in which the tasks might be completed. A complete review of the activities should ensure that there are no gaps. You can't leave any activities out—or they simply won't get done.

RESOURCE REQUIREMENTS

The resource requirements must be planned. The complexity of project management is in the coordination of the resources to ensure efficiency and effectiveness. You must plan for all the resources required to finish each activity with the project. Your resources must be available when you need them—otherwise, the progress of the project is delayed while you wait for resources to become available.

PROCEED WITH CAUTION

Resource allocation ensures that the right resources are available for the right activities. This also means ensuring that excessive resources are not available. Waste is the flip side of this issue that is generally not considered.

The resource requirements include the following:

- Human resources
- Other resources
- Financial resources

Human resources are the people that you need to get the work done. Particular attention must be paid to the skill set required to complete the project. Managers, technical people, and clerical support must be included in the planning. Any training the people need must be planned as well. You must consider who you need and how long you need them. This should include those you need both inside and outside the organization.

Numerous other resources are always needed. These will vary greatly from project to project. The most critical of these resources is time. These other resources also include all the materials that you need and the equipment that is required. Even the facilities that you will require must be included in this planning.

Money is needed for every project. Part of planning the project involves establishing a budget. With limited financial resources in every organization, you must carefully plan what these financial needs are. This often requires that you be flexible. You must obtain competitive bids if you go outside the organization for any resources (whether human resources, equipment, or facilities).

JUST A MINUTE

More firms today are using project organizations. These are temporary structures to utilize the talent and expertise in the firm to manage projects—both ongoing and new ones. During the planning stage, the team is kept very simple, and creative individuals are critical.

Planning ensures that the resources you need for the completion of the project will be available when they are needed. Part of planning includes your own planning and scheduling. You should create a grand schedule of all your projects. This, in essence, is the management of project management. You want to ensure that you prioritize the projects for which you are responsible, to be sure that you are not spread too thin.

WHY PLANS FAIL

Planning is fraught with pitfalls. Plans can be more effective if you know why they tend to fail. Plans are most likely to fail if any of the following conditions occurs:

- Those involved in the planning process don't understand how to plan. A lack of knowledge of the planning process itself leaves the team with no sense of direction—or a poor one at best.

- The plan has not solicited input from major stakeholders. Without early support and buy-in, the best plans will be blocked and cannot be effectively implemented.

- Only the project manager completes the plan. Having the appropriate people participate in the planning process increases the buy-in. This not only increases the chances of a higher quality plan (with more insights), but also smoothes the way for implementation.

- The team thinks implementation will be easy. Implementation is difficult at best. If the job is underestimated, unexpected consequences can derail the entire effort.

PHASE II: SCHEDULING

Project scheduling is an integral component of project management. The sequence of the tasks identified in the first step of planning must be scheduled. This includes the consideration of time. That is, this includes a consideration of how long each task will take. The scheduling encompasses the people (including their skill set) and the resources needed.

The specific resources identified in the planning stage are now tied to a specific activity in the project. And the relationship of tasks is identified. When determining the order of tasks, you must recognize that some tasks can be performed simultaneously.

To efficiently utilize your resources, you must determine the critical points in the project's progress. Managerial techniques available to you include Gantt charts (with milestone charts) and networks (such as PERT and CPM).

Program evaluation and review technique (known as PERT) is a project management system using three time estimates to schedule and control large projects. The critical path method (referred to as CPM) is a network technique to manage complex projects. Both PERT and CPM are discussed in more detail in the next section on controlling a project.

PROCEED WITH CAUTION

The project stages are not meant to be linear. You may need to plan, implement, and return to planning. Scheduling may indicate the need for revised planning.

The Gantt chart is a graphical depiction of the progress of your projects. It was developed by Henry Gantt, an industrial engineer who focused on productivity increases. Each task or activity on the chart is represented as a bar drawn horizontally across a time line. The chart shows when an activity starts and stops (the length of time). This enables delays and problems to be readily recognized. You can view overlapping activities (where resources are committed to more than one activity at a time).

Activities are listed vertically (along the y-axis) in chronological order. Time is denoted horizontally (along the x-axis). As the activity is conducted, the bar is filled in. The chart then enables you to see where the project activities should be and where they actually are. The bar chart summary provides an overview that helps you coordinate your resources.

The Gantt chart is popular for its simplicity to use, its low cost, and its visual depiction of progress at a glance. A Gantt chart can be hung up for everyone to see. This keeps everyone informed. The disadvantage is that the interrelatedness of activities and the sequential nature of those activities are not depicted. Instead, activities are denoted in an independent fashion without regard to which activity comes first.

The most popular tools used in the project scheduling stage include time and cost estimates, budgets, cash flow charts, and personnel charts. These tools assist you in scheduling your people and resources. Computer methods are gaining in popularity. They assist you in processing more data and doing so more quickly.

Scheduling requires updating and revising on a continual basis. You are then able to address obstacles and develop contingency plans.

PHASE III: CONTROLLING

Project controlling involves monitoring the progress of the project. It is essential that regular reports are generated and meetings are held. This enables you and the project team to evaluate the results and revise schedules as necessary.

The program evaluation and review technique (commonly referred to as PERT) and critical path method (known as CPM) are two project management techniques using networks to measure the progress of a project. The Navy developed PERT in the late 1950s to manage the development of the Polaris Missile. Remington Rand and DuPont developed CPM during the same time to use in the chemical industry. Both have been computerized and generate numerous valuable reports for monitoring the project's progress.

JUST A MINUTE

Numerous software programs are available with computerized project networks. Some of these include Primavera System's Sure Trak, MicroSoft Project, and VisiSchedule. EProject Express provides a Web-based option. Most of these software programs generate valuable reports to assist you in controlling projects.

Both PERT and CPM develop networks and use the critical path. That is, they use the longest time to complete an activity within the project. The key is to add up the time through the network. The longest route to completion is the critical path. This helps to identify tasks that need to be monitored the most closely and helps to identify where the slack in the project is. The slack is your opportunity to reduce project time. The biggest disadvantage is that there is usually over-control of the critical path—to the point of excluding other activities in the project.

Monitoring the project is all about measuring actual performance against objectives—as planned in the initial phase. These control requirements must be determined and in place before the project begins. Resources, costs, and quality are monitored. The need for revisions and updating of the plan then becomes clear. You will know when it is necessary to take corrective action by monitoring the progress.

You can use management by exception—that is, pay attention to only those activities that are not within an acceptable range of deviation from the plan. This monitoring will also enable you to know when and how to shift resources to keep the project on schedule.

JUST A MINUTE

Enrolling in an Operations and Production Management course at your local college or university can be quite helpful in providing you with detailed knowledge of more complicated project management software programs. A review of linear programming will also be included. This is recommended if you are responsible for many complicated projects on an ongoing basis.

THE PEOPLE INVOLVED

To successfully complete a project, many people must be involved. No matter how good one individual is, an entire project cannot be pulled off without the help of many others participating in a number of different roles. Some of these critical roles include the project manager, the project sponsor, and the team members.

THE PROJECT MANAGER

The project manager oversees the project. This is generally a highly visible position. The project manager coordinates the project and the work of the team—providing direction. The team starts work long before the actual work begins—with the planning of the project.

While most effective project managers tend to be generalists, they must possess a wide range of skills and attributes. Some of these include the following:

- The ability to deal with complexity
- An orientation toward task completion
- Self-confident
- A good reputation with respect to credibility
- Decisive
- Strong interpersonal skills to bring people together
- Ability to see others' perspectives
- Ability to lead, influence, and inspire others
- Excellent communication skills
- Ability to empower others
- Good sense of humor
- Ability to deal with ambiguity

- Visionary
- Well-developed facilitation skills to handle conflict
- Courageous
- Good listening skills

Some of the responsibilities of the project manager include the following:

- Know what the project involves and how to put the plan into action.
- Interact and coordinate activities.
- Select members of the project team and keep them motivated.
- Prepare the plan using a top-down approach. First examine the big picture, then break it down into smaller activities.
- Anticipate problems and develop a contingency plan.
- Keep stakeholders informed and involved—especially the sponsor.
- Use both rational problem-solving and intuition.
- Manage the team members and the project.
- Prepare periodic reports and hold team meetings.
- Take the blame when things go wrong, yet share the credit when things go well.
- Monitor, monitor, monitor. Know how the project is progressing.

THE PROJECT SPONSOR

Each project generally has a sponsor. This is the person who initiated the project. You can usually consider the sponsor the project's primary support person.

PROCEED WITH CAUTION

 You must ensure that the project is not endangered if the sponsor should leave, be promoted, or transfer. A solid plan documenting the costs, the benefits, and the rationale for the project will help.

The project sponsor has a number of responsibilities in this critical role, complicated by the fact that the sponsor and the project manager do not generally have a direct reporting relationship. These responsibilities include the following:

- Having regular communication with the project manager (both formal and informal)
- Taking part in the planning process
- Approving the project definition
- Actively supporting the project manager and acting as a champion (serving as mentor in many cases)
- Conducting the final review of the project
- Terminating the project if necessary

You do, however, need other people to make your project a success. The various stakeholders must be involved early. You usually must solicit their assistance to get them involved.

THE PROJECT TEAM MEMBERS

As the team leader (and occasionally as the team sponsor), you must generate a list of possible team members to review. You should choose people with the right skill set and those who have a desire to work on the project, because these project team members must be committed. You also need people who will get along together to work effectively. Care must be taken to ensure that the members are skilled in multiple disciplines. Not only must attention be paid to technical skills, but business skills must be considered in the mix as well.

Putting together an effective project team takes special care and consideration. It requires that several roles must be filled—and not just technical roles. The functioning of the team and its health must be maintained and nurtured with team roles. While your project goal must be your ultimate benchmark, the skill set identified in the planning stage helps you to determine who should be invited to join the team.

There are no simplistic approaches. Choosing a project team is filled with complexities and uncertainties. Your careful planning, however, can reduce these variables.

The biggest mistake is selecting team members who are just like you. That is, picking people who have the similar skills, strengths, and personality. This means that they are also likely to possess the same shortcomings. Diversity is the key. Diverse talents, skills, and personalities are needed for successful projects.

Part of this diversity is achieved today by utilizing cross-functional teams. A member of the team is selected from marketing, human resources, finance, accounting, engineering, and operations. Another piece of the diversity puzzle is achieved by selecting individuals with different personalities. Each team will thrive and be more creative with different types of people on board. It helps to have an innovator, an organizer, a troubleshooter, a communicator, and a strategist.

Stagnation can be the kiss of death. The innovator can anticipate changes in the environment (both short- and long-term), and then act in creative ways to take advantage of these opportunities. This person can be thought of as the agent of change. This is the risk taker who is willing to push your team forward.

The organizer role ensures that the details are attended to. Usually the person who works behind the scenes to ensure that everything comes together at the right time and in the right way, this person is usually only missed when not there. The need for the organizer is not always recognized when all is going well. It is only when the details don't come together that the importance of this role is fully understood. The organizer role is especially critical when addressing a consistent level of quality.

The troubleshooter is helpful when unforeseen circumstances and crises arise. This is the person who thinks fast on his or her feet and also has a contingency plan ready.

Part of completing a project effectively is the public relations function. Each project team needs a communicator—for both internal and external communication. Messages must be relayed with the greatest clarity within the team and to those outside the team to garner support and minimize resistance.

A strategist is key to the effectiveness of the project team. This role should be filled by the project leader, but may have a backup within the ranks of the project team membership. These are the individuals who look beyond today. They know that the decisions they make today are positioning the project team for success tomorrow. This is the individual most comfortable with the planning stage of the project.

CLOSURE FOR THE PROJECT

Once the project is completed, the project team is disbanded. It is critical that the team experience closure because organizations are using more projects all the time. Project team members must have a positive experience to move comfortably and confidently into the next project.

Closure can be achieved with a final report and a final meeting for the project members. The Gestaltist psychologists suggest that that this closure is critical in any effort.

Part of completing the project is getting feedback from the project team members and thanking them for their contributions to the effort. Care must also be taken to ensure that members do not check out too early as they see the project winding down and the next project on the horizon. A reminder of the ending date can be helpful.

HOUR'S UP!

You will most likely have the responsibility of managing several projects throughout your career. The effective management of these projects can make (or break) your career. Check out these questions to see how much you learned about project management.

1. Delays in projects …
   a. Come with significant price tags.
   b. Don't really cost much because they are expected.
   c. Can always be avoided.
   d. Are only found in nonrepetitive projects.

2. The phases of projects …
   a. Begin with scheduling.
   b. Begin with planning.
   c. Begin with controlling.
   d. Begin with a feasibility study.

3. WBS …

    a. Is the process by which larger activities are broken down into smaller and smaller tasks.

    b. Is grouping activities together to shorten the project time.

    c. Is the process by which resource requirements are identified.

    d. None of the above.

4. Resource requirements include …

    a. Human resources.

    b. Financial resources.

    c. Materials, equipment, and facilities.

    d. All of the above.

5. Objectives identified …

    a. Are really constraints.

    b. Ignore time and cost.

    c. Must be measurable.

    d. Disregard the needs the project will meet.

6. The Gantt chart …

    a. Provides a pie chart of your project's progress.

    b. Provides a graphical depiction of the progress of your project.

    c. Fails to identify delays.

    d. Does not consider time.

7. Controlling the project …

    a. Involves monitoring the actual performance against the objectives.

    b. Involves monitoring, but not taking corrective action.

    c. Never requires a shifting of resources.

    d. Never uses management by exception.

8. The project sponsor …

    a. Is the person who initiated the project.

    b. Is generally one of the biggest supporters.

    c. Should be kept informed.

    d. All of the above.

QUIZ

9. When selecting project team members ...

   a. Avoid creating a cross-functional team.

   b. Avoid selecting people who are just like you.

   c. Avoid selecting innovators.

   d. Avoid selecting good communicators.

10. The project plan ...

    a. Should be strictly followed.

    b. Should be flexible to allow for change.

    c. Doesn't need to include resource requirements.

    d. Disregards cost considerations.

HOUR 7

The Basics of Process Development

CHAPTER SUMMARY

LESSON PLAN:

In this hour you will learn about ...

- The importance of quality.
- Methods of productivity improvement.
- Continuous process improvement.
- Three phases of process reengineering.
- Job design in managing processes.
- Understanding the role of change.
- Overcoming resistance to change.

Most organizations are concerned with productivity and efficiency. Increased productivity means higher profits for companies. This also means improved global competitiveness.

Productivity measures how efficient your organization (or your process) is. It involves comparing the outputs to inputs by generating a ratio. You are responsible for improving productivity in your organization. To increase productivity, you can increase output, reduce input, or a combination of the two.

Productivity problems in the United States have been blamed on poor management and an unwillingness to change. Contributing to the problem is a reduced propensity for risk, government regulation, and the declining work ethic of employees (resulting in poor-quality work).

QUALITY

Poor quality costs the company money; scrapped or reworked products come with a big price tag. The high quality of imports has also eaten into the U.S. market for many products. Consumer safety groups have brought quality to the forefront of public issues. Quality is not just the concern of manufacturing firms. It is everyone's concern, in every department or unit.

Many businesses today are using total quality control, an organization-wide commitment to quality. The program names may change through the years, but the message remains the same: Make it right the first time. Don't expect to inspect in quality.

Companies are using quality circles to help. These are work groups that meet regularly to improve productivity in their areas. Today, these quality circles are being replaced, in some cases, by employee involvement teams. The group members address specific product problems. Membership in these groups is usually by management appointment. Both circles require that members be trained through in-group processes.

PRODUCTIVITY

GO TO ▶
Refer to Hour 15, "Teamwork," for a detailed discussion of the group processes necessary for effective group functioning.

The lagging growth in productivity in the United States can be addressed in a number of ways. In your organization, you can combine some jobs, improve attendance, reduce accidents, reduce machinery breakdowns, and use preventive maintenance on equipment.

Some of the methods of productivity improvement used by organizations include robotics, just-in-time (JIT) inventory control, and computer-assisted manufacturing (CAM). Robotics uses computers to program repetitive tasks; JIT inventory control ensures that raw materials arrive when needed; computers link suppliers and companies; and CAM uses computers as an aid in manufacturing different products. With minor adjustments, customization of products is possible to better meet the needs of customers.

While most of the productivity literature has traditionally focused on the manufacturing (goods-producing) sector of the economy, the service industry can also enjoy productivity gains. While it is harder to automate and evaluate the quality of service, management still can be successful in achieving productivity gains. This is often achieved by breaking down the job and recognizing that productivity increases often come from the operations function (the "front line" people).

Employee productivity in service firms can be improved by ensuring that employees have the necessary skills, knowledge, and abilities to perform their jobs. Their attitudes will also impact the firms' performance—in terms of customer service and attention to detail on the job. The selection process, then, also becomes critical in these service firms.

To improve the productivity level of employees, consider the following tips:

- Upgrade the skills of your employees.
- Clearly articulate high standards so everyone knows what they are supposed to do.
- Motivate employees to improve productivity.
- Build in quality—don't expect to inspect it in later.
- Use good measurement tools to monitor performance.

CONTINUOUS PROCESS IMPROVEMENT

When making changes in processes, you may choose to engage in continuous process improvement or process reengineering. That is, you may choose to tinker to make minor adjustments or make dramatic changes for a major overhaul.

Continuous process improvement (CPI) focuses on incremental improvements. The emphasis is on making improvements on the current process over a long period of time, which results in less disruption to the work. It is critical that your entire workforce be trained in using CPI regularly. Process reengineering is used when CPI doesn't fill the need.

PROCESS REENGINEERING

Tinkering doesn't cut it any longer in every case. When your industry is undergoing significant change or when your organization is in a crisis situation, major change is in order. This requires reengineering, not CPI. If there is little top-management financial support and little support for people, CPI is the best choice.

Reengineering results in more widespread change with ripple effects felt throughout the organization. The change is more radical in nature. Reengineering usually involves restructuring and the use of cross-functional teams. The focus is on value-added activities and sharing information with more employees. Keep in mind, though, that 70 percent of reengineering efforts don't realize the desired outcome.

Most organizations today need frame-breaking change and major improvements. It requires that you re-think the way that work is performed. Reengineering is a major overhaul, requiring that you examine the process from scratch. This means that you have no regard for how the process was completed in the past. It is the redesign of processes to achieve improved performance. The end result of process reengineering is usually a change in the structure of the organization or job redesign.

A systematic approach to process reengineering includes three phases:

Phase I: Planning

Phase II: Designing

Phase III: Implementing

PHASE I: PLANNING

The planning stage involves identifying the processes to be reengineered, the needs of the customer, and the ideal end result of the process. The focus of the effort then becomes the gap between the current results and the ideal results.

In identifying the processes to be reengineered, benchmarking can be helpful. That is, learn what other companies are doing. Learn from the best practices and then adapt these to your own needs.

JUST A MINUTE

Benchmarking requires continuously raising the bar. As you benchmark against the best practices, by the time you implement these in your own organization, the best practices that you have observed have now very likely been improved—thereby raising the bar before you have even implemented the process yourself.

PHASE II: DESIGNING

The design stage is all about the actual change management. This is closing the gap between the ideal process and the current process. The success of the design involves getting input from those who will be impacted.

A new flow chart of the process must be created. When this new, ideal process is mapped out, you must identify what requirements are needed to support it (including the people, the technology, the equipment, and the finances).

People will always be impacted by the reengineering effort. The effort may change the way they do parts of their job, or even the way they do their entire job. The effort may also eliminate their job or some portion of it. It is critical, then, that you identify the current responsibilities for people in the old process as compared to their new responsibilities in the reengineered process.

You may need to create new job descriptions or even new organizational structures to ensure the success of the change effort. This must be addressed as an emotional issue.

The technology to be used in the reengineered process must be identified along with the way in which this technology will be used. Benchmarking can be very helpful in this regard. Knowing what others have done successfully prevents your reinventing the wheel. For example, if you know that headsets were successful in speeding the time of a competitor's fast-food drive-thru service, you might choose to adopt this technology in your firm. This reengineering process should include a consideration of the documents, office equipment, people, and computers.

A cost-benefit analysis must be conducted. Both tangible and intangible benefits should be included. Two of the major categories of costs and benefits are labor and equipment. Both ongoing and one-time items should be considered.

The change management plan indicates how the change will be implemented and the method by which your plan will be monitored. The plan should include a statement of why this process was reengineered with the driving forces and benefits.

PHASE III: IMPLEMENTING

Implementation can include a pilot or trial to test the change effort. This pilot will help identify any unanticipated problems. It provides an opportunity to evaluate the new process, make adjustments, standardize the new process, and evaluate the overall change effort's performance. Standardizing the process is establishing the new process as the normal way of doing things.

To use business process reengineering, you can't think about controlling the process and you can't worry about how things have always been done or worry about making mistakes. You can no longer have inefficiencies in business. And you can't build on these existing inefficiencies. You must eliminate these tasks. Bottom line: You must ask if the process is even required today.

JOB DESIGN

Developing processes within the organization requires an understanding of job design. Job design is the process of determining the tasks that are to be performed within the organization and how they are to be arranged into jobs. This involves the specific identification of job tasks. This may even include a designation of machinery and equipment involved in the performance of the job. Job design must also include a consideration of the skills and abilities of the workforce. These job designs can be performed by time and motion experts, the employees themselves, or you, the manager.

Cross-functional integration is being utilized more today in some of the more progressive organizations. Jobs across functions are combined into one with cross-functional integration. This is thought to provide even more challenges for employees because they are learning more than one functional area of the company.

While technology has helped you increase efficiency in the workplace, it has also introduced new challenges. Ergonomics is the study of job design to fit the job to the worker. You are not looking to fit employees to the machine, but just the opposite.

An increasing amount of attention has been paid to computers in the workplace today. Workplace injuries related to computers have drastically increased with the growing use of computers. Repetitive motions at the keyboard have resulted in record incidents of carpal tunnel syndrome.

FYI A common cumulative trauma disorder (known as CTD) is carpal tunnel syndrome. Approximately one half of the workers' compensation cases in the United States are CTD-related.

Ergonomics has helped reduce the number of injuries by addressing the better fit of people to their computers and their workstations in general. Industrial engineers have paid particular attention to the placement of the keyboard, the chair height, and the screen positioning, to name just a few of the issues considered in ergonomically redesigning jobs using computers. Some companies have even revolutionized the design of the traditional office chair to better meet the ergonomic needs of office workers.

Inappropriate job design leads to worker complaints. This in turn results in lower productivity. It benefits both the organization and the individual employee to pay attention to job design.

The basic premise is that employee motivation can be improved by designing jobs that appeal more to your employees. The goal of scientific management was to design jobs to be performed in the one best way in order to maximize efficiency. Job design today focuses on both efficiency as well as ensuring that the job is an enjoyable one for employees to perform.

DESIGN CHOICES

When designing jobs, you have several major techniques to choose from. Depending upon the tasks and the employee, you may use job simplification, job enlargement, job rotation, and job enrichment.

Each presents advantages and disadvantages that you must understand when making your choice of job design.

JOB SIMPLIFICATION

Job simplification is the design choice used most frequently in mass manufacturing. This technique involves taking the large job of the organization and breaking it down into simplified tasks. Each of the smaller jobs then can be standardized.

This standardization enables the task to be performed more efficiently. This results in people performing the task repeatedly in the same way, which leads to the task being performed better over time. Ideas are also presented to improve job performance.

Job simplification has also been called job specialization. This is based on Adam Smith's concept of division of labor developed in 1776. An economist, Smith advocated breaking bigger jobs into smaller tasks that could be performed by many people.

The auto industry has capitalized on this job specialization with the assembly line. If each worker on the assembly line was responsible for making an entire automobile, it is unlikely that many would be produced even after one year's time. But by breaking the job of making an automobile into literally thousands of smaller jobs, production can reach approximately 1,000 in one, eight-hour shift.

Job simplification can be achieved in a number of ways. Simply changing the sequence of the tasks performed in a job can increase productivity and may even reduce some boredom.

Job simplification enables your employees to become very skilled at performing this task and to provide more suggestions for improvements—by very virtue of the fact that they perform this job repeatedly.

You must carefully weigh the advantages and disadvantages of job simplification. Employee satisfaction cannot be sacrificed for efficiency. It is possible to achieve both—with balance in designing jobs.

JOB ENLARGEMENT

Job enlargement is often referred to as *horizontal loading*. With job enlargement, employees can be offered the opportunity to combine two or more tasks into one job. This addresses the key disadvantage to job simplification—that of boredom. Adding additional tasks to the position may reduce the boredom of a routine job. Performing a variety of tasks helps combat boredom—at least in the short run.

The two tasks, however, have the same level of difficulty and responsibility (horizontally equivalent). You are adding a variety of tasks that are on the same level of challenge.

Generally, most companies have reported that employees experience less dissatisfaction and less boredom in the short term with job enlargement. You should, however, be aware of drawbacks to job enlargement. It generally costs more to train employees because they are performing multiple tasks now. Since no higher-level tasks are added, some boredom and dissatisfaction may be experienced.

JOB ROTATION

Job rotation is similar to job enlargement in that it addresses tasks on the same responsibility level. It differs in that job rotation doesn't combine the tasks at the same time. Instead, employees are asked to perform one task for a specified period of time, and then perform another task for another period of time. Employees are moved from job to job on a specified schedule. This schedule may involve daily, weekly, or monthly rotation.

The tendency might be to assume that workers will want more money to perform more tasks. According to Frederick Herzberg, if your employees are already being paid competitively, they will respond to the rewards of an enriched job. It is, however, up to you as the manager to help employees see that in today's competitive workplace, it is in their own best interests to acquire as many new skills as possible (without necessarily receiving pay increases every time). This keeps them marketable and employable.

FYI Research has supported the expectation that employees who are frequently rotated in jobs received promotions faster in the organization. Job rotation is important to career development.

Job rotation is an excellent technique to build worker skills. As organizations seek to build a workforce with broad-based skills, job rotation provides opportunities for cross training. More people in the organization will be able to perform a given task.

JOB ENRICHMENT

Job enrichment is an extension of Frederick Herzberg's two-factor theory of motivation. Author of *Work and the Nature of Man* in 1966, Herzberg studied 200 engineers and accountants to develop his two-factor theory. Just adding tasks of the same responsibility level will not motivate employees, according to Herzberg. Instead, you must add control and responsibility to the job. With more control over the job, the employee is likely to be more motivated. A higher-skill-level task will also increase motivational levels. For example, Volvo was one of the early, most widely publicized examples of job enrichment; they used teams of 20 workers to produce an automobile instead of an assembly line. Cars were moved from one team to another— cutting production time and increasing worker satisfaction.

The addition of responsibility to a job can provide challenge and motivation for employees. Unfortunately, job enrichment is not for everyone. This is not a universal motivational tool for every employee. Since personal characteristics vary from individual to individual, there are indeed employees who prefer to work without an enriched job.

Before enrichment can be addressed, you must ensure that the hygienes (those factors extrinsic to the work itself) have been sufficiently addressed. You can't even consider enriching a job without first ensuring that the hygienes (such as working conditions, safety on the job, company policy, or relationships with peers) are met. Otherwise, the efforts to enrich the job will be ineffective.

CHANGE

GO TO ▶
Refer to Hour 11, "Motivation," for a more complete discussion of motivators and hygienes in the two-factor theory of motivation as developed by Herzberg. This theory provides the foundation for job enrichment.

Change must be understood on both the individual and organizational level. Since organizations are collections of individuals, change on the individual level provides insight into understanding change on the organizational level. To effect organizational change, individuals within that organization must change.

A recurring theme of this book has been that change is here to stay. No business can operate exactly the same way today that it did just a decade ago. The business itself constantly changes, as do the industry and the world in which the business operates.

The impact of change is put in perspective when you realize that the source of most firms' competitive advantages will endure for less than 18 months. The time horizon for the "sustainable" competitive advantage continues to get shorter. It seems that less and less is truly sustainable over the long run.

A key component of effective management is knowing when to implement a change and how to implement it. It must also be understood that change extends beyond the intended area. As changes are made in one part of the organization, there are ripple effects felt in other parts of the organization.

THE CHANGE PROCESS

Kurt Lewin, a German social scientist, proposed a change process in 1952 suggesting that change occurs in three stages. This can be used to explain change on either the individual or the organizational level. The three stages are as follows:

Stage 1: Unfreezing

Stage 2: Change

Stage 3: Refreezing

The first stage is unfreezing. During this stage, the need for a change is recognized. You see that the current behaviors are not working. In the unfreezing stage, people are open to accepting new behaviors. Part of the unfreezing stage is demonstrating why the change is needed. At this stage you need to provide incentives for your employees to change. Employees need to see the benefits of the change.

During the change stage, the actual change is made. You are committed to trying new behaviors and changing your attitudes in this stage of the change process.

Refreezing is the final stage of change. The change must now be reinforced or instututed. This must become the "normal" way of doing things. At this stage, you must internalize the new behavior. The new behavior becomes habit now.

You can provide opportunities for your employees to practice the new behaviors. Make sure the organizational systems support the change (such as the reward and compensation systems).

RESISTANCE TO CHANGE

Resistance to change occurs when individuals are unwilling to make the change or in some cases, when they are unwilling to support the change effort. This is a very common occurrence in all organizations.

Resistance to change can take many forms. Only by understanding why people resist change can you better manage this resistance and successfully implement the change effort.

Some of the major reasons for resistance to change include …

- Fear of the unknown.
- Insecurity.
- Failure to see the need to change.
- Vested interests or self-interests are threatened.
- Working relationships change.

STRATEGIES TO OVERCOME RESISTANCE TO CHANGE

Managing change is a key component of effective management. Consider these general tips in managing change:

- Eliminate surprises. Tell people what is happening and give them time to process the change.

- Provide opportunities for employees to participate in the change design. This will help to reduce their fears because there will not be as much unknown.
- Explain the benefits of the change. Make sure that the people who are being impacted really understand the change.
- Have others who buy into the change talk with the resistors. This will help gain support. Demonstrate a positive attitude toward the change yourself.
- Provide rewards for those implementing the change effort. This also provides incentives for others to implement the change.
- Consider using trial periods to try out the change. This lets you phase in the change. You can make modifications and assess the effect of the change before full implementation. This is an opportunity to work out the kinks.
- Provide an opportunity for employees to discuss their fears about the change. Giving them an opportunity to express their feelings can smooth the way for a more effective implementation.
- Explore the reasons for the resistance. Try to gain an understanding of why people are resisting and the source of their resistance.

HOUR'S UP!

Developing processes and changing those processes is one of your ongoing responsibilities. Check out these 10 questions to see how much you learned about process development.

1. The primary message of total quality control is …
   a. Inspect in quality at all times.
   b. Make it right the first time.
   c. Zero defects when possible.
   d. Consumer groups will target you if quality is not your primary concern.

2. The productivity level of employees can be improved by …
   a. Upgrading employee skills.
   b. Clearly articulating high standards.
   c. Providing incentives and motivating.
   d. All of the above.

3. Continuous process improvement (CPI) …

    a. Is appropriate when your company is in a crisis situation.

    b. Results in widespread change.

    c. Focuses on incremental improvements.

    d. Is frame-breaking change.

4. Process reengineering …

    a. Results in a more radical change.

    b. Requires rethinking how you do everything.

    c. Uses benchmarking to identify best practices.

    d. All of the above.

5. When jobs are appropriately designed, the organization benefits with …

    a. Improved performance and productivity.

    b. More OSHA visits.

    c. Lower efficiency but happier employees.

    d. Lower efficiency but more enjoyable jobs.

6. Jobs are standardized with …

    a. Job rotation.

    b. Job simplification.

    c. Job enlargement.

    d. Job enrichment.

7. Job enrichment …

    a. Is referred to as horizontal loading.

    b. Is desired by everyone universally.

    c. Adds control and responsibility to the job.

    d. Involves adding tasks of the same responsibility level.

8. To effect organizational change …

    a. Individuals within that organization must change.

    b. You must dictate what should be done.

    c. You need not pay attention to the implementation.

    d. You must isolate the change effort from the rest of the organization.

9. All of the following are reasons why people resist change except …

    a. Fear of the unknown.

    b. Insecurity.

    c. Threatens vested interests.

    d. Don't want to keep doing things the same way they always been done.

10. Strategies to overcome resistance to change include …

    a. Eliminating surprises.

    b. Providing rewards for those implementing the change.

    c. Providing opportunities for employees to discuss their fears about the change.

    d. All of the above.

Hour 8
Relationship Management

CHAPTER SUMMARY

LESSON PLAN:
In this hour you will learn about ...

- Examining perception's role in understanding relationships.
- Understanding customer relationships.
- Managing the relationship with your boss.
- Developing relationships with your subordinates.
- Working with the marginal employee.
- Managing all relationships.

Now that you understand the context in which you manage, an understanding of individuals is in order. Effective management depends upon strong interpersonal skills to manage the many relationships.

At the heart of these skills is an understanding of individuals within and outside the organization. Human relations is more than common sense. It requires that you understand your behavior and the behavior of those with whom you interact.

Businesses have now become relationship-oriented. And these relationships are critical to the success of the organization. Managers occupy boundary-spanning positions responsible for developing relationships both internally and externally. These external relationships are established across organizational borders.

PERCEPTION

Perception is a key process in understanding relationships in the workplace. Everyone doesn't respond in the same manner to the world around them; perception is very subjective. Everyone picks and chooses different stimuli to pay attention to, and they interpret these stimuli differently. Perception is simply your interpretation of reality.

FYI Poor interpersonal skills have been cited as one of the top reasons for managerial failure in the early and middle stages of management careers.

Police officers are especially aware of the impact of perception. If a crime occurs and there are five eyewitnesses, there are likely to be five different accounts of the crime. It is highly unlikely that four witnesses are lying and only one is telling the truth. Rather, five people viewed the crime through their own perceptual lenses with five different perceptions of the event.

No two people view the world in exactly the same way. The lenses through which they view the world are different—resulting in different perceptions of reality. Effective relationships depend upon understanding these differences.

THE PERCEPTUAL PROCESS

The perceptual process is the processing of information from the world. This is the way that you decide which information to gather, how to organize it, and how to make sense of it. You use your five senses to perceive your world.

When you process information about others, the process is referred to as social perception. This is especially important to you. Because your managerial work is accomplished through others, the way you process information about the people you work with (and especially those who work for you) shapes the behaviors that your employees engage in.

Because you cannot possibly take into account and pay attention to everything, you use selective perception. Walking into a room full of people, you are able to process only some of the perceptual cues that bombard you. The rest of the stimuli are ignored.

PROCEED WITH CAUTION

 Each individual brings a unique set of personal characteristics and experiences to the perceptual process. As a result, everyone pays attention to a different set of perceptual cues. No two people view the world in exactly the same way as a result.

You may be accused of seeing only what you want to see, or hearing only what you want to hear. This may be true to a certain extent because everyone uses selective perception. Your beliefs and values influence the perceptual process and especially what stimuli you select to take into the process.

Those stimuli that are taken into the process must be organized and interpreted. That is, you assign meaning to these pieces of information. Interpretation may be influenced by your past experiences and your values.

PERCEPTION VS. REALITY

The world is really a distortion of reality that each individual builds upon. Your personal view of the world is your perception. This is generally not the reality of the world. Reality becomes nearly irrelevant in the perceptual process.

The behaviors you engage in are based on your perception of your environment. This places greater importance on perception rather than reality. Perception determines your actions and attitudes.

As you interact with others, you don't respond to the reality of a situation. You respond to your reality of the situation. You also respond to another person's perception of the situation because this is what is driving their behavior.

It would be easier if everyone perceived the world in the same way. Unfortunately, this is not the case. You, then, must become aware of the causes for these differences in perception. You can then more effectively manage your relationships and interactions with others.

PERCEPTUAL ERRORS

Due to the complexity of the perceptual process, you may easily misperceive others and the world around you. The first step toward avoiding committing these perceptual errors is to know what they are and how you may fall into their trap. Then you can work to avoid committing them. These errors include the following:

- The halo effect
- Selective perception
- Projection
- Contrast
- Stereotypes
- The self-fulfilling prophecy

The halo effect affects your ability to be objective in your perceptions of others. The halo effect occurs when you allow your perception of someone's performance in one area to flavor your perception of their performance across all other dimensions. This has been especially dangerous in the performance appraisal process.

GO TO ▶
Refer to Hour 12, "Managing Performance," for a more detailed discussion of the halo effect in the performance appraisal process.

Because you cannot pay attention to all the stimuli in your environment, you organize information in the way that makes the most sense to you. You have a unique lens or "psychological filter" through which you view your world. This also enables you to retrieve this information from memory.

Selective perception narrows the stimuli from your environment. Unfortunately, this creates problems because you may avoid some stimuli that should be taken into account.

You pay more attention to those stimuli that are consistent with what you think you already know. That is, you confirm your view of the world that you have already formed. You tend to screen out the information that may contradict your view of the world. This is the real danger of selective perception, because you need to do just the opposite to learn.

Projection is the tendency to project your own traits onto others. You may also project your own feelings onto others—thinking that others feel the same way about issues as you do. As a result of projection, you have the tendency to perceive others to be more like you than they really are. And of course, it makes everyone more comfortable with themselves to view the world more like others.

Contrast refers to the process of comparing characteristics recently encountered. This impacts the perceptual process by influencing what is perceived. The contrast effect occurs regularly in the interviewing process. When you interview an exceptionally outstanding applicant the next several applicants are readily compared to the first outstanding applicant. And, the subsequent applicants don't measure up well. They may be good applicants, but the recent comparison creates the perception of being a poorer applicant.

Stereotypes are the beliefs you hold that the members of specific groups share characteristics. Stereotypes, then, are generalizations. While you may realize that your stereotypes are not accurate, you still use them to help organize the information that you gather about your world and the people in it. Unfortunately, these may lead you to jump to conclusions. Appreciating the differences of a diverse workforce helps combat generalizing people with stereotypes.

The best defense against stereotypes is to directly address yours. You will increase your awareness of how you view others and be able to better avoid using them inappropriately.

Unfortunately, much of what you think you know about people is not accurate. And stereotypes are usually based on one single characteristic to label people. This certainly doesn't do people justice. The biases that you hold, then, interfere with your ability to accurately assess others and the world around you. Adding to the difficulty is the fact that stereotypes tend to be surprisingly resistant to change. People develop stereotypes and then hold fast to them.

The self-fulfilling prophecy is also known as the Pygmalion effect. It involves the idea that you get what you expect. Your expectations of others determine their behaviors. The self-fulfilling prophecy can be used to increase performance levels—or decrease them. Expectations of poor performance (whether accurate or not) can very likely lead to poor performance. But if you hold expectations that your employees can do more, it often causes them to perform at higher levels.

There has even been evidence that the IQs of students can be raised by as much as 25 points by communicating high expectations of their performance. The same can be expected of employees on the job in their task performance.

ATTRIBUTION

Attribution involves the assignment of causes of behavior to help interpret behavior. That is, you observe behavior and then you attribute that behavior to specific causes. You have one set of "rules" for assigning causes of others' behavior and another set of "rules" for assigning causes of your own behavior. This process is really a function of human nature.

When assessing the behavior of others, you underestimate internal causes in good situations. So when good things happen to another person, they are not explained by their skills and abilities, but rather by external causes—such as who they know or where they were. Behavior in poor situations, however, is explained by overestimating internal causes. They don't know as much—not that there was a situation external to them that had nothing to do with their abilities.

When assessing your own behavior, you reverse these underestimations and overestimations. You overestimate internal explanations for good performance and underestimate external explanations. Then when you experience poor performance, you overestimate external causes and underestimate internal causes.

If one of your co-workers is preparing a presentation on PowerPoint and is unable to get the software running properly, you are likely to think that the individual doesn't know enough about the software program or the computer to do this. If, on the other hand, you are making the presentation and cannot get the software running properly, you are likely to think that there is something wrong with the computer.

We reverse this thinking when there is a positive occurrence. If your peer comes to you and excitedly relates how a new promotion was just received, you think how the individual was just in the right place at the right time or somehow knew the right people to land that promotion. However, if you receive the promotion, you think that you got the promotion because you work hard and are smart (and you, no doubt, deserved it).

JUST A MINUTE

Attribution does not occur in Asian cultures in the same way that it does in the United States. For example, Japanese top managers have been known to stand up and take the blame for their organization's poor performance—suggesting that they are not good managers. American top managers are more likely to blame the poor performance on external environmental factors.

These errors are committed over and over. You just need to remember that these errors are alive and well. They are being used by everyone—in assessing your behavior and everyone else's. The key to managing relationships with others is to understand these errors, act on them, and try to avoid committing them yourself.

TRUST IN EVERY RELATIONSHIP

Trust is a critical ingredient in any and all relationships. The trust of employees generates loyalty and reduces turnover. The trust of customers can generate repeat business. The trust of your creditors can result in credit being extended. Trust also ensures that the company pays their bills on time and maintains their good relationship. Trust, then, is a critical resource to be nurtured in every relationship.

You must build relationships of trust by first extending it. You can't empower a workforce that you don't trust. But you must give people a reason to trust you. Without trust, there is no risk-taking and no innovation.

STAKEHOLDERS

Stakeholders are those groups that have a stake in your organization. These are generally the groups that your firm most closely interacts with. These include your stockholders (or owners), unions, the government, suppliers, creditors, customers, the competition, communities, and employees.

Each stakeholder wants something different from you and your organization. Stockholders (or owners) want dividends and a higher stock price. Unions want good working conditions and wages for their membership. The government wants you to follow the laws and regulations. Suppliers want you to buy their products and services and pay on time.

JUST A MINUTE

Partnering with suppliers and customers has become more important to organizations today as the focus turns to value-adding activities. These partnerships can be evolving relationships or formal strategic alliances. The key with either is to reduce the boundaries between the two over time. These relationships are more long-term than in the past. Some suppliers now even maintain offices at the customers' facilities to streamline operations.

Your creditors want you to pay them, while your customers want a high-quality product or service at a good price. Your community wants jobs for the local labor pool and wants your firm to contribute to the community in general. Your employees want a rewarding work environment.

All these stakeholder groups have different interests. Some of these interests may be conflicting with one another. While your shareholders expect a good return on their investment (known as wealth maximization), your customers want a good price—meaning less money for the shareholders.

PROCEED WITH CAUTION

Your competitors are a major stakeholder group that you must establish a relationship with. You must know them, know what they are doing, and what they are selling. It is important that you keep in mind that your competitors today may very well be your strategic partners tomorrow. A fine line must be walked to ensure the relationship stays positive. In addition, you must know your strategic group. These are the competitors that are most like you—with the same resources and the same general strategy.

Trade-offs, then, characterize these stakeholder groups. You are responsible for managing all these relationships effectively.

CUSTOMERS

The key is to retain the customers that you have. This means viewing each contact with the customer as an opportunity to continue and further this relationship. Finding new customers means additional costs in terms of marketing, sales, and advertising. The cost of attracting a new customer is five times the cost of retaining one. Establishing a relationship with your customers makes them more likely to stay with you.

PROCEED WITH CAUTION

The 80-20 rule is especially helpful in customer relationships. The key is to identify the 20 percent of your customers that generate 80 percent of your business.

You can't just make the customer aware of your product or service. It takes more. Customers have to want your product or service. There are a number of tips that can help you be more effective in building and maintaining relationships with your customers. Consider the following:

- Make sure that customer service is a core value of the organization's culture (starting with top management). Set the tone by being a good role model. That is, deliver excellent customer service yourself.
- Hire employees who demonstrate strong interpersonal skills and are outgoing.
- Convey to the customer that you know how important they are. Show you care and appreciate their business.
- Determine the level of customer service that customers consider superior—then try to beat that.
- Engage in continuous improvement of customer service. Deliver customer service training to employees. Don't assume that they will just pick it up.
- Reinforce customers' decisions after the sale to help them feel good about their choice.
- Contact your customers on a regular basis. Every contact with every customer is an opportunity to deliver superior service.

- Track your progress in customer contacts. Know when to quit your pursuit of a customer. It takes practice to know when it's time to quit.

- Use market research to really learn about your customers. Consider focus groups, public data, customer surveys, and test marketing.

- Don't try to be all things to all customers. Use niche marketing.

- Remember that the customer is always right. Be customer-focused. Know what the customer wants and deliver it.

- Don't be afraid to solicit feedback to find out what the customer wants. Customers can provide real insight into your business. Soliciting input and listening to it can provide innovative ideas. Keep your ear to the ground and watch buying trends.

- Reward good customer service. Walk the talk and put your money where your mouth is.

JUST A MINUTE

There is good news with dissatisfied customers. If their complaints are quickly resolved, 95 percent of them will become loyal customers.

Remember that you have both internal and external customers. Customers include anyone who receives your goods and services. Internal customers should be treated with the same respect as external customers. These internal customers are critical in the sequential interdependence of work.

INDEPENDENT CONTRACTORS, OUTSOURCING, AND ALTERNATIVE WORKERS

As businesses have concentrated more on their core competencies, noncritical functions have been outsourced. Consultants (also referred to as independent contractors) may be hired when expertise needed for the short term doesn't exist in-house. These functions may be performed by independent contractors. These relationships must be carefully managed to ensure success.

Don't assume that outsourcing is the key to reducing costs. Make sure that you don't make the process more complex (and ultimately more expensive) than it has to be. Specific demands will increase your costs. The two biggest problems are undermanaging and not effectively monitoring the relationship.

When possible, you should select the independent contractor yourself (to ensure compatibility exists between the two cultures). It is critical that you communicate your expectations (especially the service level expected) and measure his or her performance on an ongoing basis. Establish limits, deadlines, and penalties if the service level is not met. Make sure that you clearly articulate your vision.

You must also integrate the contractor into your own work unit—providing opportunities for the contractor to join in meetings with your unit and to interact with your employees. You must also stipulate the reports that you require and the time frames for those reports.

To help better manage irregular business volume, contingent workers are used. These workers may be called when needed (during peak business periods). These contingent workers may also be called contract workers (hired on a temporary basis for a specific project), leased employees, or temporary employees.

JUST A MINUTE

Temporary and leased employees are now no longer seen exclusively in the worker ranks. Now management positions are being filled by temporary and leased employees.

MANAGING YOUR BOSS

The relationship you have with your boss is critical to your performance in the organization. And there are certain steps you can take to ensure that you are effectively managing this important relationship. Consider these tips:

- Invest time to develop the relationship.
- Start to manage your relationship with your boss by knowing yourself, your style, and your own needs.
- View yourself from your boss's perspective.
- Know what your boss expects. You can't meet expectations that you don't know about. Also determine how your performance will be evaluated.
- Observe what your boss does; listen and ask questions to find out what your boss expects.

- Determine how you are going to meet those expectations. Be proactive—don't wait to be told what to do. Take the initiative.
- Support your boss—both privately and publicly. Be loyal, cooperative, and respectful to your superior.
- Find out what interests you and your boss share off the job. This can bring another dimension to the relationship.
- Develop trust. Trust must be mutual, so you must be trustworthy.
- Make sure your boss is always informed. Don't keep secrets.
- Accept criticism. Don't be defensive.
- Give credit to your boss. Be instrumental in increasing the visibility of your boss.
- Don't expect to get all the praise you need from your boss.
- Don't waste the boss's time. With many demands, you will not be viewed favorably if the time you take is not a good return on investment.

PROCEED WITH CAUTION

Check out the boss you will be working for before taking a new position. This relationship can make or break you. Know what you are getting into. If you think you can't work with this individual, don't take the position.

DEVELOPING SUBORDINATES

You have been reminded throughout this book that management is all about getting things done through others. As a manager, then, you are only as good as those with whom you surround yourself. You must carefully develop your subordinates. It is not just your employees' success that is at stake, but the organization's as well as your own.

FYI Personal qualities account for 85 percent of an employee's success while technical skills account for only 15 percent.

Developing employees can significantly increase productivity. People work at only about 65 percent of their capacity and use less than 25 percent of their brain capacity on the job. You can inspire people to give more—and much of this is accomplished through developing your employees. Your attitude toward your employees shapes their behavior. When you expect the best, you get the best. You can bring out the best in your employees by being committed to their development.

Once an organization has successfully recruited and selected its employees, they must be socialized into the organization. This is the process by which employees learn how you do things in your organization. This has been referred to as *acculturation*, that is, learning about the organizational culture.

GO TO ▷
Refer to Hour 17, "Organizational Culture," for a discussion of the role of organizational culture in orienting employees to the organization.

Formal orientation serves to further communicate the expectations you and your organization have of the new employee. Making these expectations clear makes it easier for the employee to perform well and to begin to identify with the organization.

The Marginal Employee

You will be faced with the dilemma of marginal employees many times in your career. These are employees whose contributions to the organization are considered marginal. They fail to fully meet the job requirements. Unfortunately, most managers choose not to deal with the issue (and hope that it will just go away).

Instead of going away, however, the problem festers and begins to infect all those surrounding the marginal employee. If an employee is truly not performing, they must be advised of their lack of performance. Otherwise, they may not know how to change their behavior.

PROCEED WITH CAUTION

The paternalistic relationship between the company and its employees is gone in most organizations. Some employees still yearn for these past cultures and have not made the transition to the new cultures that require contributions of employees on a regular basis. You must help employees adjust.

The decision for you is whether to salvage the marginal employee or to terminate their employment. There usually is no easy answer. It requires careful deliberation on your part to ensure that you do what is best for all parties concerned as well as for the organization.

You should consider the following factors when assessing the marginal employee:

- **Potential.** Does the employee have potential in the long term for your organization?

- **Input from others.** What have others said about the marginal employee's performance and behavior?
- **Attitude.** Does the marginal employee have a positive attitude about the job?
- **Absenteeism.** Is the employee missing an inordinate amount of time? This may indicate that he or she may have already begun his or her separation from the organization.
- **Skills.** Does the marginal employee possess skills that are highly valued by the organization?
- **History.** What is the past performance of the employee?

The employee must be kept informed of the situation. Sufficient detailed information must be provided to the employee. Soliciting the employee's input is a critical component. This is not a decision for you to make on your own, but rather with the input of the employee.

When the decision is made to salvage the marginal employee, follow-up meetings must be scheduled. The employee must clearly understand exactly what is expected and how the behavior will be monitored.

When the marginal employee cannot be saved, they should be terminated. Transferring the employee to another department is not acceptable. This almost never rectifies the situation, but rather exacerbates the problem. This transfer can be expensive and time-consuming for the organization. (Not to mention that you acquire a bad reputation for passing on your problems.) And it's unfair to the marginal employee, whose time has come to move on to another organization where there may be a better fit and an opportunity for them to truly contribute.

GO TO ▶
Refer to Hour 12 for a discussion of reinforcement strategies and how they shape behavior. A discussion of managing progressive discipline is also included.

JUST A MINUTE

The key is to avoid allowing marginal performers to develop in the organization. Creating an effective incentive system to reward good performers should prevent large numbers of employees from turning into marginal or low-performing employees.

TIPS FOR ALL RELATIONSHIPS

While there are details to pay attention to in specific relationships you have with various stakeholders, there are general guidelines to keep in mind for all relationships. You must not only be skilled technically, you must also have good human relations skills. That is, people must like you. Consider these tips:

- **Be positive.** Think and act optimistically.
- **Smile.** This communicates nonverbally that you are approachable.
- **Demonstrate concern for others.** Be sincere about this concern and be sensitive to others. (Remember that the world does not revolve around you.)
- **Engage in active listening.** Hear people out without interrupting. Draw people out.
- **Use empathy.** Make an effort to understand the feelings of others. Be open-minded about what you learn.
- **Celebrate others' successes.**
- **Show respect for others.** Be polite. Think about what you're doing and the impact of your actions. Avoid hurtful and offensive behaviors.
- **Ask for advice and input from others.**
- **Reserve judgment until you have all the information.** Avoid snap judgments.
- **Avoid complaining.**
- **Consider opinions and ideas that are different from your own.** Respect others' views. View criticism as an opportunity to make improvements.
- **Demonstrate a good sense of humor.** You will appear more approachable and likeable. Laugh at yourself.

JUST A MINUTE

Using people's names is a sign of respect. To better remember someone's, repeat it in talking to the person to ingrain it in your memory.

HOUR'S UP!

Recognizing that relationships are critical to management at all levels, review these questions to see what you've learned in this hour.

1. The perceptual process is important because …

   a. You don't know when you might be a police officer.

   b. Your managerial work is accomplished through others, and the way information is processed shapes their behaviors.

   c. You see only what you want to see.

   d. Everyone views the world in exactly the same way.

2. According to selective perception …

   a. You pay more attention to those stimuli that are consistent with what you think you already know.

   b. You pay more attention to those stimuli that are inconsistent with what you think you already know.

   c. You selectively project your own traits onto others.

   d. You selectively compare characteristics recently encountered.

3. The self-fulfilling prophecy …

   a. Is also known as the Pygmalion effect.

   b. Suggests that you get what you expect.

   c. Your expectations of others determine their behaviors.

   d. All of the above.

4. According to attribution …

   a. When assessing causes for your own good performance, you underestimate internal causes.

   b. When assessing causes for your own poor performance, you underestimate external causes.

   c. You use one set of rules in attributing the causes of your own performance and another set of rules for others.

   d. Your attributions are always accurate.

5. Managing stakeholder relationships …

   a. Is easy because everyone shares the same interests.

   b. Requires no trade-offs.

    c. Requires that you use trade-offs to balance conflicting interests.

    d. Simply requires that your company make everyone happy.

6. All of the following should be considered when managing relationships with customers except …

    a. Convey to the customer that they are not necessary to your business success.

    b. Contact your customers on a regular basis.

    c. Know when to quit in your pursuit of a customer.

    d. Remember that the customer is always right.

7. In managing your relationship with your boss …

    a. Guess at what is expected of you.

    b. Just do your best and don't worry about what is expected.

    c. Find out what your boss expects of you by observing, listening, and asking questions.

    d. Wait to let your boss tell you how to meet those expectations.

8. Managing your subordinates effectively …

    a. Can inspire your subordinates to give more.

    b. Means surrounding yourself with incompetent employees so you look better.

    c. Has no impact on your success.

    d. Means also addressing their development.

9. Marginal employees …

    a. Should be avoided at all costs and will go away.

    b. Must be kept informed of their performance.

    c. Don't hurt anyone.

    d. Won't impact the performance of others.

10. In all relationships, you should …

    a. Demonstrate concern for others.

    b. Consider opinions different from your own.

    c. Demonstrate a good sense of humor.

    d. All of the above.

QUIZ

HOUR 9
Managing Conflict

Conflict is inevitable when people come together. The potential for conflict is found everyday virtually everywhere. Conflict occurs when one person wants one outcome that will prevent others from getting the outcome that they want. As people are denied their desired outcomes, conflict results. This conflict can occur in varying degrees—being either minor or major.

IDENTIFYING CONFLICT IN ORGANIZATIONS

All organizations need some conflict. Optimal amount of conflict are needed to maintain the health of organizations. The problem, however, occurs when there is either too little or too much conflict. Therefore, you want to learn to manage conflict—not eliminate it.

Your organization needs the tension created with just the right amount of conflict. Unfortunately, if there is too much conflict, it is destructive to the organization and the people within it.

Conflict commonly occurs when people are not involved in change efforts in the organization.

FUNCTIONAL VS. DYSFUNCTIONAL CONFLICT

Conflict generally holds a negative connotation. Yet there are real benefits to be gained from optimal levels of conflict in the organization.

CHAPTER SUMMARY

LESSON PLAN:
In this hour you will learn about …

- Understanding organizational conflicts.
- Using win-win conflict management strategies.
- Finding success in conflict management.
- Discussing conflict issues.

Conflict can be either functional or dysfunctional. Dysfunctional conflict is usually emotional and involves destructive disagreement. This is more likely to be of a lose-lose nature.

When there is too little conflict, it is dysfunctional. People become complacent, and there is little or no creativity. Optimal amounts of conflict are needed for innovation. If groupthink is suspected (where conformity is stressed), you want to stimulate conflict. The key, then, is to stimulate functional conflict and resolve dysfunctional conflict.

GO TO ▶
Refer to Hour 14, "Groups," for a discussion of groupthink and the dangers it presents to creative solutions.

When there is too much conflict, it is also dysfunctional. When high levels of conflict are left unchecked in the organization, productivity decreases and hostility increases between people. The interaction and satisfaction of people are endangered with conflict that is not appropriately managed.

Energy is directed away from the work at hand and toward the conflict. More hostility is generally experienced. Energy is not focused on the work, and resources are not efficiently used. During high levels of conflict, anger tends to be focused on the individual instead of the issue at hand. Cooperation is diminished and trust is endangered. This is all destructive to the organization.

Having optimal levels of conflict (which is different for each organization) creates benefits for the organization. Healthy disagreement is actually good for the organization. This conflict is considered functional.

TYPES OF CONFLICT

There are many types of conflict that are experienced in organizations today. These types include the following:

- Interpersonal
- Intergroup
- Interorganizational
- Intrapersonal

Interpersonal conflict occurs between two or more individuals. Most of this interpersonal conflict is caused by personality clashes and a failure to communicate effectively. People have value differences that result in conflict. Conflict may also arise when people don't like each other, when no trust exists between the parties, or when there are differing perspectives. Even the very pyramid structure of the organization sets people up for conflict as they vie for the same promotions and resources in the organization.

Anger is at the heart of interpersonal conflict. You can't deny it, but rather must acknowledge it and recognize that it's not only okay, but healthy in reasonable amounts. As long as the involved parties don't act rashly on this anger, it is healthy. The parties must let their feelings out before they confront each other.

Intergroup conflict occurs between groups. The most common cause for intergroup conflict in organizations is scarce resources. When scarce resources must be allocated, it opens the door for conflict. The interdependence of tasks also sets the stage for conflict. In addition, incompatible goals have the potential to create conflict. When goals are mutually exclusive, conflict often results.

GO TO ▶
Refer to Hour 20, "Organizational Communication," for a discussion of effective communication and the barriers to effective communication.

JUST A MINUTE

Cross-functional teams help the organization manage conflict. The coordination needed for interdependent tasks is significantly enhanced.

Interorganizational conflict occurs between two or more organizations. While there is inherently a certain amount of conflict due to natural competition, this is conflict that is of a more serious nature and that goes beyond healthy competition. This interorganizational conflict may also occur between an organization and one or more environmental factors. That is, conflict can arise between an organization and its consumer groups, government agencies, or suppliers, to name just a few.

Intrapersonal conflict is conflict that occurs within an individual. This conflict can take many forms, including the following:

- Interrole
- Intrarole
- Person-role conflict

Interrole conflict occurs between different roles that one individual assumes. As you take on multiple roles, they will sometimes conflict with one another. That is, one role expects one thing of you while another role expects something else of you. As a business professional, your organizational role may expect you to work on a specific evening. As a parent, your child may expect you to attend a special school activity on that same evening.

Intrarole conflict occurs when inconsistent messages are sent concerning what is expected of you in a given role. Your superior may suggest to you that you need only work nominal overtime in your organizational role. Your superior's superior, however, may think this communicates lack of loyalty to the organization and actually expects you to work more overtime.

It is not uncommon for superiors and subordinates to send inconsistent messages concerning what is expected (from each of their perspectives) of your managerial role. Employees may expect to be supported while superiors may expect you to uphold the organizational view.

Person-role conflict occurs when the role of the individual is inconsistent with personal values. People often experience ethical dilemmas when the values expected in their organizational role are in conflict with their personal values.

CONFLICT MANAGEMENT: GETTING TO WIN-WIN

Conflict management is resolving conflict in positive ways. Three of the most common strategies for dealing with conflict involve framing the situation in terms of who "wins" (getting his or her way) and who "loses" (not getting his or her way). These strategies are referred to as the following:

- Win-lose
- Lose-lose
- Win-win

The win-lose strategy can be deceiving. The conflict is actually solved on the surface, but the party of the losing side of the equation isn't really satisfied. (Few people are actually satisfied with losing.) Over a period of time, resentment begins to build and as this surfaces, conflict is once again experienced.

 FYI The American culture tends to avoid conflict in general. The assumption is that conflict is not beneficial or healthy. Avoiding it actually involves actively removing oneself from the situation.

The win-lose strategy imposes a solution on the disputing parties, which sets someone up to lose. This strategy is not recommended unless there is an ongoing conflict that the parties themselves cannot resolve and that interferes with the actual work performance of the organization.

The lose-lose strategy is found in three different scenarios. These are as follows:

- There is a compromise by everyone involved. Each of the parties must give up something that they wanted.
- The parties involved use an arbitrator. The arbitrator then often suggests a solution that doesn't make either of the parties 100 percent happy.
- The parties are forced to stick to the rules with no room for flexibility. Both parties lose as the rules are strictly adhered to.

The lose-lose strategy is used when you need a speedy solution. In this case, there is generally not enough time for any negotiation. This strategy, however, presents a short-term remedy because it is focused only on a quick fix and not on the root cause.

Both the win-lose and lose-lose strategies set up the parties involved in the conflict for an adversarial relationship. Those involved tend to think in terms of winning and how much they are losing. The problem itself becomes almost secondary. There is seldom concern for the actual causes of the problem.

The win-win strategy addresses the root problem that is creating the conflict. The implementation of this strategy requires patience and flexibility on the part of the mediator. The key is to focus on identifying a solution that everyone can accept. Finding this win-win solution requires trust and the ability to listen. The parties cannot be competitive and focused on winning.

Win-win strategies are often depicted in terms of making the pie larger. Instead of fighting over how large each party's slice should be, the focus is on making the pie larger; then, everyone's slice is larger. This requires creative thinking and a move away from the concept of winning versus losing.

BEING SUCCESSFUL IN CONFLICT MANAGEMENT

As a manager, you spend an inordinate amount of time resolving conflict. Certain skills and abilities can make you more successful in dealing with conflict.

FYI Managers spend approximately 21 percent of their time or one day a week, dealing with conflict.

First and foremost, to be successful in conflict management, you must consider your attitude. You must keep a positive attitude. You must recognize that some conflict is actually beneficial for you, your employees, and your organization. Disagreement is healthy. In addition, you must keep your emotions in check. You cannot let your emotions rule the process. While it is recognized that anger is part of conflict resolution, it cannot be the primary emotion ruling the process.

You must be assertive to be successful in conflict management. That is, you must be able to stand up for yourself and your rights. Yet, at the same time, you cannot violate the rights of others.

The nonassertive individual (also referred to as the passive individual) lets other people's rights be more important than their own rights. This individual generally has little self-respect and is not as effective in conflict management. Moving to the other extreme, however, is just as ineffective. The aggressive individual violates the rights of others. They tend to think that their own rights take precedence over others. They focus on getting control at all costs.

Conflict management, then, requires many skills and abilities. Consider the following to more effectively manage conflict:

- Strive for a win-win solution. It takes more energy and creative thinking, but is more likely to address the root cause of the problem.
- Value everyone's viewpoint. Don't jump to conclusions, but hear everyone out and try to see each party's perspective of the conflict. It requires empathy to recognize everyone's ideas.

JUST A MINUTE

 Emotional intelligence (EQ) is needed even more than general intelligence today. This is the ability to control your own emotions and recognize emotions in others. As a manager, you need EQ to manage conflict.

- Be respectful of everyone involved. You should not let personalities influence you. Treat all parties with equal levels of respect.
- Consider personnel changes as a last resort. People can be transferred out of the conflict.

- Make a conscious choice on your part to cooperate. It is too easy to set up competitive situations. You are responsible for creating a cooperative environment with the parties.

- Exercise patience. Speedy solutions are usually not win-win outcomes. You must also exercise patience with all parties involved as they present their viewpoints.

- Part of being patient may require that you step back from the situation. Instead of rushing to judgment, it may be appropriate in some situations to gain perspective by stepping back. The process can then be restarted with a fresh view.

- Depersonalize the conflict. You must help the parties involved focus on the facts and be objective. You can be instrumental in helping the parties identify the points of agreement rather than focusing on the points of disagreement.

- Recognize that resolving conflict can be a very painful process for everyone involved. Feedback is an important part of the process of conflict resolution, but you and the other parties may not necessarily like this feedback.

When managing conflict, it is important to recognize that different conflict is created as a result of different power relationships within the organization. Understanding the power relationship may be the first step toward understanding the conflict.

PROCEED WITH CAUTION

Managing conflict is not the same as avoiding conflict. Rather, it is dealing with the conflict in a constructive way.

As the name indicates, the balance of power is even in even-power relationships. The parties involved in the conflict are at the same organizational level with equal power. The conflict is usually set up in a win-lose situation that you must restructure into a win-win situation.

A high-low power relationship is more difficult. One party is in a more powerful position than the other party. The balance is in favor of the more powerful individual, who is trying to control the other, less powerful one. Hierarchical differences often create resentment toward the authority figure.

The high-middle-low status relationship characterizes your managerial position. The middle party is being squeezed from both sides with increasing hostility from all sides.

DISCUSSING THE ISSUE

There are specific steps that you should consider when discussing the conflict issue. These are as follows:

GO TO ▶
Refer to Hour 4, "Managerial Decision-Making," for a more in-depth discussion of the rational problem solving model and the initial stage of problem identification.

1. Begin by defining the problem. Just as in the rational problem-solving model, it becomes critical to identify the cause (instead of the symptoms).

2. Gather information. This step identifies what is really involved in the situation. There is a fact-finding mission to shed light on the issue.

3. Present solutions. Brainstorming is important in this step to generate creative alternatives. This gets a lot of ideas on the table.

4. Identify what the goal is. It is critical that you be able to determine what the solution should achieve. Bottom line: You must know what is wanted by both parties.

5. Choose a solution. Starting at this step is a mistake that short-changes the process and creates the probability that the process will not be as successful. Selecting the solution requires that you keep in mind the goal. You then select the solution that is most feasible by narrowing down the alternatives that fit the goal.

6. Finally, implement the solution. This implementation also involves determining timetables, establishing measures for following up, or monitoring the implementation to ensure that the goal identified is achieved.

IDENTIFYING TECHNIQUES THAT ARE INEFFECTIVE

It can be very helpful for you to have knowledge of ineffective techniques for dealing with conflict. Learning from others' mistakes saves you from making the same mistake yourself.

Many times, people do nothing and just hope that the conflict will go away. Failing to take action will create frustration on the part of the involved parties.

A related strategy is stalling. Higher-level management may suggest that they are working on the issue in order to stall. Of course, when the involved parties find out the truth, resentment results.

GO TO ▶
Refer to Hour 14 for a more detailed discussion of how brainstorming is used in the decision-making process.

Another common strategy that is equally ineffective is keeping the issue that could create a conflict a secret. The hope is to keep the issue hidden from as many people as possible to avoid a possible conflict.

To direct attention from the real issue, some people in a conflict situation attack the character of the other party involved. Discrediting the person will then discredit his or her position.

PROCEED WITH CAUTION

While discrediting is a popular strategy for some people, it is not highly recommended. In some cases, if you try to discredit your opponent, you may be seen as the disreputable party—thereby harming your own position.

CONTROLLING CONFLICT

As a manager, you have a responsibility to help manage conflict before it gets to the stage of resolution. You can manage the environment that sets the stage for conflict and minimize the probability of conflict that must be resolved. This can be accomplished in a number of ways. It requires monitoring the organizational climate and watching for situations that are ripe for dysfunctional conflict.

By using creative methods, many times you can enlarge the resource pool. Because scarce resources and their allocation often open the door for conflict, you may manage the situation by making a larger resource pool or providing additional resources. Sometimes it can mean just transferring funds or reallocating the resources for which you have responsibility.

JUST A MINUTE

The role of integrator can be used as a liaison position. This neutral third party can help open up the communication between two departments in conflict.

Conflict is created as a result of interdependent tasks. You can improve the coordination of these interdependent tasks to minimize the possibility of conflict.

Developing superordinate goals alleviates the conflict created by competing goals. Instead of fighting over whose goals are achieved, both goals are set aside for a higher-order organizational goal. Both parties learn that they must work together to get anything—otherwise, a lose-lose situation could result. Focusing on a common goal creates the realization that both sides are more alike than originally thought.

One of the methods of controlling conflict is to pay particular attention to the fit of employee personalities. Personality testing can be used in the selection process. Care can also be taken when selecting team members and establishing work groups to ensure that fewer personality conflicts occur.

STIMULATING CONFLICT

Since organizations need some optimal level of conflict, it is possible that you may need to stimulate conflict in some situations. While conflict management is generally thought of in terms of diminishing the level of conflict, the flip side is equally important. Because some conflict is healthy for the organization, you must be able to stimulate conflict when sufficient levels are not present.

When stimulating conflict, you may need to set up competitive situations in order to create conflict. Many organizations use sales contests among units to stimulate this competition. Retailers frequently develop sales contests among stores to stimulate conflict.

PROCEED WITH CAUTION

Care must be taken when stimulating conflict. This conflict can cross the line and actually become destructive to the organization. When sales contests are used, they can easily get out of hand and generate dysfunctional levels of conflict.

Outsiders can be imported into the organization. This new blood often stimulates conflict and encourages new ideas and creativity.

Revising the way things are being done stimulates conflict. Changing procedures opens the door to challenging the status quo. Keeping things the same creates complacency, and can become dysfunctional as levels of conflict diminish to destructive levels.

Hour's Up!

As a significant amount of your time on the job is dedicated to conflict management, the principles learned in this hour can be very helpful. Review these questions to see what you've picked up about conflict management.

1. Conflicts occur …

   a. In only certain structured situations.

   b. When one person wants one outcome that will prevent others from getting the outcome they want.

   c. When people get their way.

   d. Only at high levels.

2. Your organization …

   a. Needs some conflict to maintain its health.

   b. Can never have too little conflict.

   c. Should work diligently to eliminate all conflict.

   d. Cannot benefit from conflict under any circumstances.

3. Interpersonal conflict …

   a. May be caused by personality clashes.

   b. May be caused by a failure to communicate effectively.

   c. May be caused by the very pyramid structure of the organization.

   d. All of the above.

4. Intrarole conflict …

   a. Results from conflict between two or more organizations.

   b. Occurs when inconsistent messages are sent concerning what is expected of you in a specific role.

   c. Results from multiple roles to which you aspire.

   d. Occurs when two or more groups are in conflict.

5. The win-win strategy …

   a. Can be easily implemented.

   b. Addresses the root problem that is creating the conflict.

   c. Doesn't require that everyone accept the solution.

   d. Is a short-term remedy.

6. To be successful in conflict management …

   a. You must keep a positive attitude.

   b. You must open up and be more emotional.

   c. You must be aggressive.

   d. You have to set aside the rights of others temporarily.

7. When discussing the issue creating a conflict …

   a. Try not to gather too much information to cloud the issue.

   b. Begin by defining the problem.

   c. Limit the solutions to speed the process.

   d. Avoid rational problem-solving.

8. When trying to control conflict …

   a. Watch for situations that are ripe for dysfunctional conflict.

   b. Enlarge resource pools when possible.

   c. Improve the coordination of interdependent tasks.

   d. All of the above.

9. Stimulating conflict …

   a. Is never necessary.

   b. May be necessary if not enough conflict is present in the organization.

   c. Cannot be accomplished by bringing in outsiders.

   d. Requires that the current status quo be maintained.

10. People avoid conflict …

   a. Because they are risk-takers.

   b. Because they are nonconformists.

   c. Because there is anxiety when confronting others.

   d. Because they know all conflict is unhealthy.

QUIZ

PART III

Managing People Effectively

Hour 10
Managing People

- Understanding the benefits of a diverse workforce.
- Effectively managing diversity.
- Accommodating people with disabilities.
- Avoiding sexual harassment pitfalls.
- Avoiding ineffective management styles.

It's not enough to have good technical skills. As a manager, you must be able to inspire people and create a supportive environment in which every individual has the opportunity to contribute his or her best. Because management is all about getting things done through others, managing people becomes a critical component of effective management. People are not predictable. So this further complicates an already complex process.

The new paradigm of management suggests that there is a partnership now between managers and employees. In this partnership, employees must be treated with respect and given responsibility. They want to be empowered and given an opportunity to buy in. You must get to know your employees and ask them what they think. Trust is the critical ingredient in managing people today.

Further complicating the process of managing people is the fact that people are so different. The workforce today is characterized by more diversity than ever before. This means that there is no one-size-fits-all management technique; instead, individual differences must be taken into account.

WORKPLACE DIVERSITY

Workplace diversity is one of the critical buzzwords being bandied about in management circles today. The Hudson Institute's report Workforce 2000, published in 1987, highlighted the demographic trends driving the move to the diverse workforce in America. Two of the trends identified were the increase in the number of women and the increase in the number of minorities projected in the workforce. The globalization of business with more people crossing borders also served as a driver to diversity.

FYI   Age discrimination, once thought to begin at age 50, now begins at 40.

The workforce in America is a reflection of the country's diverse population. The key today is no longer to make everyone fit the American mold, but to value differences. You must learn to utilize those differences to the fullest extent possible. You want to capitalize on the fact that people are different. Most important, you must be proactive in creating a positive work environment where everyone can utilize their skills and make valuable contributions.

Unfortunately, the term *diversity* carries different meanings for different people. Some suggest a narrow definition focusing on demographic differences found in today's workforce. Others suggest broader definitions, even including personality dimensions.

This broader definition of diversity suggests that it reflects all the differences among people. That is, you should consider all the characteristics that make each individual unique. Diversity is all about differences—all of these differences.

Surface-level diversity reflects the more observable differences that contribute to a diverse workforce. These characteristics include gender, age, race, ethnicity, and "able-bodiedness." These are also the characteristics that are most likely to lead to discrimination.

THE BENEFITS OF A DIVERSE WORKFORCE

No longer considered a soft issue, diversity can contribute to your organization's competitive position. Diversity is good business (in terms of social responsibility). And diversity certainly provides many opportunities for other benefits to the organization.

While diversity may be the right thing to do, the benefits derived by the organization go far beyond this. There are both hard and soft benefits to be derived from diversity.

A failure to effectively manage diversity costs your company money. Talented workers leave—adding to turnover costs and the costs of hiring new employees. Lawsuits may cost the firm money when employees are discriminated against. Lost productivity and missed opportunities negatively impact the bottom line.

The organization benefits from the differences of your workforce because each individual brings a unique perspective to the problem-solving process. Each person's lens through which they view problems is different—thanks to their unique personalities, personal experience, and cultural backgrounds. Heterogeneous groups produce better solutions—generating more varied and higher quality solutions to problems.

Turnover costs are generally established to be 90 percent of the employees' salary. With effective diversity management, companies can substantially trim their turnover costs. Generally, the turnover rate for women tends to be higher than for male employees.

Diversity management can improve these retention rates and thereby save the company considerable sums. For example, if just two of your female employees with salaries of $25,000 a year can be retained through diversity management, you could save $45,000 in turnover costs for your organization.

FYI It is estimated that companies lose two thirds of their discrimination cases with an average settlement of $600,000 per case.

Managing diversity effectively means fewer lawsuits—and lower costs. The effective management of diversity results in a greater awareness of differences and the skills required to ensure that more people are valued. This translates into fewer claims of discrimination.

As applicants seek their "employer of choice," those companies with a reputation for being diversity friendly are finding themselves attracting the most talented applicants. Diversity builds on itself. As your company becomes a diversity employer of choice, an even more diverse workforce will be attracted and retained—enabling the company to reap even more benefits from diversity and become even more diverse. This becomes a self-perpetuating cycle.

A diverse workforce helps the company understand and serve a diverse customer base as well. Diversity is good for business. A diverse workforce brings you greater understanding of diverse customer bases, and a better chance to gain access to these diverse consumer groups.

HOW TO MANAGE DIVERSITY

Managing diversity is really everyone's job. It is not just a responsibility for management. And it requires creativity and innovation. Many of the traditional mind-sets and ways of doing business must be reexamined and re-thought.

The key to managing diversity is recognizing these differences within a diverse workforce. You no longer want to fit each person (regardless of differences) into the "organizational man" mold. Today, you want to capitalize on these differences—including the fact that the organizational man today may be a woman.

Different doesn't mean inferior; it simply means different. You must, therefore, invest in getting to know each employee and his or her strengths in order to best utilize his or her talents. The first step is to learn more about your own biases. Your own insecurities often result in ineffectively managing diversity.

Larger numbers of immigrants from countries across the globe are coming to America for employment. This is creating a more diverse workforce than ever before. People don't leave their cultural differences at home when they accept a job in your organization. This places increasing pressure on you to manage this diverse workforce.

JUST A MINUTE

The term "cultural pluralism" has replaced the "melting pot" term to better reflect diversity in the American population.

And, the changing demographics within the United States are also impacting the workforce. America's population is aging. As the life expectancy of Americans increases, people are working for more years.

DIVERSITY TRAINING

There are two major types of diversity training: awareness and skills-based. Awareness training provides just what the name implies—an awareness of diversity. Employees receiving this training are educated in the issue of diversity. Skills-based training provides employees with the skills needed to manage a diverse workforce and work effectively in that workforce.

While you are learning about the cultures of your employees, you may also recommend courses at local colleges to help them. Introductory management or organizational behavior courses can assist them in learning about acceptable practices in American business. Your company may also consider an in-house course if your workforce is particularly diverse. These courses should only be used to improve employees' awareness of customs for doing business in America. The idea is not to rob an employee of his or her culture.

GO TO ▶
Refer to Hour 3, "The Global Environment," for a basic discussion of culture and the different dimensions of culture to help you better understand about cultural differences. Tips are also offered on doing business in different cultures.

JUST A MINUTE

You should no longer try to assimilate people into the dominant culture. This runs counter to the whole concept of diversity management.

You might consider a diversity audit. Just as a financial audit would be used in the firm, the diversity audit gives you an opportunity to measure your company's performance in regards to diversity. You are also able to measure the effectiveness of your diversity training. Even if your company does not utilize this audit organization-wide, you can conduct one in your own unit.

A diversity audit can be performed by the human resource department, by an outside consultant, or by you. The key is to evaluate your organization's (or your unit's) position on diversity. The audit might be performed with focus groups, surveys, or interviews with people in the organization. You are trying to determine if the necessary training is in place to provide opportunities to women, minorities, and other protected classes. You also want to identify networking and mentoring programs that might assist a diverse population. And finally, you should ensure that diversity training is offered to every employee on all organizational levels. This audit, then, helps you to better understand what your organization (or your unit) is doing to manage diversity.

PEOPLE WITH DISABILITIES

People with disabilities were an untapped labor pool for many years. In recent years with more legislation addressing those with disabilities, America has begun to tap into this talented labor pool. Companies are now making reasonable accommodations for people with disabilities and are reaping the benefits. But this labor pool is still being underutilized.

The Americans with Disabilities Act (referred to as ADA) was passed in 1990. According to the law's definition of disability, 20 percent of Americans have a disability. The ADA prohibits companies from discriminating against individuals with disabilities. Furthermore, companies are required to provide reasonable accommodations for those with disabilities. Surprisingly enough, a large number of employers have indicated that the cost of these reasonable accommodations is often less than $100.

Accommodations can be revisions in procedures being used (that actually cost the company nothing). Sometimes it may mean altering work hours for an employee who must take public transportation. Or perhaps the equipment used on the job can be adjusted—such as a lowered counter. Almost 70 percent of the reasonable accommodations necessary to hire a person with a disability cost the company under $500.

FYI Estimates have suggested that there are as many as 36 million people with disabilities employed in the American workforce.

Nearly three quarters of those people with severe disabilities are unemployed. When employed, the talents of people with disabilities are not being utilized. They are still under-employed. Even with ADA, the unemployment rate for Americans with disabilities has not budged from its 1991 level of just under 70 percent. Many people with disabilities are forced to take part-time positions or positions with lower salaries just to get employment.

Ironically enough, it is the employers' negative stereotypes and discomfort concerning people with disabilities that prolong this underutilization. As with most diversity issues, the key once again is awareness. You must be aware of your stereotypes and your prejudices to be able to address them and reeducate yourself and your employees.

A Special Challenge: Sexual Harassment

Nearly one third of the Fortune 500 companies have already been involved in sexual harassment lawsuits. Each of these lawsuits is said to have cost the company approximately $7 million in related losses. This amount is in addition to the costs of litigation itself. These claims are only growing. The years between 1990 and 1996 saw an increase of 150 percent in sexual harassment claims.

Unfortunately, there has been a disparity between the number of women entering the workforce and a corresponding sensitivity of men in dealing with those women.

Well-publicized lawsuits have made American companies think more about their own approach to sexual harassment. The Anita Hill-Clarence Thomas hearings in 1991 brought this issue to the forefront of American businesses' agendas.

JUST A MINUTE

Employment Practices Liability Insurance enables your company to purchase insurance to cover you in claims of discrimination and harassment.

The concept of sexual harassment is much broader today than originally perceived. Victims are not just females. Males can be sexually harassed. And today, same-sex harassment is an issue to be considered.

The presence of any one of the following conditions is cited as necessary for sexual harassment:

- Where activities of a sexual nature are a condition of employment
- Where activities of a sexual nature have consequences for employment (such as termination, promotion, or demotion)
- Where activities of a sexual nature create a hostile work environment

It is the third of these conditions that has been the most difficult to manage. The first two conditions are referred to as quid pro quo. This is known as an exchange of favors. The third condition is known as environmental harassment and has been defined by the Equal Employment Opportunities Commission as follows:

"Unwelcome sexual advances, requests for sexual favors, and other verbal or physical conduct of a sexual nature constitute sexual harassment when

… such conduct has the purpose or effect of unreasonably interfering with an individual's work performance or creating an intimidating, hostile, or offensive working environment."

It is the responsibility of the firm to educate employees and monitor their behavior. The organization is held accountable for the actions of its employees. This message was clearly conveyed in the Supreme Court case of *Meritor Savings Bank v. Vinson*.

JUST A MINUTE

As the number of women in the workforce continues to increase, approaching half the total number of workers, their impact must be closely examined. Women are no longer short-term employees marking time, but are building careers and making valuable contributions in the workplace.

There is a clear recognition that unwritten policies that are "understood" are not sufficient in today's environment. Companies must have clearly written policies concerning sexual harassment. The EEOC has also suggested that failure to write a policy on sexual harassment places the company at a clear disadvantage when defending court actions.

Discrimination (of all types) is no longer just first generation (at the point of hiring), but now is also second generation (at the point of promotions and on-the-job). In all cases of discrimination, the company has the burden of proof. The company is responsible for sexual harassment committed by managers. The company, then, must quickly respond to investigate complaints of sexual harassment.

PROCEED WITH CAUTION

You are responsible not just for your own employees (and yourself), but others who you know are harassing employees (such as customers or suppliers). This is referred to by the courts as situations where you "should have known" and taken action to stop the situation.

To better protect yourself and your firm your company should …

- **Create a zero-tolerance policy.** Take a hard-line approach to offenders and clearly articulate this zero tolerance.
- **Develop a written policy.** The policy should include a simple definition of sexual harassment. This policy itself communicates that his or her offense is a serious issue for the company.

- **Develop a policy, but also ensure that it is clearly communicated and understood by all employees.** It is a good idea to include this policy in an employee handbook that employees sign upon receipt. Your company is then protected to a certain legal extent.

- **Provide an example of what is inappropriate.** Sometimes employees don't realize what behaviors they engage in until they see them acted out by someone else. Role plays can be especially helpful in providing these examples.

HOW TO AVOID MANAGING INEFFECTIVELY

While there is no one best way to manage, there are management mistakes that you want to avoid in developing a management style. You tend to develop an overall technique that characterizes your overall style.

On top of general management mistakes, there are management types that can be dangerous for you and your organization. Too often, managers fall into traps from which they cannot easily extricate themselves. The best approach is to learn how to avoid these pitfalls early in your management career.

GO TO ▶
Refer to Hour 1, "What Is Management?" for a detailed list of some of the management mistakes that you may want to avoid to be more effective in managing people.

THE MICROMANAGER

You've all witnessed the micromanager. But have you closely examined your own management style to ensure that you are not micromanaging your employees?

At the heart of the micromanager's behavior is a lack of trust. Those managers who micromanage often feel that no one else can do the job or no one else can do the job as well as they can. Therefore, they fail to delegate. And on those rare occasions when they do delegate, they dole out small pieces of a larger project and then check up at frequent intervals to ensure that the work is being completed exactly the way they want it done. They tend to communicate minute details of just how the work should be performed.

In today's work world, your employees generally want more autonomy. Knowledge able workers want to use the knowledge they have acquired. The micromanager leaves no room for autonomy—thus demoralizing the staff.

Additionally, the knowledge, skills, and abilities of the employees are not being utilized. So not only is the employee dissatisfied (and likely to leave the job), but the micromanager is losing the opportunity to implement improvements, and the company is losing as well. The organization loses the untapped potential of the employee and productivity from the micromanager.

The micromanager loses the opportunity to take on other responsibilities and is likely to miss out on promotions. Doing your subordinates' jobs means you can't take on higher-level tasks. It also means you are probably not learning new things.

Micromanaging is ineffective, inefficient, and less productive. The micromanager is certainly not concerned with employee satisfaction (half of the dual track of effective management). Time spent over managing the employees is inefficient. And the micromanager will not be as productive as possible because time is invested doing and/or supervising lower-level work instead of performing the true management tasks that cannot be delegated.

AVOID BEING A MICROMANAGER

Because a lack of trust lies at the root of the micromanaging personality, the best strategy is to develop trust in people—especially those who work for you. Some of the ways this can be done include …

- Getting to know the people who work for you.
- Knowing their strengths and weaknesses.
- Delegating based on those strengths and weaknesses.
- Getting your employees the training they need.
- Knowing what the position requires and hiring good people.
- Picking your replacement and beginning training immediately.
- Letting go and realizing you don't have to do everything yourself.

Effective delegation means accepting the risks that accompany it. You may not get exactly the results you expected, but you must accept them and accept the mistakes.

Delegation means being willing to let employees make mistakes. This helps employees learn and develop into better, more productive employees. It takes a strong, confident manager to delegate and let mistakes happen.

THE LAZY MANAGER

As a manager, you are a constant role model for your employees. The lazy manager sends numerous nonverbal messages to the staff—all of which result in poor task performance and poor levels of employee satisfaction.

The lazy manager tends to over delegate—to have time to do nothing. This often results in a staff that is overworked. Employees gripe, "This isn't my job," or "This isn't in my job description." The quality of the work performed in this unit is generally very poor. Those employees doing the work for a lazy manager usually lack the appropriate skills and training to perform the job correctly. And, the lazy manager doesn't take the time to provide this training.

JUST A MINUTE

Procrastination often is the result when you wait for the "right" time. You tend to evade and avoid problems. This causes you to be reactive (instead of proactive) and may be perceived as laziness.

The employees of a lazy manager receive a message loud and clear that they too, can be lazy. If staff members perceive that a manager is surviving in the organization with a poor work ethic, they will question why they should work hard. The longer they work for a lazy manager, the more likely they are to come to the realization that they, too, can "get away with it."

AVOID BEING A LAZY MANAGER

The lazy manager often is a poor planner with few, if any, goals. To avoid becoming a lazy manager …

- Always have a to do list.
- Include short- and long-range projects with time frames.
- Develop a good work ethic.
- Try to model the behavior of other "good" managers.
- Plan for your next job—by working to get there.
- Remember that you are constantly "on" and being evaluated.

THE POWER-HAPPY MANAGER

The power-happy manager abuses the legitimate authority found in the organizational position that they occupy. This is generally seen in new managers who have not learned sensitivity in management.

The power-happy manager generally fails to understand the new workplace. Today's manager gets things done through other people—using interpersonal skills and personal power. The command-and-control manager who relied upon legitimate authority is disappearing from the organizational ranks. Those who abuse their power will soon become obsolete and find themselves unable to adjust to the current environment in which management operates.

The greatest damage done by the power-happy manager is to the relationships with people in the organization—and sometimes outside the organization as well. With the shift in the importance of power from position power to personal power, those who rely on (and abuse) the power they gain from their position will find that they alienate people. Those who are alienated are the same people who they need to get their work done tomorrow.

PROCEED WITH CAUTION

 The concern should be on results. Those managers that place more concern on being right commit a grave error.

The power-happy manager assumes the mentality of "do it because I said do it" and generally gives little reason for what is being directed. Employees are not only offended and thinking of how to gum up the works, but they are less likely to give 100 percent. The manager loses out when those closest to the work being performed fail to offer suggestions for improvement and deliver only what is minimally acceptable.

AVOID BEING A POWER-HAPPY MANAGER

GO TO ▶
Refer to Hour 18, "Organizational Politics and Power," for a detailed discussion of the types of power available to managers and how to successfully build a power base.

While power can be a heady experience, the abuse of power must be avoided at all costs. It only comes back to haunt you. To avoid becoming a power-happy manager, try to …

- Remember that power is more evenly distributed throughout the organization than what you may have thought.

- Think about your pre-management days and how you felt about power-happy managers.

- Consider that the trend is toward empowerment of all employees—not just you.
- Weigh getting ahead versus destroying relationships.
- Take a long-term view instead of being shortsighted. You need these people you are alienating.

HOUR'S UP!

A great deal of attention has been given to diversity in today's workforce. See if you have learned enough to now walk the talk.

1. Diversity ...
   a. Reflects all the differences among people in the workforce.
   b. Covers only demographic differences.
   c. Covers only personality differences.
   d. Is a management fad that won't last.

2. Surface-level diversity ...
   a. Receives little attention.
   b. Isn't readily observable.
   c. Reflects only ethnic differences.
   d. Refers to the observable differences that contribute to diversity.

3. Benefits of diversity include ...
   a. Improved retention rates.
   b. Decreased turnover costs.
   c. Access to diverse consumer bases.
   d. All of the above.

4. The key to managing diversity is ...
   a. Ignoring differences.
   b. Capitalizing on differences.
   c. Assimilating everyone into the dominant culture.
   d. Determining which culture is superior.

5. Diversity training ...
   a. Can include awareness programs.
   b. Can include skills-based training.

    c. Helps better manage diversity.

    d. All of the above.

6. The Americans with Disabilities Act (ADA) …

    a. Prohibits companies with 15 or more employees from discriminating against people with disabilities.

    b. Has resulted in a significant change in employment rates.

    c. Has dispelled all negative stereotypes concerning people with disabilities.

    d. All of the above.

7. Which of the following conditions is necessary for sexual harassment?

    a. Activities of a sexual nature create a hostile work environment.

    b. The hiring of a female employee.

    c. The hiring of a male employee.

    d. All of the above.

8. To protect yourself and your firm with regard to sexual harassment …

    a. Create a zero-tolerance policy.

    b. Create a written policy.

    c. Provide examples of appropriate and inappropriate behavior.

    d. All of the above.

9. The best strategy to avoid micromanaging is to …

    a. Develop trust in people—especially those who work for you.

    b. Do everything yourself.

    c. Avoid delegating.

    d. Distance yourself from your employees.

10. The power-happy manager …

    a. Generally does not offend anyone.

    b. Assumes the mentality of "do it because I said do it."

    c. Relies on personal power bases.

    d. All of the above.

QUIZ

HOUR 11
Motivation

CHAPTER SUMMARY

LESSON PLAN:
In this hour you will learn about ...

- Using motivational theories.
- Identifying the needs that drive human behavior.
- Structuring rewards to meet those needs.
- Influencing employee behavior with positive assumptions.
- Understanding the social comparisons that employees make.
- Using money as a motivator.

Motivation is a critical issue for you, and it is at the heart of your success. Because management is all about getting things done through others, the ability to get others to perform is critical. The workplace motivation that you are concerned with is the high level of performance that results in meeting (or exceeding) organizational objectives.

With downsizing and restructuring becoming commonplace in organizations, employee morale has been negatively impacted. Some have even gone so far as to suggest that employee morale is at a critical low point. This has made the motivation of the workforce even more important.

The old techniques of motivating no longer work in today's environment. The old hierarchy using command and control are not effective with the team concept. Providing one-size-fits-all rewards no longer works with a diverse workforce.

You must use sound concepts to more effectively motivate your employees. This begins with an understanding of how the motivation theories can be applied to better motivate your workforce. These theories can provide you with the motivational levers to pull in order to increase the motivation of your employees.

Motivation is not a personal characteristic that people possess. Rather, motivation varies as the situation changes. Your motivation and your employees' motivation will vary from situation to situation.

JUST A MINUTE

Research has indicated that the average employee works at only 60 percent of their capacity. Effective motivation techniques can improve this statistic by tapping into the 40 percent of unused potential.

Motivation refers to the processes that determine how much effort will be expended to perform the job. Motivation is a very complex issue, and people's behaviors are driven by more than one motive at a time.

PROCEED WITH CAUTION

No one motivational theory explains the behavior of all people. You need to understand as many theories as possible to use them with different people and to use them in combinations to be more effective.

Your organization must be productive to be globally competitive. This requires that each individual give 100 percent. The success of the organization depends upon the success of each individual within the organization. Motivation is a critical driver of organizational performance.

A lack of motivation costs the company money—in terms of lost productivity and missed opportunities. People are more inclined to deliver performance that is minimally acceptable. Some have even wondered today if Americans are still in search of excellence or if they are in search of mediocrity instead.

Motivation is a complex issue requiring an understanding of individuals. It is no longer answered with just money. In the past, a manager might be able to throw additional money at an employee to improve motivation. Money doesn't get the same mileage in today's workplace.

In the past, the motivation technique was a scare tactic. "Do it or else …" was the refrain of the command-and-control manager. That tactic no longer works in today's environment of empowerment and teams.

LEARNING FROM MOTIVATION THEORIES

No single theory captures the complexity of motivation in its entirety. You need to understand multiple theories, and then integrate them to get a more complete understanding of how to better motivate your employees.

The key is the application of these theories. It is important for you to be able to apply the concepts from the theories in order to structure rewards that better meet the motivational needs of your workforce. By learning what needs are likely to drive your employees' behavior, you will be more effective in selecting the rewards that will meet these needs.

While everyone is motivated, you want your employees to be motivated such that their performance goals are consistent with the organization's goals. The motivational theories help you to align individual and organizational goals.

Understanding these motivational theories also provides you with insight into yourself. You learn more about yourself and perhaps gain a better understanding of why you may do some of the things that you do. With an emphasis on self-management, this self-understanding becomes even more important.

MASLOW'S HIERARCHY OF NEEDS

Abraham Maslow was a clinical psychologist who developed a theory in 1943 to explain what drives human behavior. Referred to as the hierarchy of needs theory, he explained human behavior in terms of needs.

His theory's underlying premise is that people must have their needs met in order to function effectively. The fulfillment of needs suggests that there is tension within the individual that must be met. This is what drives human behavior. The needs that Maslow identified are ordered in a hierarchy:

- Physiological needs
- Safety needs
- Social needs
- Esteem needs
- Self-actualization needs

He suggested that human behavior is first motivated by basic physiological needs. That is, you need food, water, and air. These are basic biological needs. Providing your employees with a sufficient salary and breaks during their workday enables them to meet some of these basic physiological needs. Wellness programs also assist your employees in meeting these needs.

Once these needs are fulfilled, people are motivated by safety needs. This would include having a secure environment. You can provide fulfillment of these needs for your employees by offering them a safe work environment and some degree of job security.

Many of the benefits that companies offer work to fulfill the safety needs of employees. These include savings plans and profit sharing programs. There are many creative programs being offered now. Even outplacement services to assist laid-off employees can address the safety needs. These services can ease the pain of the layoff and fulfill some of the safety needs.

FYI The importance of Maslow's needs (i.e., the order he identified) may vary from culture to culture. For example, security is a higher level need in the Japanese culture than in the United States.

As this need is fulfilled, people progress up the pyramid to be motivated by social needs. Maslow also referred to this as belongingness. These reflect the need for affiliation and the need to have friends. Social aspects of the job become very important in the fulfillment of these needs—especially because people spend so many hours of their day on the job.

Your company's social events (such as holiday parties and the sports teams) provide opportunities for socialization. Getting to know people helps satiate the social need. Corporate sponsorship of some community events also provides an opportunity for employees to socialize while giving something back to the community.

As these needs are satiated, people are motivated by esteem needs. These needs involve gaining approval and status. You can help your employees fulfill these needs with recognition awards such as plaques, trophies, and certificates.

Recognition given to employees to address the fulfillment of esteem needs does not necessarily have to be big or expensive. You can be very creative while still fulfilling your employees' needs. This involves knowing each of your employees enough to understand what pushes his or her buttons and what he or she may value.

And finally, the need for self-actualization drives people's behavior. Self-actualization is the need to reach your full potential. In the words of the Armed Forces, this is "being all that you can be." This is the area where you can be the most creative. These rewards are most often nonmonetary and just require you to think about what people would value. You want to provide opportunities wherever possible, for employees to reach their full potential. Addressing the development of skills for your employees helps them to reach self-actualization.

While the first four needs can be fulfilled, the need for self-actualization cannot be fulfilled. Once you move toward your potential, you generally raise the bar and strive for even more. As people move up to the next level, these new needs become the dominant drivers of their behavior.

JUST A MINUTE

Maslow suggested that only a small percent of the population really is able to reach the level of self-actualization.

There are key points from Maslow that can help you better motivate your employees. You are provided with a good starting point in addressing the needs that drive your employees' behavior.

First, you should realize that each individual is unique. Each individual is motivated by a different set of needs. One of your employees may be fulfilling basic physiological needs (being right out of college with school loans and trying to get a place of their own). An older employee may be motivated by esteem. Therefore, what works to motivate one employee may very well be ineffective in motivating another employee.

Second, your employees' needs change over time. Maslow identified the frustration-regression component of the hierarchy of needs. That is, if you are motivated by a higher order need and the fulfillment is lost, you will regress back down the pyramid to the first level need that remains unfulfilled. You can change upward or downward over time—depending upon your situation. Your employees likewise change.

The key issue for organizations is to ensure that individual and organizational goals are aligned. This way, the individual effort expended to fill the individual needs also meets organizational objectives.

HERZBERG'S TWO-FACTOR THEORY

Frederick Herzberg developed the two-factor theory in 1959. His theory is also known as the motivator-hygiene theory. His theory's basic premise is that dissatisfaction and satisfaction are not opposite ends of a single continuum. Rather, the opposite of dissatisfaction is no dissatisfaction and the opposite of satisfaction is no satisfaction.

PROCEED WITH CAUTION

These theories of motivation are specific to the U.S. workforce. The research for these theories is based upon the American workforce. Any application of these theories across other cultures may require some adaptations.

The way to move an individual from dissatisfaction to no dissatisfaction is by utilizing *hygienes*. These are factors that are extrinsic to the work itself. Hygienes are factors concerning the environment within which the work is performed like the color of the walls, the temperature of the room, company policy, or the paving in the company parking lot.

Management generally uses hygienes inappropriately because they are referred to as the quick fixes. They are the factors that can be easily manipulated. Unfortunately, they are not the factors that can move your employees toward satisfaction. These factors simply placate employees, but do nothing to truly motivate them.

The key for management, then, is to ensure that the hygienes are sufficient. If they are not, employees will be dissatisfied. And before the real motivation can be addressed, employees must have sufficient hygienes so as not to be dissatisfied.

Instead, to move employees from no satisfaction to satisfaction, motivators must be used. These are the factors that are intrinsic to the work itself. Examples of motivators include more autonomy, opportunities for advancement, and more responsibility. These obviously take more of a commitment on your part to offer to employees. But these are the only factors that will move your employees toward satisfaction.

McGREGOR'S THEORY X AND THEORY Y

Douglas McGregor proposed that managers use one of two different assumptions concerning people. His theory is called the Theory X and Theory Y view of managers, which reflects these two different sets of assumptions. The key is that these two sets of assumptions influence the behavior of managers.

The Theory X view is the negative set of assumptions. The Theory X manager believes that people are lazy. This manager thinks that people must be forced to work because it does not come naturally to people.

The Theory Y view of people holds that people will look for responsibility. Theory Y managers believe that work comes naturally to people. These managers hold the view that people can control themselves. This is seen as the positive assumption about people.

Generally, Theory Y managers will have more motivated employees. That is not to say that there are not times when the Theory X manager can be effective when used in the appropriate situations. But today's workforce, as a general rule, seeks more challenging work and a more participative environment in which to work. This is more closely aligned with the assumptions of the Theory Y manager.

GO TO ▶
Refer to Hour 7, "The Basics of Process Development," for a discussion of how job enrichment is used. This job design technique builds upon the work of Herzberg.

McClelland's Learned Needs Theory

David McClelland's learned needs theory is also referred to as the acquired needs theory. According to the theory developed in the 1970s, needs are developed or learned over time. McClelland suggested that there are three needs that are important in the workplace. While all three are present in everyone, one need is dominant. These are the need for achievement, power, and affiliation.

The need for achievement is the drive to achieve. People who have a dominant need for achievement generally are seeking ways to improve the way things are done. These are individuals who like challenges and excel in competitive environments.

An employee that you identify as having a dominant need for achievement should be provided with challenging jobs with lots of feedback on his or her progress. And, you should keep giving him or her new responsibilities.

FYI McClelland's research suggested that only about 10 percent of the American population has a dominant need for achievement.

The need for power is the need to control others. Those people who have a dominant need for power like to be in charge of the situation and like to be in charge of others. Those with a dominant need for power tend to enjoy jobs with status.

If you believe that an employee has a dominant need for power, it is best to give him or her some control over his or her jobs. You should allow these types of employees to participate in decisions that impact them.

JUST A MINUTE

Generally, managers will have a dominant need for power. This is an important requirement in managing others.

The need for affiliation is the need to have close relationships with others. People who have a dominant need for affiliation want to be liked by others. They generally do not want to be the leader because they want to be one of the group.

Employees with a dominant need for affiliation should be assigned to teams. They are not as motivated working alone as they are working with others. You might also let them train new employees or act as mentors because this addresses more of their needs for this interaction that is dominant within them.

EQUITY THEORY

Equity theory is a social comparison theory that was developed in 1963 by J. Stacey Adams. The underlying premise of this theory is that people will correct inequities:

$$I \; ? \; I$$
$$O = O$$

The ratio of your inputs to outputs is compared to the ratio of another's inputs to outputs. You can compare your ratio to other employees with comparable positions. You might also compare your ratio (especially with regards to the output) to your organization's pay policies or past experience. It is also possible that you might perform your comparison with a standard instead of an actual person. Annual industry surveys can serve as the comparison.

Inputs involve all that you bring to the job. This includes your education, the hours you work, level of effort, experience, and general performance level. The output portion of the equation is generally measured in terms of the salary and benefits that you receive. Anything else that you get from the relationship is an output to include. In some cases this could include prestige, approval, and status.

Any inequities in the relationship will be corrected as soon as they are detected. The only variable that can be manipulated is your input. So if you believe that the relationship is not in balance and that the ratio of your inputs to outputs is greater than the ratio of the comparisons, you will work to bring the relationship back into equity by reducing your inputs.

You can correct inequities in a number of ways. You can make the correction by changing the perception of the inputs or outputs. You may somehow begin to rationalize your perception of the inequity. Because equity is a function of perception, it can be manipulated.

You may actually change your inputs or outputs, or get others to change their inputs or outputs. You might try to obtain a pay increase. You are also likely to change your inputs. You may minimize your inputs by increasing your absenteeism or performing at lower levels.

GO TO ▶
Refer to Hour 8, "Relationship Management," for a detailed discussion of the perceptual process.

You may choose to change the comparison person or standard. Or, you may remove yourself from the situation (such as quitting your job).

For example, keeping salary compensation secret in organizations often negatively impacts the company. As these social comparisons are made, people usually see others as making more money than they do; thus, creating an inequitable relationship that will be corrected by the employee giving less to the organization.

This inequity motivates people to restore equity. People will therefore alter their work effort (such as changing inputs) or they will change jobs.

The perception of fairness is critical in equity theory. It becomes critical that you reward high performers to maintain this perception of fairness. This is the underlying foundation of this theory.

EXPECTANCY THEORY

Expectancy theory is actually rooted in goal setting theory (which will be addressed in the next section). Developed by Victor Vroom in the 1960s, expectancy theory is comprised of three links. The major premise is that behavior is based upon the expectation that this behavior will lead to a specific reward and that reward is valued.

According to expectancy, you must decide how hard you have to work to get an upcoming promotion. Then you must decide if you can work at that level (to get that promotion). Finally, the third link is deciding how much you value that reward (the promotion).

All three pieces of this equation determine the level of effort that you are willing to expend. That is, all three determine your motivational level. What is particularly critical is the view of these three pieces as a multiplicative relationship. You can think of expectancy as the following equation:

$$M = E \times V \times I$$

Where:

M = Motivation	V = Valence
E = Expectancy	I = Instrumentality

Expectancy is your view of whether your efforts will lead to the required level of performance to enable you to get the reward. *Valence* is how valued the reward is. *Instrumentality* is your view of the link between the performance level and the reward. That is, whether you believe that if you do deliver the required performance, you will get the valued reward.

Because this is a multiplicative relationship, if any one of these links is zero, motivation will be zero. Therefore, it is important that you address all three links for your employees.

You must be clear about telling your employees what is expected of them. It is critical that you tie rewards to specific performances. You must also be careful to offer rewards that your employees will value. Rewards should address the employee's dominant need driving his or her behavior. Critical in this process is the employee's perception of his or her performance. Employees will become de-motivated when their performance does not produce the valued outcome.

You must be especially careful about building trust. Your employees must know that if they perform at the required level, you will follow through with the desired reward. Your credibility becomes a key component in this theory.

USING GOAL SETTING TO INCREASE INDIVIDUAL MOTIVATION AND PERFORMANCE

Goal setting has become critical in the motivation process. You must know how to set goals for yourself and how to work with your employees to set their goals. The process of goal setting is determining performance objectives, which guides future actions. Goals you set should be realistic, attainable, and specific. The type of goals you set will impact the behavior that results.

You always want to be specific in the goals that you set—whether for yourself or for others. Vague goals do not result in the best performance levels. It is only by specifying exactly what is to be done that high levels of performance can be reached. If you tell an employee to "do your best," he or she has no clear idea of what his or her performance should be.

JUST A MINUTE

Goal setting is based upon concepts from scientific management. According to Frederick Taylor, the father of scientific management, the setting of performance standards is critical to improving performance.

An example of a specific goal is to produce 10 percent more widgets each week for the next three months. This leaves little room for doubt. And more importantly, this is measurable. So when the three months are up, the production can be measured.

You must also be realistic in the goals set. These goals cannot be too high or too low. If goals are set too low, the performance that results will be extremely low. If goals are set too high, frustration results and performance is likely to be quite low again. Only realistic, obtainable goals result in higher performance levels.

People relax and tend to do what is minimally acceptable when given low goals. These goals often leave employees underutilized. They don't work to their full potential, believing that they have delivered what is expected of them. You can't set low goals and then hope that employees will exceed them. It just doesn't happen in most cases. You must decide what is realistic and attainable.

You must also give your employees feedback on their progress toward meeting their goals. Just as the example of the specific goal was measurable, you want to encourage your employees to likewise measure their progress. This way, you both know how the employee is doing in meeting his or her goal.

Using MBO (management by objectives) gains buy-in. If you sit down with your employees and set goals together, they will be more likely to own those goals. This will enhance their performance in working toward meeting those goals. Your employees tend to work harder toward the attainment of goals that they helped establish. They take ownership.

Determining the Role of Money in Motivating

GO TO ▶
Refer to Hour 12, "Managing Performance," for a discussion of the role of goal setting in the performance appraisal process.

Money is not the only motivator. In fact, money is not the prime motivator any longer. While in the past, money was used as the quick fix by management, today your employees want more than just money. Adam Smith, the economist, suggested in 1776 that the self-interest for monetary gain is the primary motivator of people. While some still adhere to this assumption, most researchers agree that money is not the primary motivator for most people. Job satisfaction has become more important today.

Many of the highly paid employees of Microsoft Corporation have served as prime examples of this. These people have remained exceptionally productive as a result of their job satisfaction—instead of additional money.

Herzberg suggested that money is a hygiene. That is, money is extrinsic to the work itself and does not really move people toward satisfaction. Instead, people are said to desire autonomy, challenging work, and more creative rewards.

JUST A MINUTE

In Eastern Europe, money is a more effective motivator for young workers than in the United States. The American workforce reflects the societal trend toward placing more value on noneconomic rewards.

The value of money as a motivator is generally in what it can buy. Once basic needs have been met, more money is not necessarily a primary motivator for people. There is also a symbolic meaning of money that can be the actual motivator rather than the money itself.

Hour's Up!

Effectively motivating others pays off in numerous ways for you and your organization. Check out these questions to see what you picked up about motivation in this hour.

1. Motivation …
    a. Is not a personal characteristic.
    b. Varies from situation to situation.
    c. Refers to the processes that determine how much effort will be expended to perform the job.
    d. All of the above.

2. Learning from motivation theories ...

   a. Means you pick one that answers most of your questions.

   b. Doesn't help in today's workplace.

   c. Requires that you integrate them to understand what drives your employees' behavior.

   d. All of the above.

3. Maslow's basic physiological needs can be met by ...

   a. Developing wellness programs.

   b. Offering a safe work environment.

   c. Scheduling lots of company picnics and parties.

   d. Giving employees recognition awards such as plaques.

4. Hygienes ...

   a. Simply placate employees, moving them from dissatisfaction to no dissatisfaction.

   b. Always motivate employees.

   c. Are intrinsic to the work itself.

   d. Are rarely seen as quick fixes.

5. Theory Y managers ...

   a. Let assumptions influence their behavior.

   b. Believe people will look for responsibility.

   c. Hold positive assumptions about people.

   d. All of the above.

6. According to the equity theory ...

   a. Your employees never compare themselves to others.

   b. Your employees will compare the ratio of their inputs and outputs to a fellow worker's ratio of inputs and outputs.

   c. Your employees only care about what is fair for them, regardless of what anyone else gets.

   d. Pay never enters the equation.

7. In applying expectancy theory ...

   a. You should be clear about your expectations of your employees.

   b. You must ensure that the rewards offered will be valued by your employees.

c. Rewards should address the employee's dominant need.

d. All of the above.

8. The goals you set should be …

   a. Specific and realistic.

   b. High and vague.

   c. Low and specific.

   d. Stated in terms of "do your best."

9. Money …

   a. Is still the prime motivator for all people.

   b. Is the only motivator for most people.

   c. Is no longer the prime motivator.

   d. Is intrinsic to the work itself and therefore an important motivator in Herzberg's terms.

10. Building a motivated environment …

   a. Requires flexibility.

   b. Requires creativity.

   c. Means moving beyond "one-size-fits-all" rewards.

   d. All of the above.

QUIZ

HOUR 12
Managing Performance

CHAPTER SUMMARY

LESSON PLAN:
In this hour you will learn about ...

- Understanding the role of the performance appraisal.
- Effectively conducting a performance appraisal.
- Identifying errors to avoid in evaluating performance.
- Using reinforcement strategies in shaping behavior.
- Rewarding employees.

Once you have a good understanding of how to motivate your employees, you must continue to manage their performance. Your employees are one of your organization's greatest resources. They continue, however, to be one of the most mismanaged resources in most organizations. The benefits to be gained from effective performance management are tremendous.

REVIEWING THE PERFORMANCE APPRAISAL

Feedback is a key component of the management of your employees' performance. As you learned from Hour 11, "Motivation," employees must be given constant feedback. This information tells them how they are progressing toward the attainment of their goals.

The most common formal tool used for this feedback in organizations today is the performance appraisal. The performance appraisal is the systematic evaluation of employee performance. Formal appraisals should not be the only tools used. You should still provide your employees with informal feedback concerning how they are doing.

The formal performance appraisal system usually spans a period of six months to one year. This is too long for employees to go without any feedback. The performance appraisal should be used in combination with informal feedback. Using this strategy ensures the results of the formal performance appraisal never come as a surprise to the employee.

Performance appraisals are utilized today for two major reasons: to provide feedback and for evaluation purposes.

 FYI While employees in the United States are usually willing to provide a rebuttal to their appraisal, Japanese employees are generally not comfortable with offering rebuttals. They tend to let the appraisal stand.

When the performance appraisal is used as feedback, it provides information concerning development needs. The coaching and training needs of employees are given specific attention. As a feedback mechanism, the key objective of the process is to give the employee feedback on current performance levels and address future development.

In addition, appraisals are used to make evaluative decisions concerning employees. Decisions about promotions, transfers, demotions, and terminations are made as a result of the information provided during the performance appraisal process. In addition, decisions about raises are tied to performance appraisals that are conducted for purposes of evaluation.

JUST A MINUTE

 More organizations are beginning to separate the performance appraisal process from pay increases. This places more emphasis on employees making adjustments to improve their performance rather than placing the focus of the process on money.

IDENTIFYING TYPES OF PERFORMANCE APPRAISAL SYSTEMS

There are two major categories of performance appraisal systems: comparative and absolute.

Comparative appraisals determine an employee's performance relative to others. These methods include ranking systems and forced distribution.

Ranking systems require that you rank order your employees relative to one another. That is, if you have 10 employees, you would rank them 1 through 10, denoting who is the highest performer. Unfortunately, this type of appraisal does not provide employees with a lot of information concerning their performance.

They know where they rank in comparison to their fellow workers. But, they do not know what kind of gap exists between them and the next higher ranking. To really effect change in the performance of your employees, they need to know what they are doing right and what needs to be corrected.

A ranking system does not provide them with the type of information they need to be able to make adjustments in their behaviors.

A forced distribution comparative appraisal requires that you "rate" a predetermined percentage of your employees in each ranking category. For example, the following forced distribution system might be used in an organization:

- Outstanding performance: 10 percent
- Above average performance: 20 percent
- Average (meets expectations) performance: 40 percent
- Below average performance: 20 percent
- Poor performance (unacceptable): 10 percent

You would then be required to fit your employees into this distribution. This distribution is once again relative to the performance of fellow employees.

The absolute methods include graphic rating scales and behaviorally anchored rating scales (BARS). These tend to be among the most popular of the performance appraisal methods used today.

The graphic rating scale utilizes a numerical scale to rate employees on several dimensions. You are generally required to provide some commentary to explain the numeric rating. For example, if you rated an employee an 8 on a scale of 1 to 10 for ability to complete projects on time, you would provide an explanation of why an 8 was given (as opposed to a 10). You might describe a project that was one day late along with a commentary on the usual timely performance citing specific projects and dates.

BARS tend to be a grander version of graphic rating scales. Instead of just providing numbers, each rating along the scale is given a description of the behaviors at different performance levels. While the BARS is a more expensive tool to develop, it provides more detailed feedback on employee performance.

The trend today is toward the 360-degree performance evaluation. No longer is the appraisal given exclusively by the immediate supervisor. This makes sense given that this is now an information society with knowledge workers. Too often, the direct supervisor is not as aware of the work of an employee as in the past. Feedback from others is a valuable contribution to the process.

Both employees and managers have a dislike of the performance appraisal process. Managers believe the process is too time consuming and that there are more important issues to address with their time. Many also believe that they are not good at delivering the performance appraisal. Training can help with this complaint.

As the 360-degree name implies, this appraisal is conducted by a full circle of people interacting with the employee. This includes the boss, subordinates (in the case of managers), customers or clients, suppliers, peers, and the employees themselves. This method provides a more complete picture of an employee's performance.

CONDUCTING THE APPRAISAL

It is not easy to conduct a performance appraisal. It requires good written communication skills and a keen ability to observe human behavior.

An effective performance appraisal also requires that you determine expectations in advance and identify how these will be measured. Thought has to be given even to the environment within which the appraisal is to be conducted.

GO TO ▶
Refer to Hour 7, "The Basics of Process Development," for a discussion of using job descriptions as criteria for the measurement of performance.

You want to ensure that you are familiar with your organization's appraisal form. Be sure to utilize the comments section to expand on any ratings that you give the employee. This is also your mechanism to "tailor" or customize the appraisal form to your employee's specific job—because most companies use the same form organization-wide across all job categories.

The performance appraisal is a critical document and should be written with a considerable amount of reflection. Set aside some quiet time to think about the employee's performance, and then actually compose the evaluation. You should keep notes on the employee's performance throughout the evaluation period so that you are not just trying to write the appraisal from memory.

Do not place any of these performance notes in the employee's personnel file. This could create a legal minefield. Anything placed in the personnel file becomes part of the employee's permanent file.

You should always provide details. Vague generalities do not tell the employee anything. Vague statements cannot be used to accomplish real behavior changes. They don't provide the employee with enough feedback. You should use your notes to cite specific dates and situations.

You must focus on behaviors. Personal attributes cannot be the focus of the appraisal. Citing specific incidents enables you to focus more on the behaviors rather than personal attributes. (This is also critical from a legal standpoint.)

The actual appraisal interview should be delivered in a quiet environment without interruptions. Calls and visitors should not be allowed to interrupt. Many companies have conference rooms where the interview can be conducted. Often times, your office allows for too many interruptions so another setting should be considered.

A sufficient amount of time should be allocated for the interview as well. Allotting too little time or just being "fit in," communicates that this is not as important to you as it should be. You should ensure that there is time for your employee to ask questions and discuss the appraisal with you.

You should use this interview to solicit feedback from your employee. Your employees should always be asked how they think their performance can be improved (even in the case of a good performer). This not only puts the ball in their court, it enables you to find out what they think and get their input. For those who are not performing well, you are allowing them to participate in outlining their improvement.

You should then ask them how you can assist them in meeting their performance goals. This forms a partnership with the two of you working together to improve performance. Each of you has a role in this improvement. This is especially important for poor performers to know that they are not in it alone, but that you are actively partnering with them.

JUST A MINUTE

The sandwich technique can be used effectively in delivering news of poor performance. You should start with a positive comment about the employee's performance; discuss areas for improvement, and then close with a positive comment. You must, however, be careful to ensure the employee hears the important areas for improvement.

The performance appraisal, while generally dreaded by most managers, should be viewed as a positive experience. You can gain valuable insights from your employees during this process and shape their work behaviors—if you manage effectively.

RECOGNIZING ERRORS TO AVOID

Just as it is human nature to fall prey to some perceptual errors, there are errors easily committed in the performance appraisal process. The best way to guard against these errors is to be aware that they exist and to know how they are committed.

The halo effect occurs as a direct result of the perceptual process. As you "rate" an employee on one dimension, you broad brush other dimensions with a similar ranking—whether accurate or not. For example, if you rate an employee high on interacting successfully with peers, you may erroneously rate them high across all dimensions on the performance appraisal. One dimension does make an appraisal.

GO TO ▶
Refer to Hour 8, "Relationship Management," for an in-depth discussion of the halo effect from the perspective of the perceptual process.

You can easily commit the "recency" error. This occurs when you remember what happened most recently with your employees. This is particularly critical with an annual performance appraisal.

Employees are astute enough to realize this aspect of managers as humans and use it to their advantage. There is often a yo-yo effect of employee performance. As the month or two before the appraisal approaches, the employee's behavior improves, and then this is what is remembered when the appraisal is written.

Once the appraisal process is over, the employee's behavior returns to the "normal" level. Then again, just before the next appraisal, the employee's performance improves. And, this cycle will continue as long as you base your appraisal on recent performance, rather than the entire period covered in the appraisal.

The leniency error occurs when you take what you believe to be the easy way out. Some believe that rating every employee leniently creates fewer problems. It really doesn't, but initially it seems easier than explaining performance differences to employees. In reality, it only creates more problems in the long run.

Leniency provides employees with high performance appraisal ratings for mediocre or marginal performance. This marginal performer is then "rewarded" in organizational terms. This will increase the likelihood that his or her marginal performance will continue—because they have no incentive to improve.

PROCEED WITH CAUTION

The leniency error creates morale problems as well. Those employees working at high performance levels become less motivated as they see there is little difference between their rewards and the rewards of those not working at the same high level.

The strictness error is the flip side of leniency. You rate everyone very strictly. While it is acceptable to maintain high standards, performance appraisals should be an accurate reflection of performance. Appraisals that are too strict will de-motivate employees and frustrate them. They will begin to think that no matter what they do, it will never enable them to achieve the rewards that they value.

REINFORCING EMPLOYEE BEHAVIOR

Reinforcement centers on the consequences that result from the behavior that is engaged in. The key as a manager is to reinforce the appropriate behaviors that your employees engage in. Equally important is to not reinforce inappropriate behaviors.

GO TO ▶
Refer to Hour 11 for a discussion of expectancy theory. According to this theory, you must reward employees for good performance and enable them to see that their performance will lead to the rewards that they value.

If you work late and your behavior (working late) is followed by your boss's praise, you will increase the probability that this behavior will be repeated. That is, once your boss praises you (a positive consequence), you are more likely to engage in this behavior again, that is, you are more likely to work late again when asked. If however, you work late and it is not even acknowledged (a negative consequence), then you are less likely to work late again when asked. The consequences that follow your behaviors shape your behavior.

REINFORCEMENT STRATEGIES

There are four main reinforcement strategies for you to use when reinforcing behavior. You can use the following:

- Positive reinforcement
- Negative reinforcement

- Punishment
- Extinction

Positive reinforcement occurs when positive consequences follow behavior. This ensures that the behavior will be repeated. To be effective, the positive consequences (also referred to as rewards) must be administered as soon as possible after the appropriate behavior. This ensures that the behavior is closely tied to the reward. There is no mistaking the connection between the behavior and the positive consequence. Positive reinforcement strengthens the behavior.

Also critical is another law that helps you better apply positive reinforcement. This is the law of contingent reinforcement. This law suggests that your employees have to actually engage in the appropriate behavior to receive the reward. While this may seem to be a given, in reality this is often misused.

Negative reinforcement is also referred to as avoidance. Not to be confused with punishment, negative reinforcement is used to get people to engage in appropriate behaviors by avoiding the negative consequences of not doing so.

You try to avoid your boss's criticism, being placed on probation, and termination. As a result of trying to avoid these negative consequences, you engage in appropriate behavior. With avoidance, it is the threat of punishment that is the source of control.

Punishment is used to decrease the probability that people will repeat undesirable or inappropriate behaviors. Punishment is the administration of unpleasant consequences when inappropriate behavior is engaged in.

There are, unfortunately, many reasons why punishment is not always the most effective of the reinforcement strategies. Most of the time punishment causes people to focus on the person administering the punishment—instead of the behaviors that need to be changed. This is a major consideration today with the rise in workplace violence. Resentment toward the punisher becomes the focus. In addition, those who are punished don't change their behavior permanently. It is usually just a temporary halt to the inappropriate behavior in order to remove the negative consequence.

You are cautioned against the overuse of punishment or the inappropriate use of this strategy. Whenever possible, one of the other reinforcement strategies should be used.

Extinction can be particularly effective when used in combination with positive reinforcement. Extinction approaches reinforcement from a little different perspective. The key with extinction is to remove whatever consequences are keeping the behavior in place.

An example may clarify this. If you reprimand an employee for inappropriate behavior in front of co-workers and they find this situation amusing, then joke with the employee—who enjoys the attention—you must remove the positive reinforcement (the co-workers' attention) to extinguish the behavior. You could achieve this by reprimanding the employee privately where others cannot witness the exchange.

JUST A MINUTE

Organizational behavior modification (referred to as OB Mod) is a program using the principles of conditioning to change behavior in the work place. It is based upon rewarding those behaviors that you want repeated and punishing those behaviors you do not want repeated.

REINFORCEMENT SCHEDULES

Reinforcement can be offered to employees continuously or intermittently. The choice of schedules can influence the effectiveness of managing behavior.

Continuous schedules provide for rewards to be offered continuously. That is, each and every instance of the behavior is rewarded. Each time an employee engages in the appropriate behavior, a positive consequence is administered. This can become very costly. Furthermore, as soon as the consequences are removed, the behavior will be extinguished.

Intermittent schedules provide rewards intermittently. The appropriate behaviors are rewarded, but on an intermittent basis. People do not know when these rewards will be delivered. Slot machines are a good example of intermittent schedules—no one knows when the payoff is coming. The behavior is continued (putting in the coins) in the hopes that the payoff will soon occur.

PROGRESSIVE DISCIPLINE

Part of managing your employees' performance is to administer discipline. Discipline does have an appropriate role in the shaping of behavior. Just as rewards are effective in motivating people, discipline, if used appropriately, can be equally effective.

Due to the increased litigation in the workplace today, you must ensure that you are careful in the administering of discipline. It is best to meticulously document everything. Should you be asked to recall any events, you can rely upon your documentation rather than your memory.

Discipline must be administered fairly and consistently. Each employee engaging in inappropriate behavior must be treated the same. And most important, each incident of a given behavior must be addressed.

The key to effective discipline is communicating the policy in advance. Employees must clearly understand what the policy is. This should be incorporated into the Employee Handbook distributed to all employees. It is critical that the disciplinary process be written and received by every employee. Employees are often asked to sign a statement that they have received their employee handbook. This is a measure of protection for the company should litigation arise. The company can then prove that they did indeed distribute the policy to the employees.

Employees may not like what happens to them as a result of engaging in inappropriate behavior, but they will perceive a measure of fairness if they understood the consequences up front. To spring a disciplinary action on an employee creates a feeling of unfairness—and rightly so.

Progressive discipline provides progressively harsher discipline for repeated instances of inappropriate behavior. The program begins with a verbal warning at the first infraction. It should be given calmly as an opportunity for the employee to correct the behavior before there are any serious consequences that result.

JUST A MINUTE

You must also consider the reason behind the poor performance of the employee. In some cases, the poor performance can be the result of a system within the organization and not the individual. Poor performance can be viewed (in some situations) as a symptom rather than as a root cause. You need to diagnose the situation.

The focus of the warning must be on behavior. The inappropriate behavior must be clearly discussed. Equally important, you must outline what the appropriate behavior is and reinforce this as the desired performance. In reshaping the employee's behavior, it is important that he or she be told what to do to replace his or her inappropriate behavior.

It also helps if you explain why you need the employee to change his or her behavior. They need to know that this is not merely whimsy on your part, but that a real purpose is served with the prescribed behavior. Discussing the interdependence of their work on others often helps in this respect. Sometimes people simply do not realize how their own behavior impacts others and the work of others.

If the inappropriate behavior continues, a written warning is the next step in progressive discipline. This warning must very specifically articulate what the inappropriate behavior is. This meeting should take place in a quiet environment that communicates the critical nature of the situation.

A key part of this warning must also include a follow-up plan of action with a statement of how the behavior will be monitored. There should be a specific date set for the follow-up. It is your responsibility to ensure at this point, that your employee knows exactly what the consequence of continuing this behavior will be. Any further disciplinary action should definitely not come as a surprise to the employee.

The employee should be asked to sign the warning. At the end of the discussion, your employee is given a copy and the original is placed in the employee's personnel file. Your employee can then refer to the warning as a reminder of the specifics. Every attempt should be made to end the discussion on a positive note with you indicating that you have every confidence that the behavior will be corrected.

Generally, if the behavior continues, another more serious written warning is issued. This warning stipulates that if the behavior continues, the employee faces termination. Again, a time frame is established with specific measures for monitoring the performance. It is a good idea to consult with representatives from the human resource department at this point. The documentation should be reviewed to ensure that everything is in order should termination result.

The last phase of the progressive discipline is usually not necessary. This is termination. The specifics of the inappropriate behavior are once again addressed. The termination should not come as a surprise to the employee if the stages of the progressive discipline have been handled effectively.

While disciplining your employees may be an unpleasant task, it is crucial that it be done. To fail to discipline employees creates a poor work environment. Those employees who are following the rules feel somehow cheated and become demoralized if others are not held to the same standards.

REWARDING EMPLOYEES

Appropriately rewarding employees is a key component of effectively managing the performance of your employees.

Consider these tips in rewarding your employees:

- Use nonmonetary rewards creatively. Think about how to build in more autonomy and responsibility to their jobs as a reward.
- Know your employees and tailor their rewards to meet their needs.
- Consider flexible benefit plans, whereby your employees can select the benefits that best meet their needs.
- Use team rewards where appropriate.
- Consider creative pay plans such as skill-based pay, whereby your employees are rewarded for the acquisition of new skills.
- Consider employee recognition programs to reward top performers. Signs designating the employee of the month, special parking spaces, or special dining privileges can be used quite effectively.
- Don't overuse rewards. Ensure that employees actually engage in the appropriate behaviors prior to receiving the rewards.
- Provide rewards immediately. This helps make the link between the performance and the reward.
- Make sure that performance is tied to the rewards.

HOUR'S UP!

Recognizing that the management of people's performance is critical in meeting your own goals and those of your organization's, check to see what you have learned.

1. The most common tool used for the feedback of employee performance …
   a. Is the pay increase.
   b. Is the performance appraisal system.
   c. Is the informal comments made by superiors on a regular basis.
   d. Is self-appraisal.

2. A forced distribution ...

    a. Requires that you rate a predetermined percent of your employees in each ranking category.

    b. Requires you to force employees to perform at higher levels.

    c. Requires that you force employees to rate themselves.

    d. Requires that you distribute raises equally.

3. The 360-degree performance evaluation ...

    a. Is conducted by a full circle of people who interact with the employee.

    b. Is always conducted exclusively by the direct supervisor.

    c. Is used less frequently today.

    d. Doesn't really make sense in an information society with knowledge workers because you are the only one who knows what your employees really do.

4. Conducting a performance appraisal ...

    a. Is not an easy task.

    b. Requires that you determine expectations in advance.

    c. Requires thought as to when and where the interview will be conducted.

    d. All of the above.

5. The recency error ...

    a. Occurs on every performance appraisal due to human nature.

    b. Occurs when you evaluate an employee based on what happened during the entire course of the performance appraisal period.

    c. Occurs when you evaluate an employee based on what happened most recently.

    d. Occurs when you forget the most recent information.

6. The law of effect ...

    a. States that behaviors that are followed by positive consequences are more likely to be repeated.

    b. States that behaviors that are followed by negative consequences are less likely to be repeated.

    c. Can be used to help shape behavior.

    d. All of the above.

7. To be effective, positive reinforcement …

   a. Should be administered as soon as possible after the appropriate behavior.

   b. Should be administered only when the appropriate behavior is actually delivered.

   c. Is used to increase the probability that appropriate behavior will be repeated.

   d. All of the above.

8. You should avoid the overuse of punishment because …

   a. Punishment never works.

   b. Those who are punished usually don't change their behavior permanently.

   c. Employees will only focus on the behavior and never you as the punisher.

   d. Administering punishment is not a pleasant experience for you.

9. Progressive discipline …

   a. Can be as effective in shaping behavior as rewarding employees.

   b. Seldom requires documentation.

   c. Must be kept secret to be effective.

   d. Requires terminating employees immediately for inappropriate behavior.

10. When rewarding employees …

   a. Consider creative, nonmonetary rewards.

   b. Use team rewards for team efforts.

   c. Provide rewards immediately to establish the link between the performance and the reward.

   d. All of the above.

QUIZ

HOUR 13

Career Development: Your Responsibility

A career is broader than a single job. A career is really a package of jobs and the movement that occurs between those jobs. Today, careers must be carefully and skillfully managed.

Career management is not passive. As the name implies, it requires active management. If you are not actively involved in developing your career, the chances are very great that you will go nowhere.

CAREER DEVELOPMENT TODAY

Career management has always been important, but it has become even more critical today. Yet the very nature of how these careers are managed has seen significant changes. Career management today doesn't resemble the career management of just 10 or 15 years ago.

Just a generation ago, a career implied a job with just one company. Now a variety of jobs, organizations, and even industries are involved in a career. Today, managing a career means managing movement from one organizational opportunity to the next. Job switching has become commonplace in today's workforce.

CHAPTER SUMMARY

LESSON PLAN:

In this hour you will learn about …

- Career development in today's world.
- Benefits to the organization of managing careers.
- Traditional stages of career development.
- Contemporary approaches to career development.
- Alternative career tracks.
- Signs of trouble in your career.
- Steps for effectively managing careers.

PROCEED WITH CAUTION

The failure rate of new managers during the first 18 months on the job is estimated to be approximately 40 percent. Job switching may contribute to this high failure rate because managers are now spending so little time on the job before they move on. It doesn't even provide a chance for managers to build relationships and get a feel for what is expected of them. And, there's no chance to see one job opportunity through before moving on to the next one.

With the new contract between managers and employees, there has been increased responsibility placed on employees. The organization is no longer responsible for the management of your career. Now, you have the primary responsibility for managing your career.

And this management of today's careers has been further complicated by the demise of the more traditional career path of upward mobility. Today's career path is more characterized by lateral and crisscross moves throughout the organization. You are also given more options for nonmanagerial positions.

Some organizations approach career development from a formal perspective. They may offer a wide array of courses on a continuing basis for employees to select those they need or want. The company provides the training and development opportunities, but the individuals must assess their own needs and take advantage of the opportunities.

Companies are utilizing more creative options to compensate for the loss of the traditional upward mobility. Job revitalization and broadbanding are two of these options. They require that employees take on new responsibilities and acquire new skill sets.

Job revitalization breathes a breath of fresh air into a "stale" job when a promotion is not available for an individual. Revitalization is renewing a job and giving it a face lift. Even moving the location of the job-holder can revitalize a job. *Broadbanding* is a compensation option to reward employees. Employee salaries can be increased without a promotion.

PROCEED WITH CAUTION

Career planning must be tied to the organization's strategic human resource plan. This ensures that the organization's human resource needs for the future will be better met.

BENEFITS TO THE ORGANIZATION

If your organization manages career development well, the following benefits can be reaped:

- Your organization will be considered an "employer of choice." This puts you in a better position to hire talented people because they will be more attracted to your organization.

- The organization will develop a larger talent pool. Time and attention will be paid to developing the talent needed to achieve strategic objectives.

- You will experience a higher retention rate. Managerial talent is critical for all organizations. If organizations wisely manage the careers of managers, they are likely to remain with the organization longer and become important talent for the organization.

- Properly managing career development often results in higher motivation levels. As your organization helps you identify your next job move, the skills you need to acquire, and your overall development, you are more likely to be motivated in your job.

If poor career planning is conducted (or if no career planning is done), there is likely to be an erratic talent pool in the organization with periods of feast or famine. That is, there may be large amounts of talent (perhaps with no opportunities to utilize this talent) or very little talent as a result of no planning efforts. A lack of career planning also generates a dissatisfied workforce.

JUST A MINUTE

As employees realize the importance of planning career moves, those organizations that are willing to work with employees will be chosen as "employers of choice."

To be effective, career-planning programs must have the support of top management. The organization should have a human resource philosophy concerning career progression. In addition, employees must be encouraged to take responsibility for their career development. This can be accomplished in part by encouraging the use of self-help books and workbooks.

TRADITIONAL STAGES OF CAREER DEVELOPMENT

Careers generally proceed through a set of stages. These stages are as follows:

1. Exploration
2. Organizational entry
3. Establishment
4. Maintenance
5. Disengagement

The traditional model of career development begins with the stage of preparation for work. During this first stage of exploration, people prepare to enter the workforce. The focus is on the acquisition of the skill set needed to enter the workforce.

FYI College students are a prime example of those people in the exploration stage. As more students seek to acquire the skills necessary for the work force, there has been an increase in the number of students changing majors. As students explore their interests and the opportunities available in the workplace, they make more changes in their major courses of study.

A number of tests have been widely used to identify individuals' interests to help identify career choices. Two of the most popular tests are the Strong Interest Inventory and the Campbell Interest and Skill Survey.

The organizational entry stage occurs next. The individual is now ready to choose a job from the offers of employment made. The match of interests and skills (developed during the exploration stage) should be taken into consideration when making this choice. The person-job fit becomes a critical factor to consider.

Establishment is concerned with the early career. Individuals are identifying the occupation that they are interested in pursuing. This also requires the acquisition of additional skills so that advancement can continue in the chosen field.

A mid-career assessment of goals occurs in the maintenance stage. In this stage, individuals analyze the talents they are using and examine the need to learn any new skills to remain marketable.

The final stage involves disengagement during the late career. Preparation for retirement is the focus at this stage. Individuals must seek other avenues of fulfillment to replace the job.

CONTEMPORARY APPROACHES

More contemporary views of careers recognize that most people have multiple careers (on average three per individual) with various employers throughout their working years. These contemporary approaches recognize that employees don't necessarily progress straight through these stages, but can regress to prior stages. One of these approaches suggests that a career be simply viewed in stages from early, mid-, and late-career with specific issues that are addressed in each.

The early career stage is characterized by new entry into a job. Generally, the key issue to be managed is the inconsistency between the glamorous vision of the career and the actual entry-level position occupied. Employees may feel that their skills are being underutilized. This disappointment then results in dissatisfaction with the job. This disappointment is further exacerbated as performance appraisals are not as good as expected. Most superiors focus on the areas of improvement for early career stage employees (versus strengths), and the result is an average or below average performance appraisal, which is disappointing to the individual.

The organization can take steps to help minimize the early career issues. The best step is the use of realistic job previews that will reduce the inconsistencies between the vision of the job and the actual job. Applicants receive a more realistic view of the job they will be taking. Some more progressive organizations are moving extremely talented new hires with impressive skill sets into more challenging jobs after short orientations. Early career individuals are also assigned a mentor in some organizations to help with the initial adjustments of the job and reduce dissatisfaction levels.

The mid-career stage occurs in higher-level jobs. The mid-career plateau is one of the primary issues experienced in the stage. There is a leveling off of opportunities and further advancement is not probable. Resentment is often experienced and blame for the lack of advancement is often placed on the organization. Without challenges, employees tend to become stagnant and unenthusiastic. They lose interest in most aspects of life as the job becomes stagnant. The danger now is that of job loss. These are the individuals that are generally the first to be named in a downsizing or workforce reduction.

The organization can provide career counseling to help the individuals understand the issues of this plateau. They may also provide different alternatives for career paths. More lateral moves and transfers can be utilized to provide new challenges to stagnant careers—usually at the same rate of pay. In some cases, a demotion may also be used just to provide a fresh opportunity for the employee experiencing stagnation and a plateau.

It has been suggested that not all plateaus are alike. Three different plateau types have been identified: structural, content, and life:

- The structural plateau occurs when no more promotions are available in the current organization. Any upward movement will have to be found in another organization.

- The content plateau is experienced when job responsibilities have been mastered and boredom sets in. There are no challenges for the employee continuing with the current job responsibilities.

- The life plateau threatens the individual's sense of identity (due to lack of success), and threatens his or her self-identity. Who these individuals are is tied to the job they hold.

PROCEED WITH CAUTION

 The life plateau does not necessarily have to be experienced as a result of a job plateau. Any factor in a person's life that is tied to his or her identity can create this effect. People often describe divorce in this way. The divorce represents a "failure" and loss of their identity as a spouse.

Most experts recommend that you keep your job in perspective. You don't want your identity and self-worth to be tied exclusively to your job. If these are tied too closely, job loss or loss of status can be a detrimental blow to your ego. In addition, an undue focus on the job results in neglecting other areas of your life that can be very fulfilling.

In the late-career stage there is anxiety over retirement. For many individuals, this stage can be quite traumatic. As organizations engage in downsizing and workforce reductions, they may offer programs for voluntary early retirement to some more mature employees. This would ensure that younger employees would not have to be laid off.

Organizations need to be sensitive to the fact that this is an emotional issue for many people. The organization can ease this transition with a gradual retirement schedule. The late-career individual may reduce the hours they work gradually, until they enter full retirement. Some companies have even developed retirement rehearsals where employees can experiment with retirement for a specified amount of time (usually three months).

The organization can also ensure that counseling is offered—especially in the area of financial planning. The key is to ensure that employees plan early for retirement. People should not wait until they get to retirement to begin their planning. Pre-retirement planning programs help in the preparation—often offering seminars to inform people of their options.

ALTERNATIVE CAREER TRACKS

There is more than one career track today. In the past, the term career track referred to upward mobility through the management ranks. Today there are additional options available to provide opportunities for those who are not interested in the traditional career track:

- **Upward mobility.** This is upward movement through the ranks to the executive management levels. This requires an interest in developing strategy for the organization. There are, however, just a small number of these opportunities available in each organization.

- **Project managers.** These individuals manage the projects that make significant contributions to the organization. They tend to be highly visible and can be powerful positions if managed appropriately.

- **Resource provider.** Resource providers obtain financial and human resources that are needed for the projects of the organization. They may also need to develop the resources needed.

- **Talent pool.** This career path is often referred to as the dual path with movement on the technical side of the organization. The talent pool is that group of employees that actually performs the work of the organization. These are the experts possessing the knowledge, skills, and abilities to implement the strategies to contribute to the organizational goals.

GO TO ▶
Refer to Hour 6, "Project Management," for a detailed discussion of how projects can be more effectively managed.

JUST A MINUTE

Changes in strategy require revisions in the skill set required by the workforce. Maintaining a skills bank or skills inventory for your employees helps to ensure that the skill set of your workforce is monitored and will be prepared to meet the challenges of the future.

Steps to Effective Career Management

Just as any project can be managed, your career can be managed with the same concepts. As you manage your business, you determine first where the organization is, and then where you want that business to go. The same applies to your career.

You must decide where you are now and where you are going. Then, you can chart a path by which you will get there. That is, you must set career goals and identify how you will achieve them.

GO TO ▷
Refer to Hour 11, "Motivation," for a discussion of goal setting. You want to ensure that your goals require you to stretch while still being realistic.

Consider these questions:

- Do you have a vision of where you'd like to go? Where do you want to be in five years? Ten years?
- What industry do you envision this future job in 10 years? Will you continue in your current industry or make a change?
- What kind of organization do you want to work in? Small? Large? What does the corporate culture look like?
- Are your goals realistic?

JUST A MINUTE

The person-job-organization fit must be carefully examined. You want to ensure that you identify the type of company that fits your personality best to be the most effective. Some people feel more at home in smaller organizations where they can perform a wide variety of tasks.

There are, however, some limitations to career planning that should be considered. Above all else, it must be recognized that there are no absolutes. You and your organization cannot be certain what the future holds. People change, companies change, and industries change.

PROCEED WITH CAUTION

Every career plan is subject to change. This is not a contractual agreement. It must be prepared to be flexible, and should be considered a living document that is revised periodically to reflect current conditions.

The human resource staffing needs may change in response to environmental changes. That is, a company may change strategic direction to take advantage of opportunities in the external environment, and this change may require different skill sets. Sometimes others can just be wrong about your performance on the job, and opportunities that were promised do not materialize. As new people enter the organization or your organization develops new relationships with other organizations (such as mergers and acquisitions), your career plan will be affected.

USING A PERSONAL SWOT ANALYSIS

While your organization probably utilizes a SWOT analysis to help create strategy, your personal career strategy can benefit from use of the same tool—just tailored to your personal needs. The SWOT analysis involves identifying your ...

- Strengths.
- Weaknesses.
- Opportunities.
- Threats.

FYI There are a number of career planning workbooks to help you identify your interests and potential to aid in your SWOT analysis. One of these tools is highly recommended to guide the process. *What Color Is Your Parachute?: A Practical Manual for Job-Hunters and Career-Changers* by Richard Nelson Bolles is an example of one of these resources.

You must know what your current skill level is. That is, you must be able to identify your competencies. These are the tools that will get you where you want to go or prohibit you from getting there.

Most people have an easier time determining what their strengths are. You want to identify what you do best—better than others. Be specific in identifying your knowledge, skills, and abilities that give you a competitive edge in the workplace. This is what sets you apart from your fellow employees.

This may also require input from others around you. You may ask your current supervisor for assistance. Review past performance appraisals and any letter of commendation that you may have received.

Identifying strengths involves gaining a greater understanding of your interests. That is, determining what you enjoy. Remember, you won't be successful in a job field that you don't like.

It's much harder to assess your weaknesses. And it's not just you, it's human nature that people have difficulties examining their weaknesses. Weaknesses are the areas in need of improvement. You need to know the critical success factors for a field and be able to improve any areas in which you are weak. A good starting point is with your performance appraisals.

JUST A MINUTE

It's human nature to preserve self-esteem and to bias self-assessments. It is critical to evaluate yourself objectively and honestly just as you would another. Listing out strengths and weaknesses objectively on paper can help overcome some of this bias.

Opportunities are found when assessing the environment. This is determining what is available. You must examine the long-term health of the field to match your strengths with the opportunities available. The key is to look for trends. Refer to trade journals in the industry to check the long-term outlook for jobs.

Threats are obstacles in the environment. Recognizing these threats allows you to minimize the risks they present and your exposure to them. The industry outlook and changing technology can signal the demise of specific positions. The key is to identify these jobs being eliminated before they occur—especially if you currently occupy one of the these positions.

FORMULATING A CAREER STRATEGY

Once the SWOT analysis is completed, your next step is to formulate a career strategy—based in part on what you learned in the SWOT analysis. This is formulating the roadmap that leads you to the attainment of your career goals. Care should be taken to ensure that the steps to be taken are specific and utilize a variety of resources at your disposal.

Your career strategy choices should consider the following options:

- Increased responsibility in the existing position
- A lateral move
- A promotion to a job with increased responsibility
- Retraining to acquire a new skill set

This may mean locating a mentor, attending workshops or seminars, reading, taking advantage of lateral moves, attending in-house programs, and using the corporate tuition reimbursement program.

Mentors are individuals that influence you. These people guide and support you in your career. The mentoring programs can be informal or formal.

JUST A MINUTE

Mentoring circles have been organized in some companies. Instead of being paired with an individual mentor, a circle of mentors can provide the coaching and support.

MANAGEMENT DEVELOPMENT

Management development consists of training and development specifically designed for managers. To be effective and ensure that the organization gets the most mileage out of this training, the management development programs must be aligned with the strategic goals of the organization—as all training should.

The organization may identify the development needs of management in the firm for either current or future positions. This is generally accomplished by use of a needs assessment. Managers who are being groomed for succession are specifically identified at this point.

PROCEED WITH CAUTION

Most organizations focus their management development programs on group needs. That is, the specific needs of individual managers are not the focus. As a result, you need to fill in the gaps with your own assessment of your developmental needs to progress in your career.

Management requires a variety of skills. There is no cookbook recipe because management is both art and science. There is not a standardized approach to management development. Standardization doesn't work because management focuses on dealing with people—an unpredictable entity at best.

A key component of management development today is international assignments. International experience has become essential to career advancement. This experience is critical for organizations in developing global management talent to direct operations in the global arena.

GO TO ▶
Refer to Hour 2, "Management in the New Workplace," for a more detailed discussion of the global arena.

SIGNS OF TROUBLE IN YOUR CAREER

In the past, you could easily tell that your career was going south. If the promotions stopped coming, you could tell that your career was in trouble. Today, it is not as easy to tell when there is trouble.

The new benchmarks that you might consider are the following:

- **If you are not still learning.** A failure to continue learning is the greatest danger sign.
- **If you are falling behind in acquiring new skills.** To just stay current in your job, you must be continually updating your skills.
- **If you are not regularly contributing to your organization.** Your organization requires you to contribute on a regular basis.
- **If you are not marketable or employable.** If you have no other place to go, your career is in trouble. You should always have other options.

JUST A MINUTE

Early philosophers have suggested "Know thyself." This adage is particularly important in management. You must know how to manage yourself before you can manage others.

TIPS TO EFFECTIVELY MANAGE YOUR CAREER

There are general guidelines you should consider to more effectively manage your career. Review these tips:

- Stay positive. Project a positive attitude. Others will notice you and be more likely to consider you for opportunities.
- Recognize that you are primarily responsible for your career management. If you sit around and wait for someone else to manage your career, you may have a long wait—and a poor career.
- Know where you are going. Use goal-setting principles.
- Know what it takes to achieve those goals. Be systematic about acquiring the skills and resources needed to meet those goals.
- Be political. Recognize the importance of visibility and cultivating important networks.
- Seek out a good mentor to help guide you in your career.

HOUR'S UP!

Career planning is important for yourself, your organization, and your employees. Review these questions to see how much you learned about career planning in this hour.

1. Career management …

   a. Is a passive process.

   b. Is an active process.

   c. Is your organization's responsibility.

   d. Just happens on its own.

2. Today's career path is more characterized by …

   a. Lateral and crisscross moves throughout the organization.

   b. Fewer options than ever before.

   c. Upward mobility only.

   d. A refusal to take on new responsibilities.

3. Benefits to the organization for managing its employees' career development include …

   a. Your organization will be considered an "employer of choice" and will attract a more talented workforce.

   b. The organization will experience a higher retention rate.

   c. The organization will experience higher motivation levels.

   d. All of the above.

4. During the preparation for work stage of career development …

   a. The focus is on landing a job.

   b. The focus is on avoiding a career plateau.

   c. Exploration occurs whereby individuals focus on the acquisition of the skill set needed to enter the workforce.

   d. Everyone decides upon the career that they are committed to for lifetime employment.

5. Contemporary approaches to career development …

   a. View careers in stages of early, mid, and late.

   b. View careers as one stage of a plateau.

   c. Are the same as the traditional stages.

   d. See career development as the responsibility of the organization.

6. A career plateau …

   a. Occurs at the mid-career stage.

   b. Is a leveling off of opportunities.

   c. Is likely to result in stagnation and boredom.

   d. All of the above.

7. Progressive organizations are helping people in the late-career stage prepare for retirement by …

   a. Kicking them out of the organization at earlier points in their career to help with workforce reduction efforts.

   b. By providing gradual retirement and retirement rehearsals.

   c. Avoiding financial planning that depresses those considering retirement.

   d. Not handling this stage as an emotional issue, but rather as a business issue.

8. Some of the alternative career tracks include all except the following …

   a. Project managers.

   b. Resource providers.

   c. Talent pool.

   d. Mentors.

9. A personal SWOT analysis …

   a. Involves identifying your strengths, weaknesses, opportunities, and threats.

   b. Involves identifying your skill set and where you are going in the organization.

   c. Is helpful in picking out your next mentor.

   d. Is very easy to perform.

10. You know your career is in trouble when …

   a. You stop learning.

   b. You have a lot of job options.

   c. You are overqualified for your own job.

   d. You contribute regularly to your organization.

QUIZ

Hour 14
Groups

Chapter Summary

LESSON PLAN:

In this hour you will learn about ...

- Understanding the role of interdependence in groups.
- Knowing the advantages and disadvantages of using groups.
- Working with the stages of group development.
- Identifying the norms shaping the behavior of group members.
- Group decision-making techniques.
- Understanding technology's role in groups today.

Groups surround you. Your life is full of groups—some with stable membership, and some with constantly changing membership. You are a member of many groups. While these groups are all around you, they are still not easily understood. We tend to take these groups for granted—seldom aware of the role that they play in organizational life.

Organizations today are utilizing groups more frequently to perform the work traditionally assigned to individuals. This use of groups is rapidly changing the very structure of your organization.

Most organizations today still use the traditional pyramid structure to depict their company. The very nature of this pyramid suggests the importance of groups. Your organization is a house of cards, so to speak. The organization's success depends upon the success of each of the groups within the organization. As groups are successful, the organization will achieve success. Should the groups not be successful, the organization cannot meet its goals.

The key to groups is their interdependence. That is, the members of a group are mutually dependent on one another. Generally, a *group* is defined as a collection of two or more individuals who work together in order to achieve a common objective.

JUST A MINUTE

The physical environment of a group impacts its effectiveness. Seating during meetings has become a critical issue in understanding the dynamics of groups. You are more likely to be perceived as the leader of the group if you sit at the head of a table. You will also interact more with the people seated across from you.

It is absolutely critical that you understand how groups work. *Group dynamics* refer to the processes that occur within groups. Because groups are more than just the collection of the individuals within that group, the group takes on a life of its own.

This is seen with the wilding of groups. That is, groups often engage in behaviors that the individuals within the group would never engage in themselves as individuals. This is due to the loss of individual identity in groups.

This is simply one example of many in which you can see that groups are entities to be studied and understood as unique entities. It is not enough to understand individuals. You must understand how individuals interact within a group and how groups interact with one another.

Groups operate concurrently on two levels in order to be effective. They must constantly be focused on task performance and human resource maintenance needs. While it may be obvious that groups must focus on the achievement of the task at hand, equally important is the attention paid to the interpersonal issues. Should the group pay attention to only the task and ignore human resource maintenance needs, the group is likely to become stalled on the task achievement. Until the interpersonal issues are attended to, the group is not going to be effective.

ADVANTAGES TO GROUPS

Groups offer the opportunity to achieve *synergy*. Defined as a whole that's greater than the sum of the parts, synergy is one of the key advantages of using groups. Consider how much you could achieve alone—versus how much you can achieve as a member of a group. Society is filled with groups that provide the opportunity for synergy.

Groups generally perform better than the average individual member's performance. Groups are used in organizations, then, to improve performance levels with complex tasks. Groups does accomplish more than individuals.

And what's more, groups generally can accomplish the task in less time than one individual can achieve the same objective.

Groups also greatly influence the individual members' behaviors. It is through group membership that behavior is often shaped. Your membership in groups defines for you what is acceptable and unacceptable behavior.

JUST A MINUTE

It has been estimated that nearly one third of the time that people spend in meetings is actually wasted. This has been estimated to cost American businesses more than $37 billion. Learning to be more productive while working in a group can decrease this wasted time and ultimately save money.

In the organization, groups help people learn how to perform their responsibilities while providing the support they need to succeed. Members are given the opportunity to learn from one another in a group setting.

These groups also provide the opportunity for the fulfillment of the social needs as identified by Maslow's hierarchy of needs. Individuals are driven by a need for social interaction. Groups give us this interaction. Some people prefer to work as a part of a group—regardless of the performance level. The group can provide greater satisfaction than working as an individual.

DISADVANTAGES OF GROUPS

Working as a part of a group requires greater resources from the organization. Group work takes more time and energy than working alone. If the time spent working as a part of a group is not productive, it costs the company significant amounts.

Groups have the potential for conflict. Too often, bringing people together in and of itself sets the stage for conflict. Conflict, then, tends to be inevitable as people work together. Where it becomes dangerous is when conflicts of interest and competitiveness are not addressed. This weakens the cooperation needed by the group members. Conflict is actually beneficial when effectively managed.

One of the biggest challenges for you in managing groups is that of social loafing. Identified by a German psychologist, Max Ringelmann, *social loafing* recognizes that not every group member pulls his or her own weight. Rather, some group members believe that their contributions will not be singled out and they prefer that someone else does the work.

GO TO ▶
Refer to Hour 11, "Motivation," for a more complete discussion of Maslow's hierarchy of needs and McClelland's need for affiliation.

When providing group rewards, you must guard against this. Should you reward the social loafer, they will continue to repeat this behavior (that is, not contributing) because this is the behavior that has been rewarded.

Individuals are often thrown together to work in groups without the appropriate training. People must understand how to work effectively together. Organizations that fail to provide this training doom the group members to poor performance.

GO TO ▶
Refer to Hour 12, "Managing Perform-ance," for a discus-sion of the law of effect. This law sug-gests that those behaviors that are followed by positive consequences are more likely to be repeated. This is why only appropriate behaviors can be rewarded.

Groupthink prevents a group from arriving at the best solution. Researched by Irving Janis, groupthink is more common than you might think. *Group-think* is an agreement (whether conscious or not) by the group not to dis-agree. This very agreement sets the group up for failure. It is through conflict that the best ideas are often generated.

STAGES OF GROUP DEVELOPMENT

While groups vary tremendously, there have been certain patterns of growth identified that groups move through. According to an American researcher, Bruce W. Tuckman, the stages of development are as follows:

Stage 1: Forming

Stage 2: Storming

Stage 3: Norming

Stage 4: Performing

Stage 5: Adjourning

The forming stage is the initial stage of group development. This is referred to as the orientation. There is discomfort and members are on their guard as they come together with people who they do not know. Tension character-izes the group at this point in time. As the members begin to identify as part of the group, they recognize their dependence on one another and try to understand the task at hand.

The second stage is that of storming. As the name implies, storming tends to be more emotional, and is characterized by high levels of conflict. Disagree-ments are common and are actually productive for the group if they occur at manageable levels. Optimum levels of conflict enable the group to move on to the next stage of development.

Storming is followed by norming. In this stage the group has achieved a newly discovered balance. They have developed standards and procedures by which to operate. The group has bonded in this stage and is experiencing a high level of cohesion. As a result, the group members hesitate to introduce conflict again. The group at this stage tends to be characterized by stability and a pressure to conform.

Performing is the stage characterized by the mature group. This is the stage where the group is performing at its optimal level. Unfortunately, some groups are unable to reach this stage because they are unable to resolve the issues in each of the prior stages.

The final stage is that of adjourning. In this stage, the group prepares to disband. It is important that the group disband on a positive note so that they can work together again if the need arises to reconvene.

PROCEED WITH CAUTION

 As organizations restructure and people are transferred from one unit to another, they change groups. The addition of new members or the loss of members creates a new group that must start over in the stages of group development.

TYPES OF GROUPS (FORMAL VS. INFORMAL)

There are both formal and informal groups in your organization. Both are equally important. While you are generally aware of the formal groups, you must be equally aware of the informal groups because they can impact your unit's performance.

Formal groups are officially designated as part of the organization. Your unit or your department is a formal group. It has been officially designated and appears on the formal organization chart of your company.

Many of the formal groups in the organization follow functional lines. For example, one formal group may be the accounting department, another the human resource department, and yet another, the research and development department. All are officially designated by the organization and may even have other formal groups within these formal groups.

Task groups are temporary work groups created by the organization. Special project committees are examples of these task groups. Members are usually formally assigned roles. As a rule, once the task (that is, the special project the group has been assigned) has been achieved, the group is disbanded. Some task groups can be permanent. For example, the curriculum committee found on college and university campuses is a permanent task group that exists to oversee curriculum on an ongoing basis.

Informal groups are not officially designated by the organization, yet can be just as powerful. It is critical that you understand what these groups are and how they are formed.

JUST A MINUTE

Formal leaders are generally assigned to formal groups. Informal leaders usually emerge in informal groups.

Informal groups are an inevitable part of organizational life. As people spend so much time together, informal groups emerge. These groups have voluntary membership (as opposed to the involuntary membership found in most formal groups).

The key is for you to learn to use these informal groups to your advantage. Even if the informal group signals there is a problem in the formal organization, this is an opportunity for you to take advantage of. It points out a potential problem that you may be able to head off and address at an early stage.

Friendship groups are formed by people who like each other. These are some of the most common of the informal groups. Because these groups' memberships cut across formal group lines (such as, formal departments), these groups often present the opportunity to expedite the actual work of the formal organization as members of the informal group call upon these "friends" for help in getting their work accomplished.

Common interests are the foundation for the formation of special interest groups. The softball teams that your organization sponsor brings people with a common interest (recreational softball) together. Once again, these informal groups represent an opportunity for you to plug into yet another network in your organization.

NORMS

Norms are the shared ideas of what group members should and should not do. Norms, then, shape the behavior of the group members. These norms can be written or unwritten.

Written norms are all around the organization. The employee handbook stipulates exactly what the organization expects in the way of employee behaviors. This may include such behaviors as work hours, parking, sexual harassment, gifts from customers, and interaction with others, to name just a few. Specific units within the organization may further stipulate what behaviors are expected of their employees. Committees often write rules of procedure that document what is acceptable behavior.

JUST A MINUTE

While most groups require conformity to their norms, the degree of conformity varies—especially across cultures. There is a high level of conformity to norms expected in the Japanese culture.

Unwritten norms are just as powerful as written ones. You can easily see this when examining motorists' behavior. The written norm specifying driving behavior may be posted as a 55 mile-per-hour (mph) speed limit. Seldom do people actually drive 55. Instead, there is an unwritten norm that takes precedence. This is the norm that you can drive up to 10 mph over the speed limit and not get a ticket. Another unwritten norm that is generally understood is that you can drive with the flow of traffic (and not get a speeding ticket). Yet, neither of these norms that are generally accepted are written anywhere—least of all in any state's motor vehicle driving manual.

Each group operates with these norms. They cover behavior from how to address members (by first name or surname) to who pays for lunch. Again, these may not be written, but they still shape the behaviors of the group members.

To effectively operate within a group, it is important to gain an understanding of what these norms are. You can only conform to those norms that you know about. If you do not conform to the group norms, you will be viewed as an outsider and not be accepted.

GROUP DECISION-MAKING

A key function of groups is to make decisions. But, the process by which alternative courses of action are selected for implementation are very different for groups than they are for individuals.

Group decisions provide you with more information and generally with more alternatives than individual decision-making. As a rule of thumb, you can expect more ideas and more varied ideas with groups as opposed to individuals. Perhaps the greatest advantage of group decision-making is the commitment that is generated. Members tend to be committed to decisions that they helped to generate. They will also better understand the decision that they participated in. Group decision-making provides the opportunity for many individuals to participate in the decision that affects them.

There are, however, drawbacks to group decision-making that you should also be aware of. It takes longer for a group to make a decision as opposed to an individual. In addition, there are often pressures at play to move the group away from the best decision. Politics and social pressures can influence a member's decision as part of a group. Seldom are group facilitators actually trained in group processes to improve decision-making or the effective utilization of the talents of individual group members.

Too often, group decision-making is a waste of time and resources. This causes a negative perception of group decision-making to result. Many times this lack of performance is a result of poor selection of group members and little or no preparation of the members. If care is not taken to ensure that the right members have been included, you cannot have high expectations of group performance.

PROCEED WITH CAUTION

As the leader of a group that is charged with decision-making tasks, you can impact the effectiveness of the group. It is important to encourage the participation of all group members and to withhold criticism of ideas. You set the tone for the rest of the group.

You should be especially aware of this as you participate in group decision-making with some of your employees. They may feel a pressure to conform to your suggestion by very virtue of the fact that you are their manager. You can encourage your employees to be more independent.

BRAINSTORMING

Brainstorming has gained tremendously in popularity. It is especially effective in generating creative solutions. This decision-making technique requires that all criticism be withheld. The key is to create a freewheeling session whereby a large quantity of ideas is generated. Each member then generates more ideas by piggybacking on the ideas of others.

Even self-criticism is avoided in brainstorming. That is, you cannot censor your own ideas and withhold any suggestions. The key is to throw out any and all ideas that come to mind without any censor. The wilder the idea, the better with brainstorming.

Brainstorming works best when members of the group have actually been trained in the brainstorming technique. Research has also shown that it is best to have periods of silence during the session to provide an opportunity for all the members to think and reflect.

Brainstorming can overcome issues of domination. Everyone participates in brainstorming. It also builds accountability and provides an opportunity for an enjoyable experience for people.

Brainstorming is often uncomfortable for people the first few times they engage in the process. It runs counter to traditional group process. As a result, you must know how to effectively facilitate a brainstorming session to maximize its performance. The following tips may be helpful:

- Let the group practice the process of brainstorming before tackling the actual task at hand.
- Make sure a scribe is appointed by the group to write down all the ideas presented.
- Make sure that all group members understand the ground rules: no criticism, time limit for keeping the floor.
- Encourage members to build on each other's ideas. They don't necessarily have to come up with brand new ideas, they can piggyback on other ideas.
- Limit people to one idea each time around the group.

Ensuring that group members know the rules of the brainstorming process will go a long way toward improving the effectiveness of the decision-making process.

THE DELPHI TECHNIQUE

The Delphi technique uses a panel of experts. This technique does not require face-to-face interaction. Information is solicited from each expert and then summarized. This new information is then shared with the experts to be used in making the next decision. This process is repeated until the final decision is made.

This technique is an especially efficient use of time. The experts are given reflection time while avoiding interpersonal problems inherent in face-to-face interactions. The result is usually a lot of ideas with high accuracy levels.

NOMINAL GROUP TECHNIQUE

The nominal group technique involves a number of steps. They proceed as follows:

- The problem is introduced with members writing down their ideas.
- Ideas are shared in a round robin technique.
- Each idea is then discussed.
- All of the ideas and solutions to the problem are then ranked. The rankings are averaged to arrive at a group decision.
- Further discussion could take place at this time to determine a final ranking and averaging to arrive at a group decision.

Once it has been decided that the group will make the decision (instead of you), this must be communicated to the group. The way that the decision is to be made must be agreed upon and communicated prior to the actual decision-making process.

You may select from the following decision-making methods:

- Simple majority rule
- Consensus
- Unanimous decisions

While this list is certainly not exhaustive, it presents the major choices that are used most frequently in organizations today.

Simple majority rule is the decision-making method that most people are most familiar with. It can be used very simplistically in groups. Generally, it is suggested that only minor decisions be made with this process. It only garners acceptance with the majority that voted for the choice. So just under half of the group members may not agree with the choice—and not accept the solution.

Consensus is often misunderstood. It does not require a unanimous decision. It only requires that everyone discuss the decision and agree to abide by it. Support of consensus decisions tends to be higher than decisions made with other processes.

While consensus is time consuming, members feel that they have been given the opportunity to influence the decision. Consensus requires that everyone have a chance to share their perspective and to be heard. This process uses conflict constructively to arrive at high-quality decisions. The value of consensus is that with members supporting the decision, implementation is often smoother.

When facilitating meetings using group decision-making, clearly define the problem for the group and revisit this definition when the group strays from the problem. When possible, avoid letting any members move toward an early solution. And by all means, avoid making the decision yourself. This is intended to be a group decision. Voicing your solution could bias the process. Finally, learn that disagreement and conflict are valuable contributions to the group decision-making process. These lead the group to better decisions.

THE ROLE OF TECHNOLOGY

Groups today do not have to meet face-to-face. With modern technological advances, group members can be geographically dispersed while meeting together. Through computer advances and telecommunications technology, you can meet with people half way around the world.

These technological advances have reshaped the way that group members interact with one another. The richness of face-to-face communication is lost and much of the emotional element is lost. Yet many benefits are gained, as technology links people together that otherwise would not work together.

GO TO ▶
Refer to Hour 20, "Organizational Communication," for discussions of the use of technology in electronic meetings and the impact on the communication process and of the communication process and the richness of the face-to-face communication channel.

With electronic brainstorming, people can be geographically dispersed as freewheeling ideas are typed into a computer. A list of ideas appears simultaneously on each group member's screens. Some people are more comfortable with this anonymous participation.

Computers have likewise influenced the Delphi technique, as experts can share their ideas electronically as well. It must be acknowledged, however, that the richness of face-to-face communication is lost.

A Special Challenge: Groupthink

Groupthink is spawned by the presence of specific conditions within the group. These create a ripe ground for the seeds of groupthink to be planted. Groupthink is found in groups that believe that they are not vulnerable, and that they are morally right. There is a misunderstood perception of decisions being unanimous. In fact, the decisions are not unanimous, but censorship created this misperception.

As a result of these conditions, groupthink leads a group to faulty decisions. The decision-making process itself becomes flawed. The group does not consider all alternatives or objectives. In addition, it does not gather sufficient information or appropriately process information. And interestingly enough, they do not develop any contingency plans because there is absolute confidence in the correctness of their decision. Therefore, there is no need for contingencies.

Now that you understand how dangerous groupthink can be to the effectiveness of a group, consider these tips to avoid groupthink:

- Formally assign a devil's advocate for the group. Ensure that disagreement is valued and encourage members to tactfully challenge each other.
- Consider a variety of viewpoints. Make sure that everyone is heard.
- Use smaller groups that break off from the larger group to make suggestions. As each group reports to the larger group, its ideas can then be evaluated.
- Use experts when appropriate. Invite them to voice their views to the group.
- Constantly evaluate all the alternatives and double check the solutions presented.

FYI One of the classic examples of groupthink from history is the Bay of Pigs invasion in Cuba. President Kennedy and his advisors made a faulty decision to invade Cuba in the 1960s. As a result of groupthink they failed to explore any information that pointed out the flaws in their plan.

HOUR'S UP!

Groups have become a critical component of business life. Check out this hour's quiz to see what you learned about group life.

1. The key to groups is …
   a. To know who is in them.
   b. Their success in meeting their objectives.
   c. Their interdependence.
   d. All of the above.

2. Groups operate concurrently on two levels …
   a. Task and human resource maintenance needs.
   b. Task and goal needs.
   c. Both focused on just the task.
   d. Neither of which addresses people issues.

3. An advantage of using groups is …
   a. The opportunity for synergy.
   b. That groups perform better than the average lone individual can perform.
   c. That groups achieve more than a lone individual can achieve.
   d. All of the above.

4. A big challenge of using groups is …
   a. Social loafing.
   b. Need to increase conflict.
   c. Learning everyone's name.
   d. Structuring members' break time.

QUIZ

5. During the storming stage of group development you would expect …

    a. Emotional issues.

    b. High levels of conflict.

    c. Productive disagreements.

    d. All of the above.

6. Norms …

    a. Are only powerful when written.

    b. Are powerful in shaping group behavior—whether written or unwritten.

    d. Must be written to shape behavior.

    d. Are generally not agreed upon by group members.

7. Group decision-making …

    a. Generally provides more ideas and a bigger variety of ideas.

    b. Is seldom effective in getting buy-in from members.

    c. Adds nothing to an understanding of the process.

    d. Is usually a tremendous waste of time.

8. The use of brainstorming requires that you …

    a. Assign the role of scribe.

    b. Avoid criticism.

    c. Build on each other's ideas.

    d. All of the above.

9. Decisions by consensus mean …

    a. Everyone agrees unanimously.

    b. Everyone agrees to support the decision.

    c. A majority rules.

    d. Support is usually low for the decision made.

10. To avoid groupthink you should …

    a. Use bigger groups to increase cohesiveness.

    b. Assign a devil's advocate.

    c. Discourage disagreements.

    d. Never invite outside experts to confuse the issue.

QUIZ

HOUR 15
Teamwork

CHAPTER SUMMARY

LESSON PLAN:

In this hour you will learn about ...

- How to distinguish between groups and teams.
- Interdependence of team members.
- Characteristics of high performance teams.
- How to build high performance teams.
- Self-managed teams in organizations today.
- How to handle special human resource challenges in teams.

Teams can enhance your organization's performance. Working with others can also improve employee satisfaction levels. But teams have to be understood to reap the numerous organizational benefits. The team-based organization is here to stay. It may very well end up being the design of choice for the majority of successful organizations in the twenty-first century.

DISTINGUISHING BETWEEN GROUPS AND TEAMS

While some people use the terms "group" and "team" interchangeably, the two are not the same. Teams are a special type of group with different characteristics and properties.

Some of the differences between groups and teams are identified as follows:

- Team performance depends upon collaborative achievements as well as individual achievements while group performance depends only on individual performance. Team members work together to pool their resources (usually skills in this case) to achieve their goals.

- Group members can be rewarded for their individual contributions. Team members are mutually accountable and rewarded as such.

- Team members share ownership of their purpose while group members measure their progress with their individual goals. A team focuses its efforts on its common goal.

- Teams tend to be more autonomous than groups; a supervisor generally oversees the work of groups. Most teams today manage their own work. Any supervisory personnel used do more coaching than actually supervising the work activities.

- A team must be small in number. A group can be large. The coordination necessary for team success cannot be achieved with a large number of members.

- Teams use just a few broadly defined job categories with its team members skilled in multiple areas. All the team members perform these few job categories. Groups generally use many highly defined job categories. With a high level of specialization, the group members occupying these positions don't always see how their work contributes to the final group effort.

- Teams often operate without a leader (often managing themselves) whereas groups usually have leader. Though this group leader may be formally appointed or emerge informally.

UNDERSTANDING TEAMS TODAY

Teams are generally defined as a highly committed group with a specifically defined task. The team members have specific roles that are well understood by each member. The level of interdependence is extremely high in a team. Each and every team member must contribute for the team to be successful—due to this high level of interdependence.

A surgical team is often held up as a prime example of a team. Without the contributions of each of the team members, the team's success is at risk. That is, if each member does not perform his or her given role, a patient could be threatened or die. Organizational teams work in the same way.

JUST A MINUTE

The work of the Tavistock Institute in the 1940s initially brought teamwork into the limelight. Located in London, they studied the workplace as a social system. This work provided the foundation for the later study of socio-technical systems.

Mutual accountability is one of the key issues in teams. This accountability is all about each member contributing his or her best effort to make the group successful. Mutual accountability, then, requires the commitment of each member to every other member to do everything he or she can to meet the team goals.

The team itself is accountable for the overall task accomplishment. Team members are accountable for carrying their load. In addition, each member agrees to be held accountable for these team goals. This mutual accountability also helps the team members bond with one another and develops the trust that is critical to their ongoing success.

Specific goals are the basis for this accountability. These team members, then, must be specific in stating goals so the team can measure its progress. The common purpose becomes the center for the team—providing the focus for all decisions and activities. The actual goals are developed from this carefully crafted purpose.

Learning is a key component of teams. Only by gathering information and using it to improve their team processes can they become more effective. This learning is a long process—usually lifelong.

GO TO ▶
Refer to Hour 11, "Motivation," for a discussion of the most effective ways to set goals.

Teams provide organizations with some of the flexibility that is needed today to be more responsive to environmental changes. The rigidity of some organizational structures is overcome with the use of teams. Teams are generally seen in the more organic structures today.

RECOGNIZING CHARACTERISTICS OF HIGH-PERFORMANCE TEAMS

While teams are being used extensively in American business, not all of these teams are effective. To be more successful in using teams, it is important to examine what characteristics a high-performance team possesses. Getting a handle on these characteristics then puts you in a better position to build a more effective team.

GO TO ▶
Refer to Hour 16, "Organizational and Structural Design," for a discussion of the organic versus the mechanistic structure. Organic structures are less rigid and provide more opportunities to be responsive to organizational changes.

FYI By 1996, it was estimated that nearly three quarters of American businesses were using teams. This number is only expected to increase.

High-performance teams generally are driven by their team's core values. These values are the center of who they are and what they do. These values drive their team performance and provide the framework for all they do.

Team members must believe that they can succeed. To achieve this belief they must support each other. Part of this is also the knowledge that management also supports them in their work.

Teams who perform at extraordinary levels set specific goals. They are not vague about what they want to achieve. These specific goals help provide them with purpose and direction. They also develop rules of acceptable team behavior.

High-performance teams are generally heterogeneous. That is, the teams reaching high levels of performance are not comprised of people who are exactly alike. Instead, these teams are composed of members who have skills that complement each other (rather than duplicate skills another member possesses).

The skills required of team members include technical, problem solving, and interpersonal. Technical skills are also referred to as functional skills. For example, a lawyer must have legal technical skills to succeed. Team members need more than technical skills, however.

They need problem-solving and decision-making skills. Members must be able to identify problems and opportunities, and then select solutions. Interpersonal skills are needed to communicate, resolve conflict, and interact effectively with team members. As the team develops, you must ensure that members have more of each of these skills.

This team membership with complementary skills is critical in achieving creativity. With a heterogeneous team, different perspectives and ideas are brought to the table. This introduction of new information can lead to more creative solutions.

There are some common behaviors that are generally observed across the majority of effective teams. Some of these behaviors include …

- **Problems are carefully considered prior to taking any action.** There is seldom a rapid jump to act without careful consideration.
- **There is distributed leadership.** All members are responsible for effective leadership, and the role is easily shared among team members.
- **Effective teams generally use consensus decision-making.** All members are heard and all support final decisions.
- **Effective team members display a high level of trust for one another.** This mutual trust is crucial to the performance of the team because they depend upon one another.
- **The team is continuously improving.** The team can never rest on its laurels, but must continuously learn and improve.

- **Team members are honest in communicating with one another.** This includes constructively criticizing one another and dealing with conflict.

It's not enough to know the characteristics and behaviors of effective teams. You also need to be prepared by understanding the most common reasons for the failure of teams. This knowledge helps you to decrease the probability of failure.

Because collaborative effort is vital to team success, a lack of cooperation by even one team member can set a team up for failure. Sharing a commitment to goals helps foster the cooperation so necessary to success. And this applies to interactions between teams. An inability to cooperate is a prelude to failure.

Without top management support, teams cannot achieve their goals. They rely on management to provide the various resources to succeed. If management is not truly committed, these resources will be withheld. Lack of top management support is also demoralizing to the team.

Managers who continue to exert control over the team and its members doom the team to failure. The command-and-control manager is out of step with the team concept. Coaches are more needed for team success.

GO TO ▶
Refer to Hour 14, "Groups," for a discussion of what consensus decision-making is and how it is used. Also see Hour 4, "Managerial Decision-Making," for an examination of types of decision-making.

UNDERSTANDING TEAM BUILDING

Team building is a technique from organizational development (known as OD) that seeks to address the functioning of teams within organizations.

The ability to build high-performance teams is critical in today's changing workplace. With teams being used more extensively, becoming adept at building these teams becomes a more integral part of your success in effectively managing people.

Following are some tips to consider when building a team:

- **Clearly articulate high standards for your team.** Be specific in communicating these standards so there is no room for doubt. These standards should require the team members to stretch and be challenged. This pursuit of excellence and high standards is not just talked about, but sets the tone for all the team interactions.

GO TO ▶
Refer to Hour 19, "The New Leadership," for tips on how to lead self-managed teams today.

GO TO ▶
Refer to Hour 7, "The Basics of Process Development," for a discussion of organizational development and other interventions that can be utilized on the group level.

- **Be the ultimate role model for your team.** The rules you set must reflect the high standards embraced by the team. And, these rules must be the rules that guide your behavior at all times. You cannot expect your team members to do more than you are willing to do.
- **Carefully assess the skills of the team's membership.** Only members with the needed skills should be asked to join the team. There is no room in a high-performance team for members who are nice to have around. Every team member must bring a critical set of skills to the table. The key is to bring members with complementary skills. Only with a diversified membership can different skills be brought to the table. Homogenous teams are not as successful as heterogeneous teams.
- **Consider the size of the team.** Teams over 12 members are too cumbersome and too difficult to coordinate.
- **Reward your high performance team members well.** You must remember to praise them and provide them with rewards commensurate with their performance levels. The rewards must be linked to the team performance. This garners commitment as team members share in the rewards of the team's success.

GO TO ▶
Refer to Hour 12, "Managing Performance," for a discussion of the use of positive reinforcement. The use of rewards in increasing the likelihood that good performance will be repeated is examined.

Team building requires that members examine their processes—that is, how they work together. This diagnosis is the beginning of building a more effective team (and ultimately, a more successful organization). The team identifies problems and gathers information to address them. Then, the team can also eventually learn more effective problem-solving techniques. This enables the team to more effectively diagnose and solve its own problems.

Team building is not a one-time event. Instead, this focus on continuous improvement is ongoing. The job of team building is never done. A team must be delicately nurtured and maintained over its lifetime.

Team building is the responsibility of each team member. This collaborative process can use a facilitator, but the team is ultimately responsible. Processes focusing on task accomplishment and interpersonal relationships are examined during team building.

In team building, process consultation becomes an important component. Through this process, team members examine team behaviors and gain a better understanding of how they work together. Some teams may even assign a member the formal role of process consultant. This team member then coordinates the examination of the team and helps the members learn about themselves. Some researchers have described this position as the one who holds the mirror of self-assessment up for all the members of the team to see themselves.

Critical to team building is the use of feedback. Continuous improvement of the team is only accomplished with feedback. Information that the team learns is fed back into the team processes to improve performance and the effectiveness of the team.

Teams use multi-skilling, which is where part of their flexibility comes from. Team members learn to perform more than just their own job. They learn to move from one job on the team to another as needed.

Team building does not have to be performed off-site. As a matter of fact, the method of choice today is actually more informal and onsite. This communicates the collaborative ongoing nature of the task.

Formal Retreat

The formal retreat is usually conducted off-site with a facilitator or a consultant present. This facilitator generally assumes the role of process consultant. This individual (usually an outsider) observes behavior and records these observations.

For team building to be effective in helping the team develop, you must create the right environment. Goals must be specifically stated, with you as the leader taking ownership and the team members sharing that ownership.

The formal retreat is losing popularity today with the increase in the use of teams. It requires substantial financial resources as well as time away from the job. Most organizations take exception to both these today.

Continuous Improvement Meetings

More teams today are using periodic meetings to address team building. This is reflecting the ongoing nature of the team building process. There is no need to wait for a formal retreat or have an outdoor experience. The work of team building can be conducted nearly daily and right on the company grounds.

This is a move to making team building an integral part of the team's operations. It has become more of an integrated activity rather than a separate activity to be undertaken in addition to the work of the team.

CREATIVE TEAMS

Self-managed teams are the most popular type of teams used in organizations today. These teams reflect the enrichment of a job on a team level. That is, the team members have been empowered with the responsibility to make decisions concerning their work that previously were made by management.

GO TO ▶
Refer to Hour 7 for a discussion of job enrichment on the individual level.

Self-managed teams have also been referred to as self-directed teams. Their use in organizations is expected to continue to increase with more emphasis being placed on participation in the workplace. This is not to say that these teams are overnight successes. Culture changes are often required in the organization in order to support these teams. Even management positions are changing drastically as a result of the increase in self-managed teams.

There are a number of advantages to using self-managed teams. The organization is able to increase their flexibility and be more responsive. Members of self-managed teams generally have a lower absenteeism and turnover rate as a result of their greater commitment to the company. In addition, these team members usually experience greater job satisfaction. Productivity has been estimated to increase by 30 percent with the use of self-managed teams. The products produced and the services delivered are also generally of higher quality.

Unfortunately, there are some disadvantages to self-managed teams. Because implementation takes so long it's generally measured in years. Due to the commitment required from the organization, self-managed teams cannot be implemented overnight. To achieve multi-skilling requires a large training budget. The efficiency of the team suffers early in its development as members try to learn the various job responsibilities. Training for self-managed teams is quite expensive. This training also includes interpersonal skills to improve the members' ability to work together and to be comfortable as part of a team.

Self-managed teams have flattened out the organizational pyramid with reduced layers of management. This has created emotional issues as some management positions have been eliminated, and others have been drastically revised. These structural changes are being addressed throughout American businesses.

Cross-functional teams are so named because they form across functional lines. While on the same organizational level, the members come from various functional units. This helps combat the functional silo mentality and brings a certain amount of diversity to the team—especially in the area of technical skills.

MANAGING TEAMS

Part of managing teams is to know when to use teams and when they are not the most appropriate structure for the work to be accomplished. When the task in question is highly interdependent, a team is the better option. Teams are not appropriate when the culture of the organization and the policies in place are not aligned with teams. For teams to be effective, the environment of the organization and the culture must enhance their effectiveness. For example, compensation systems must be aligned with teams. Rewards must be tied to team performance rather than individual performance.

GO TO ▶
Refer to Hour 16 for a more detailed discussion of the functional silo mentality in organizations.

To more effectively manage teams, you might consider the following tips:

- Help to create an organizational culture that values teams and the work they produce. Part of creating this culture means reassessing the reward structure and policies and procedures used in the organization. Everything you do must reinforce the importance of teams.

- Look for proven team skills in job applicants. Don't just assume that people can learn to work together if they have the right technical skills. Members must have technical, interpersonal, and decision-making skills.

GO TO ▶
Refer to Hour 17, "Organizational Culture," for a discussion of the role of organizational culture and how you can take a part in creating this culture.

- Make sure that you clarify the mission of the team. Because this is central to the ongoing success of the team, this should be done periodically.

- Don't force people to join a team who prefer to work alone. These individuals are not likely to cooperate.

- Provide training to develop or enhance team skills in your employees. This training is critical for the cross-training and multi-skilling of team members. The training should not just include technical skills, but also decision-making skills and interpersonal skills.

- Practice letting go. Teams don't need command-and-control managers. You must provide the team with opportunities for autonomy. This might even include letting team members select their own new members. Give them as much room as they need to manage themselves.

- Ensure that all team members participate in the decision-making process so that they will take ownership of these decisions. Involving members will improve commitment.

Addressing Special Human Resource Problems in Teams

While teams provide numerous benefits for organizations, they also can provide new challenges for you in managing people. The very nature of teams and teamwork presents opportunities for new problems to be addressed.

Sometimes a team member will become removed or uninvolved in the work of the team. This certainly threatens the effectiveness of the team because interdependence is at the core of the team's performance. Reassign tasks so that the uninvolved member performs critical tasks that will inherently involve the member with the other team members. Rewarding the team as a whole will cause other team members to solicit the involvement of the uninvolved member.

If a member becomes more independent, ensure that the task is structured such that it is impossible for the member to work independently. This may mean limiting the resources of the team so that resources are not available for the independent member.

Teams cannot tolerate any uncooperative members. Every member must share ownership and commitment to the purpose. This means cooperating with the other team members.

Hour's Up!

Understand that teams are not a management fad of the month, but that they are here to stay. Take a minute to see what you have learned about teams in this hour.

1. Groups and teams …

    a. Refer to the same concept and the terms can always be used interchangeably.

    b. Differ in that team members share a common purpose that is the center of their focus.

    c. Differ in that groups are more autonomous that teams.

    d. Differ in that only groups depend upon collaborative achievements while teams depend upon individual performance.

2. Team members …

    a. Have specific roles.

    b. Work with a high level of interdependence.

    c. Must all contribute for the team to be successful.

    d. All of the above.

3. Mutual accountability …

    a. Is not critical in the team concept.

    b. Requires that the team is accountable to the manager alone.

    c. Requires the commitment of each member to every other member to do everything they can to meet the team goals.

    d. Does little to help develop trust among the team members.

4. Teams provide organizations with …

    a. Some of the rigidity that is needed to get the job done quickly.

    b. Some alternative ways of grouping work.

    c. Some of the flexibility that is needed to be more responsive to environmental changes.

    d. All of the above.

5. One of the following responses is not indicative of the behaviors generally observed in high-performance teams …

    a. Leadership by one individual team member is always carefully determined.

    b. Consensus decision-making is generally used to ensure members are heard and the final decision is supported by all.

    c. A high level of trust is displayed for one another.

    d. Problems are carefully considered before any action is taken.

6. When building a team, you should consider the following …

    a. Clearly articulate the high standards for your team.

    b. Carefully assess the skills of the team's membership to ensure that the members have complementary skills.

    c. Be sure that there is a reward system to provide team members with rewards commensurate with their performance.

    d. All of the above.

7. Team building is …

   a. A one-time event.

   b. Always conducted off-site (generally using a formal retreat or an outdoor experience).

   c. Never conducted with a process consultant examining and recording team behaviors.

   d. Is a collaborative process critical to the ongoing success of the team.

8. Self-managed teams …

   a. Have also been referred to as self-directed teams.

   b. Require a corporate culture that embraces participation and empowerment.

   c. Generally have a lower absenteeism and turnover rate.

   d. All of the above.

9. In managing teams, you should remember that …

   a. It is not necessary to train if you did a good job of selecting the right people for the team initially.

   b. You don't need to let go because you are the manager.

   c. You can't be responsible for creating a corporate culture that is aligned with the team concept.

   d. You should not force people to join a team who prefer to work alone.

10. In selecting team members, you want those members who possess …

    a. The best technical skills, regardless of other skills possessed.

    b. The best interpersonal skills, regardless of other skills possessed.

    c. Possess strong technical skills, interpersonal skills, and problem-solving and decision-making skills.

    d. Possess both strong technical skills and interpersonal skills.

QUIZ

PART IV

Business as an Organization

Organizational and Structural Design

CHAPTER SUMMARY

LESSON PLAN:

In this hour you will learn about ...

- How organizational design is defined.
- What factors influence design.
- The role of the environment in shaping design choices.
- Span of control decisions.
- Departmentalization choices.
- How to manage within the five major organizational forms.
- How to overcome barriers using creative structures.

The design choice of your organization impacts its effectiveness. The poor performance of an organization may signal the need for the redesign of the organization. Companies should regularly diagnose the organization's structure. And, you should likewise diagnose your unit's structure to ensure there is an appropriate fit with the factors influencing your design choice.

There is no one-size-fits-all design choice. Instead, according to the contingency approach, the company must carefully match major factors in the company's environment with the structure that best fits its needs. Adaptations must be made to ensure that the most effective design choice is made.

Design is further complicated by the fact that it must be revisited periodically. As the organization changes and the factors that influence design change, the structure of the organization may need to be revised. Changes in the environment are especially important here. To improve organizational performance, some changes may be in order.

DEFINING ORGANIZATIONAL DESIGN

Organizational design is the choice made of how to structure the organization. That is, design concerns decisions of how to organize the work that is to be performed within the organization. This is the decision of how to configure the company.

This choice is generally depicted on an organization chart. This is a graphical depiction with the boxes representing positions in the organization. These boxes are identified with their reporting relationships. Sometimes the name of the person holding the position is included. This chart, then, provides you with insight into how the organization is configured and how the jobs are grouped together in both vertical and horizontal relationships.

UNDERSTANDING WHAT INFLUENCES DESIGN

The most effective design is unique to each organization—based upon a number of factors. The best design choice for your organization will take into account the technology you use, the environment in which you operate, the strategy of the firm, and the size of your organization. Each of these influences will be covered in the sections that follow.

TECHNOLOGY

Technology refers to the process used to transform the inputs of the firm into outputs. The technology your organization utilizes will impact the design choice. If you use a relatively routine technology, you will structure more rigidly to better utilize this technology.

For example, those automobile manufacturers using assembly lines (mass manufacturing technology) tend to design more rigid (or mechanistic) structures reflecting the use of routine technology. Think tanks tend to structure more openly (or organically) to reflect the lack of routine found in their business. This organic structure better meets the needs of their dynamic technology.

The rate of change in the technology being utilized in the transformation process will influence the structure as well. If the technology is rapidly changing, the structure must be adaptable enough to make adjustments. If the technology is relatively stable, then the structure can be more rigid—which encourages routines. The technology utilized by automobile manufacturers tends to be more stable. The assembly line encourages routine jobs.

ENVIRONMENT

The environment within which the organization operates will influence the structural choice. Both the societal environment and the task environment should be examined.

The societal environment is the broader of the two. This is also known as the general environment. While very similar for most organizations operating in the same industry, the impact of each component of the environment will vary with the individual firm. The components of the societal environment include the political and legal, economic, technological, and sociocultural elements.

The political and legal environmental component is comprised of legislation on the federal, state, and local levels, as well as the general political climate. Some of the variables included in the political and legal environment include tax laws and incentives, general attitudes toward business, antitrust regulation, and government stability.

The political climate has shifted drastically back and forth for the last century. Sentiment has shifted between pro- and anti-business sentiment with legislation reflecting these climates through the years. This sentiment will impact the structuring of your organization.

JUST A MINUTE

When conducting business on an international level, the political environment of each country in which you conduct business must be carefully evaluated. A key variable here is the political risk of doing business in different countries or regions of the globe. The State Department is one source that provides this information for American businesses.

Some of the variables to be considered in the economic environment include unemployment levels, the rate of inflation, interest rates, wage controls, and trends in Gross Domestic Product. The economic forces of the external environment influence every company. While the specific impact on each company may vary, the same variables apply.

Unemployment rates determine the labor pool. With low unemployment rates, there is generally a tight labor pool. You may need to consider more flexible structures to better meet the needs of employees and attract new applicants.

The technological environment encompasses technological advances. The technological forces include such variables as research and development (R&D) expenditures by the industry, patent protection, and technological transfer. With the accelerated pace of change in the environment today, businesses must carefully monitor this environment.

The socio-cultural environment includes the demographic shifts that have occurred in the United States. More women and older workers have impacted the structure of organizations, causing them to adapt to the changing environment. Flexible structures have been used to better meet the needs of the changing demographics.

The task environment is also called the industry. This is the environment that more closely impacts the company, and is in turn impacted by your company. This is generally thought of in terms of your competition, but is also expanded to include your suppliers, your customers, the government, the local community, and unions. The task environment includes all the stakeholder groups that are directly impacted by your organization.

Managing the uncertainty in the environment is one of your greatest challenges. The less information you have about your environment, the more uncertainty exists. Monitoring these environments will help you to reduce the uncertainty and better structure your organization.

The complexity of the environment is also important. This refers to the number of components in the environment that the organization must take into account when making decisions. As the complexity of the environment increases, the need for more decentralized decision-making also increases to enable the organizational members to respond appropriately to these external changes.

A key characteristic of the environment that influences design decisions is the stability of the environment. Stable environments do not have a high degree of change. Unstable environments are dynamic and characterized by constant change. Organizations that operate in more dynamic environments, then, need more organic structures to adapt to the changes.

STRATEGY AND SIZE

Alfred Chandler suggested that "structure follows strategy." Strategy outlines the plan by which the organization intends to achieve its goals. According to Chandler, who studied 70 large organizations in 1962, once an organization has decided what it intends to do, a structure can then be designed to support the achievement of those goals.

Alfred Chandler conducted a classic study and made significant conclusions concerning the link between strategy and structure. He suggested that as organizations grow and change strategies, their structure must also change.

Chandler further proposed that in the early stages of development, a company should use a centralized functional approach to structure. As the organization grows and becomes more complex, it must shift to a decentralized structure.

FYI *The Wall Street Journal* coined the phrase "dumbsizing" to reflect the questionable results of the downsizing strategy. While the expected result of downsizing was supposed to be cost reduction, this did not materialize in many organizations. In many cases, just the opposite occurred.

The size of an organization will impact the choice of structure. Intuitively, it makes sense that larger organizations will have more complex structures. This includes more layers in the hierarchy of the company and usually more formalization. The organization becomes more heterogeneous as it becomes larger in size.

As the organization grows, there is generally a greater degree of specialization. People in smaller organizations tend to wear many hats. But as the organization gets larger, employees will become specialized in doing one specific job.

MAKING STRUCTURAL DECISIONS

Once you have a handle on some of the factors that impact your design choices, you must know some of the specific decisions that you can make in structuring the organization and your unit. Some of these decisions include the following:

- Span of control
- Centralization
- Division of labor
- Departmentalization

SPAN OF CONTROL

Span of control refers to the number of subordinates that can be managed. The span of control (also referred to as the scalar principle) will determine the size of your work unit—as in the number of people that will report to you.

As the trend today has been for organizations to downsize, the organizational pyramid has been flattened. As this has occurred, the span of control has increased. That is, the span has broadened such that managers generally supervise more employees.

If your subordinates perform routine jobs with detailed procedures manuals and require little interaction with you, a larger span of control may be effective. If, on the other hand, your subordinates perform very different specialized jobs and require a great deal of interaction with you, a narrower span of control may be effective. With increased interaction you cannot effectively supervise as many people.

You can maintain closer control of your employees with a narrow span of control. Of course, the trend today is toward more empowerment, which would suggest that broader spans of control might help you avoid over-controlling your employees.

CENTRALIZATION

Centralization refers to the place in the organization where the decisions are made. In a highly centralized organization, the vast majority of the decisions are made at the top of the pyramid. In a highly decentralized organization, employees at all levels participate in the decision-making process. This is consistent with an empowered workforce.

There may be degrees of centralization and decentralization based upon the types of decisions made. That is, programmed decisions (those of a routine nature) may be made throughout the organization. Nonprogrammed decisions (or nonroutine decisions) may be made at the top of the organizational pyramid.

DIVISION OF LABOR

GO TO ▶
Refer to Hour 7, "The Basics of Process Development," for a more detailed discussion of division of labor from the aspect of better designing individual jobs within the organization.

Division of labor refers to the way in which the organization divides up the work of the organization into jobs. A high degree of specialization will take a large job and divide it up into numerous specialized jobs to be performed by different people. The automobile assembly line is a prime example of the specialized division of labor. Each individual performs his or her specialized task.

Adam Smith (an economist who wrote *The Wealth of Nations* in 1776) proposed the economic advantage of the division of labor in organizations. After observing workers in a pin factory, he determined that employees' performance could be significantly improved by having them specialize in the tasks they perform rather than working independently.

With industries that experience extraordinarily high turnover rates (like the fast food industry), the high degree of specialization in jobs helps to ensure the least amount of disruption in service. Highly specialized jobs are very narrow in terms of the responsibilities performed and are easily learned.

DEPARTMENTALIZATION

Departmentalization refers to the way in which jobs are grouped together. This is one of the coordinating mechanisms used to link the jobs divided up in the division of labor. (Span of control is the other coordinating mechanism.) The major choices for departmentalization include the following:

- Departmentalization by function
- Departmentalization by division
- Departmentalization by customer
- Departmentalization by geographic area
- Matrix approach

Departmentalization by function is the most popular method of grouping jobs today. It is based on the major functional areas of the company—accounting, marketing, human resources, operations, and so on. All accounting employees are then grouped together into one department, and so on, with each major functional area. The advantage is that employees can learn from others who perform the same job.

The problem encountered with departmentalization by function is the silo mentality. Employees see the organization through their functional lens. They fail to see the "big picture," and decisions reflect their narrow view of their functional world. There is little coordination across functional groups. People don't always interact with others outside their functional unit and may not even think about them when making decisions.

Departmentalization by process is similar to the functional departmentalization. People are grouped by the job that the group members perform. They are then able to share information with one another about the specialized process they perform. They, too, though, must overcome their narrow perspective of their own unit just as the functional departmentalization must do.

Departmentalization by product or service reflects grouping by the product being worked on or the service delivered. A consumer products company might group personal care products in one division and household sap products in another. While coordination across functional areas is improved (with representation by each functional area in the group), the unit members become product or service specific.

Departmentalization by customer or geographic region provides flexibility to respond to changing customer needs. Many specialty retail apparel companies group their departments by geographic region served to enable buyers to better meet the regional tastes of consumers. This avoids putting exactly the same apparel in each geographic region. Unfortunately, there is little opportunity for experts to share their knowledge across other customer or geographic units.

With geographic departmentalization, the firm can better respond to regional differences, but the focus is often on a specific geographic area—sometimes to the detriment of the loyalty to the larger organization. Communication is not always optimal with headquarters, either. This will further isolate the department.

The matrix approach is a combination of the departmentalization of two other departmentalization choices discussed earlier. This structure combines the departmentalization by division and function. Realizing that neither one type of departmentalization fits the organizations needs, a combination is chosen to achieve the best of both options.

The matrix violates the unity of command (by having more than one boss). Members of a matrix report to a functional superior and a product or project superior. There are a number of benefits to be gained, however.

Choices must also be made concerning the rigidity of the adherence to rules and the degree of job specialization. These are reflected in the choice of mechanistic or organic structures.

Mechanistic vs. Organic

Jobs can be standardized in a stable environment (because there is little or no change). On the other hand, highly specialized jobs do not make sense in a dynamic environment with a lot of change. These two approaches reflect mechanistic and organic designs.

As long as there are no (or at least few) environmental changes, a mechanistic structure can be best. The mechanistic organization is characterized by very rigid rules with most decisions made at the top of the organization. Each employee's work tends to be highly specialized.

Organic organizations generally do not rely on rigid adherence to rules or a formal chain of command. The flexibility needed in their changing environment comes from avoiding the formulation of rigid rules. Instead, they use broad parameters to guide the behavior of organizational members. There is also more lateral communication in the organic structure with less reliance on the formal chain of command. Job specialization is at a minimum to ensure that employees are not constrained by what their job description says.

In a highly volatile and dynamic environment, an organic structure is often most effective. Specialization of jobs is not possible with the constant change. Rules are not appropriate because they have such short lives with dynamic conditions. Flexibility is required to respond to the environmental changes and as a result, decentralized decision-making is used.

JUST A MINUTE

 The mechanistic versus organic design choice can be applied to departments or units as well as complete organizations. As a result, some departments within the same organization may be organic while others are mechanistic—each adapting to its own unit's needs.

MANAGING IN DIFFERENT STRUCTURES

There are a number of different structures to select from today. While many are more traditional, the need for intrapreneurship, reengineering, and the move to acquire properties of the boundaryless organizational type must be considered as well.

Henry Mintzberg suggested that there are five major structural forms:

- Simple structure
- Machine bureaucracy
- Professional bureaucracy
- Divisionalized
- Adhocracy

The simple structure is generally the choice for smaller companies operating in a dynamic environment. The owner-manager makes most of the decisions. This individual oversees all the operations of the firm. This simple structure enables the business to respond quickly to environmental changes.

The machine bureaucracy is seen more in larger organizations that operate in more stable environments. This structure is highly centralized and uses a high degree of formalization. Because these organizations operate in a stable environment, the tasks can be standardized.

The professional bureaucracy is seen in hospitals and organizations that have employees who have trained in specialized professions, such as doctors and nurses. The professional training provides the standardization.

Big companies operating in more than one industry generally use the divisionalized form. This is similar to the machine bureaucracy, but on a grander scale. The environment is stable, and the firm uses a high degree of standardization. Many of the conglomerates today still use the divisionalized form.

 The divisionalized form was modeled after the organizational structure adopted by General Motors in the early 1900s. Each division represented a different car model.

The adhocracy is the design of choice for newer organizations operating in highly complex environments. A highly organic structure, this structure is used to encourage creativity.

Encouraging Innovation

Larger companies have become especially concerned with innovation. Smaller companies generally are reported to produce almost 25 times as many innovations for each dollar spent on research and development as their larger counterparts.

Rigid organizational structures (including strict adherence to rules, the chain of command, and formal communication channels) tend to stifle creativity and innovation. Nurturing innovation requires decentalization and room to make mistakes.

Intrapreneurship has become a concern for more organizations in the quest to be more creative and innovative in business. *Intrapreneurship* is the term used by some to reflect innovation within the organization. Creative approaches can be taken in structuring the organization to encourage more innovation.

More freedom is often needed to encourage innovation. This may require a new department, unit, or division. A total spin-off is also a consideration. Sometimes it's not enough to try to work within the confines of an existing structure. A new structure for the creative unit is sometimes more effective. This enables the new unit to be separated from the "old" ways.

The Impact of Reengineering

A critical process today in organizational design is that of reengineering. This is the process whereby each process within the company is examined. This is the radical redesign of the processes within an organization whereby streamlining results.

PROCEED WITH CAUTION

The failure rate for reengineering efforts is estimated to be nearly 70 percent of all efforts undertaken. Surprisingly enough, employee resistance is cited as the most common reason for the failures. People and the impact of the changes on these people must be included in the reengineering effort.

As processes are redesigned, structures may have to be altered to support this streamlining. When BancOne Mortgage reengineered their mortgage application process, they restructured to support the team approach whereby a team of specialized employees handled the complete application process. This replaced the process of handing off the application to one department after another in a series of steps to complete the processing of the application.

The Boundaryless Organization

The boundaryless organization overcomes the rigidity of some of the traditional organizational forms. The boundaryless organization may also be called the barrier-free organization. Suggested by Jack Welch (the Chief Executive Officer of General Electric), the boundaryless organization is more fluid with self-managed teams.

Barriers are thought to impede organizational performance and decrease innovation. The boundaries represent restrictions to coordination across units within the organization and between those inside and outside the company.

The virtual organization is a variation of the boundaryless organization. There is a fluid network of linked firms. These companies have combined their talents and skills to achieve a specific common goal—and then will move on to their next alliance.

There is little control over other partners in the virtual organization. The nature of the structure is such that it exists for a limited time only. Each company contributes what it does best to link all the skills needed to achieve the specified goal. It gives each company the opportunity to concentrate on what they do best and outsource the rest. This will enhance each partner's chance for success, and they can share the risk of the project.

With the many benefits that the virtual organization offers, like all other design choices, it is not for every firm. It is important that you know when a virtual organization is appropriate.

Only those functions that are not critical to the core business of the firm should be outsourced. If the function is not central to the company's competitive advantage, then it can be outsourced.

HOUR'S UP!

Recognizing that organizational design choices can impact your organization's performance and your unit's performance, take a minute to check what you have learned in this hour.

1. According to the contingent approach …
   a. There is no one-size-fits-all design.
   b. The company must carefully match major factors with the structure that best fits its needs.
   c. Adaptations must be made to ensure the most effective design choice is made.
   d. All of the above.

2. Organizational design …
   a. Cannot be graphically depicted.
   b. Is the decision of how to configure the company.
   c. Disregards the actual work to be performed in the organization.
   d. Is done once in an organization's lifetime.

3. Design is influenced by ...

    a. Technology, environment, strategy, and size.

    b. Span of control and centralization.

    c. Division of labor and departmentalization.

    d. None of the above.

4. Unemployment levels ...

    a. Are a variable in the economic environment.

    b. Influence every company—though in varying ways.

    c. Determine the labor pool.

    d. All of the above.

5. The task environment ...

    a. Is the broader, general environment.

    b. Is commonly referred to as the industry.

    c. Includes the political/legal environment.

    d. Includes only your competitors.

6. As organizations grow ...

    a. Structure becomes irrelevant; it is already set.

    b. There is generally a smaller degree of specialization.

    c. There is generally a greater degree of specialization.

    d. Their structure becomes less complex.

7. Span of control should consider ...

    a. How specialized subordinates' jobs are.

    b. How you empower your employees.

    c. How much interaction each employee needs with the supervisor.

    d. All of the above.

8. One of the disadvantages of departmentalization by function is ...

    a. The silo mentality.

    b. That employees only see the "big picture."

    c. That there is too much coordination across functional groups.

    d. That it is not a popular method.

QUIZ

9. In a highly volatile and dynamic environment …
    a. Flexibility is unnecessary.
    b. An organic structure is often most effective.
    c. A mechanistic structure is often most effective.
    d. Centralized decision-making is best.

10. The boundaryless organization …
    a. Is also called the barrier-free organization.
    b. Is more fluid.
    c. Eliminates barriers.
    d. All of the above.

HOUR 17

Organizational Culture

CHAPTER SUMMARY

LESSON PLAN:

In this hour you will learn about ...

- Defining culture.
- Defining subcultures and countercultures.
- Recognizing the link between culture and organizational performance.
- Identifying the characteristics of "excellent" companies.
- Understanding the aspects of culture.
- Learning the typologies of culture.
- Building, reinforcing, and changing culture.
- Merging two cultures.

Much of the research in organizational behavior and management borrows its foundations from the behavioral sciences. Researchers have borrowed heavily from anthropology. It is possible to study the culture of an organization just as the culture of a society can be examined.

The mere mention of some company names conjures up an image—sometimes a name may bring to mind just one characteristic. This is the essence of organizational culture. It helps you understand how organizations do things.

Culture can be thought of as the glue. Culture holds your organizational members together and separates it from other organizations' members.

Culture also plays a critical part in your organization's success. It is the culture of your organization that can be at the core of your organization's competitive advantage.

WHAT IS CULTURE?

Culture reflects differences that you can feel from one organization to the next. You may not even be able to always put your finger on it. Sometimes you just know that the organization is different. Culture also influences how people behave. It also identifies who is in and who is outside of the organization.

3M is a company known for its innovation. This focus is recognized both in and outside the organization—reflecting the organizational culture.

The initial definitions of culture were quite broad. Some suggested that culture was, "the way we do things." Culture is defined as the "mental programming" of the organizational members according to Geert Hofstede, a researcher who developed a framework on the dimensions of culture in 1980 after surveying IBM employees in 50 countries. Numerous definitions have been subsequently offered to substantially narrow the definition. There are common threads in all these definitions, which suggest what culture is.

Culture reflects values that are understood by the organizational members. These values are not always written down in an employee handbook. Some organizations do, however, ceremoniously record their core values. These values have to be taken further, though. Organizational members must internalize them, they can't just be written down and referred to periodically; members must live by them.

Some organizations have even had their core values printed on wallet size cards for employees to carry with them and be reminded of their commitment to those values.

Culture, then, can actually be thought of as the glue that holds your organization together. It is the system of shared beliefs and values that serves as a guidepost for behaviors of organizational members. Culture is the shared system of assumptions or feelings that are taken for granted. Organizational culture basically identifies who you are as a member of your organization.

Just as personality is unique to each individual, culture is unique to each organization. While there may be common characteristics from organization to organization, the complete package is a unique culture. Even companies operating in exactly the same industry will have unique corporate cultures.

These unique values and shared expectations outline how the organization conducts business. It is the culture of your organization that determines how your organizational members will address customer relationships, creativity, and risk.

An instrument known as the organization culture profile or OCP uses rankings on 54 dimensions to identify shared values in an organization.

Those companies that are well known for customer service have cultures that place a high value on their customers. The culture also determines whether the climate is ripe for creative ideas (or proven methods are more highly valued) and whether risk taking is encouraged. Generally, those cultures that encourage creative ideas also tolerate high levels of risk. It is often through the willingness to take risk that creativity is fostered.

SUBCULTURES

Larger organizations may have more than one culture. While there is usually a dominant culture (also referred to as the macro culture), there are likely to be cultures found throughout the organization. Referred to as subcultures, these pockets of culture can embrace the values of the dominant culture or reject them.

Subcultures can be the result of hierarchical differences. That is, status differences in the company can lead to different cultures. This is especially found in highly centralized organizations where a distinction is made between the general workforce and top management.

With a diverse workforce (common in organizations today), there are subcultures that reflect the cultural differences of this population. Groups are bound together by their common cultural backgrounds.

The different functional areas of a firm usually develop cultures that reflect their focus in the organization. These group members perform the same job, filling the same occupation. In a university, there are usually at least two subcultures—one on the faculty side and one on the administrative or staff side. While both may embrace the values of the overall university (as in, the dominant culture), each of these subcultures will reflect its own unique focus—the faculty focus and the administrative focus. Each may operationalize the values of the dominant culture in different ways.

COUNTERCULTURES

In addition, the subculture may reject the values of the dominant culture. In this case, the subculture is called a counterculture because it runs counter to the overall corporate culture. There may be pockets of resistance within the organization that do not embrace the dominant culture's values.

FYI Organizational culture did not become a focus in the popular business literature until the 1980s. It is still considered a relatively "new" management area.

Organizations must be careful to monitor these countercultures. Their danger is when they impede the progress of the company or diminish the organization's performance levels. If the macro culture's values reflect high performance and the counterculture's do not, care has to be taken to ensure that the counterculture is turned around. The opposite situation could also occur, which could be beneficial to the organization. In this case, the counterculture should be cultivated to eventually become more dominant.

As can be seen, these subcultures can be conflicting in the values that they reinforce. When this occurs, they can fragment the organization. Culture and subculture must be constantly revisited to ensure that they are not harming the organization.

INTERNAL INTEGRATION AND EXTERNAL ADAPTATION

Corporate culture serves two major functions. It is the culture of the organization that tells people outside the organization who you are and what you stand for. Culture also prescribes the behavior and working relationships of those inside the organization.

Your corporate culture communicates to those outside the organization what you do. All members of the organization are given a common identity with culture. When the culture is strong, all the organization's employees know exactly who they are and identify with the mission of the organization. Each person knows the purpose of the company. With a strong culture and readily identified sense of purpose, the organization is also likely to have a lower turnover rate.

PROCEED WITH CAUTION

 The rise in popularity of the boundaryless organization with a contingent workforce is creating fuzzy boundaries between organizational cultures. As temporary employees move back and forth between companies, they bring pieces of other cultures with them.

Culture can generate a sense of commitment by each employee. As you buy into the corporate value system, you become more committed to the organization. You are also less likely to leave the organization as this sense of commitment is developed.

Internally, the culture of your organization prescribes the acceptable behavior. Organizational members understand what is expected of them and how they are to work with another. Stability is generated as organizational members embrace this common value system.

CULTURE AND PERFORMANCE

Organizational culture is particularly critical in dealing with change within any organization. Cultures themselves may change over time. And, as organizations recognize the need to change, these changes must be reflected in changes in the culture as well.

In a classic management work, *In Search of Excellence,* Tom Peters and Robert Waterman (Macmillan Library Reference, 1997) suggested that those companies deemed "excellent" (that is, top performers), shared eight core characteristics. These characteristics were at the center of their culture.

See how many of these characteristics are found in your organization's culture:

- **Action oriented.** These excellent companies are swift to act—making decisions way before their competition.

- **Value customers.** These organizations place a high value on customers. They really walk the talk and go beyond just meeting the needs of their customers.

- **Encourage innovation.** Excellent companies use smaller units to build a climate encouraging innovation and creativity.

JUST A MINUTE

 General Motors created the Saturn division to try and set the right climate for creativity. To encourage innovation that was not an integral part of the GM culture, a separate division was created to encourage this innovation. The Saturn automobile is still known for its innovation.

- **Believe people are their most important asset.** They have respect for the employees. Managers and employees in these organizations share a mutual respect for each other.

- **Use MBWA.** Excellent companies use "management by walking around." The management rubs elbows with employees. They can't be informed sitting at a desk in the ivory tower. There is substantial interaction between management and employees.

- **Focus on core competencies.** These companies stick to what they do best and do not get spread too thin. They don't try to be all things to all people.

 Outsourcing enables an organization to stick to what they know best. Peters and Waterman called this the need to "stick to the knitting." Organizations then should outsource the other functions. Refer to Hour 16, "Organizational and Structural Design," for a discussion on outsourcing.

- **Build lean organizations.** The high performing companies are not top-heavy structures. They are not concerned with building units with many people, but rather focus on the impact that their people are making.

- **Rigid adherence to organizational values.** This rigid adherence to values causes fewer rules to be necessary throughout the organization. The values guide the behaviors and decision-making process of employees; therefore, they do no need rigid regulations.

Culture impacts the performance of the organization. Both employee satisfaction and customer satisfaction are influenced by culture. It is, therefore, important to build a strong organizational culture.

Strong Organizational Cultures

A strong culture is related to high organizational performance. A strong culture is reinforced and taught to new employees. While it may not always be possible to articulate the core values, appropriate behavior can be modeled. Employees don't consciously think about values in a strong culture, they just engage in the appropriate behaviors. This provides the organization with a measure of uniformity and more effective communication.

Strong organizational cultures clearly communicate to members what their company stands for and what their common identity is. They focus more on people instead of rules. The organizational members who "walk the organizational talk" are celebrated as heroes. Employees and managers in strong cultures usually have a healthy sense of respect for each other.

This strong culture, though, must have high performance norms. The acceptable behaviors reinforced must encourage high performance. A strong culture also develops commitment on the part of the organizational members as they embrace these core values.

Care must be taken to recognize there is a downside to strong organizational cultures. Strong cultures create blinders for an organization. They fail to identify opportunities as they maintain a singular view of their own organization and what it does. They maintain the status quo, and no changes are made in what the organization does or how it does it.

ASPECTS OF CULTURE

Organizational culture is passed on to the generations of corporate employees just as society's culture is passed down from one generation to the next. The various aspects of culture must be understood in order to pass it on, however.

There are components of culture that are highly visible, and some that tend to be more hidden. You can experience culture by working in it or learning about the products and services offered by the company. Observing how the company deals with its environment, knowing how communication is handled, and identifying the symbols and logos provide insight into the culture and what is valued in the organization.

Culture is created with the founders of the company. The founders' values become the foundation for the values of the organizational culture. The first employees of the company accept these values to guide their behavior. This can be clearly seen in the example of Disney. The core values that were created by the Walt Disney Company are still the guiding principles by which the company operates and conducts its business.

The industry within which the organization operates may also shape the development of the culture. As companies seek out their markets within their industry, they become committed to certain values.

Changing dress code can reflect a move to change corporate culture. As more companies have changed from formal, rigid organizations with traditional dress codes, they have adopted the business casual dress code as a reinforcement. The revision in dress code is usually mirrored in other aspects of the organization as well.

There are a number of aspects of culture. Some of these aspects are referred to collectively as artifacts. These may include sagas and founding stories, symbols, rites and rituals, jargon, and values and beliefs. These aspects will be covered in the following sections.

Sagas and Founding Stories

The stories told throughout the organization help to socialize new employees and communicate culture. It is through these sagas that new employees discover what the organization values and what behaviors are expected of them.

Employees in many organizations are told the founding story that communicates the early years of the firm. This is the beginning of the creation of the culture. And this usually clearly captures the values of the founding fathers.

The stories may be somewhat embellished to make the point (especially with the telling over a long period of time). This is the way you can teach members how to fit in and become a part of the organizational community.

Symbols

Symbols are visible aspects of culture that communicate core values and corporate identity. Symbols are objects that convey meaning. Companies may use corporate logos or slogans to communicate this identity. The building itself and the decorations used communicate to those outside the organization who it is.

JUST A MINUTE

The pink Cadillac of Mary Kay Cosmetics is a very visible and widely recognized symbol of the corporate culture. This is the organizational reward given to top salespeople in the company at a large ceremony steeped in tradition and ritual.

Rites and Rituals

The official ceremonies of the firm also communicate something about the organization. These rites are recurring at regular intervals. A special rite at colleges and universities is that of the formal graduation ceremony. Special recognition banquets and ceremonies in many companies are used to communicate what is valued in those organizations.

Organizations may be able to copy strategy or processes from a competitor, but they cannot copy culture. This may very well be the source of an organization's competitive advantage because it cannot be duplicated.

Even your performance appraisal is considered a rite in your organization. This is a regularly scheduled ceremony of your firm. And, it certainly communicates what is valued in your organization. You are rewarded and rated high on those issues valued by your company.

JARGON

Each organization has its own jargon. This jargon can also extend to the industry within which the organization operates. There is a special language understood by the organizational members. This is generally characterized by use of acronyms that provide shorthand talk for members that is readily understood by those considered "insiders." Understanding this jargon further helps to bond the organizational members together.

Jargon can even include gestures. This really includes any means of communication that is used by those "in the know." It is a means of creating a sense of membership. The use of jargon and gestures is clearly observed in the stock exchange, for example, most of the gestures are only understood by those considered "insiders."

VALUES AND BELIEFS

Values and beliefs are at the very heart of the culture of your organization. These values are often the glue bonding organizational members together. These are the shared beliefs that guide the performance and the attitudes of members. This can often be the source of your company's competitive advantage.

Some organizations have strong core values focused on quality. This emphasis on quality shapes the actions and the work of the organizational members. This focus on quality can also give these companies a competitive edge in the marketplace.

JUST A MINUTE

 Watson of IBM is a prime example of the founding father's beliefs and values guiding the actions of organizational members. Watson's quest for innovative people guided the actions of those within the organization for years. Hewlett and Packard of HP also provided the foundation for the core values of their company. Their "garage rules" to avoid bureaucracy and its inherent problems permeated the actions of HP employees for decades.

A Typology of Culture

Cultures can be categorized based on a number of different dimensions. One popular categorization of culture is the double S cube. It is so named because it "measures" culture along two dimensions: sociability and solidarity.

Sociability refers to the level of friendliness found in the organization. Those organizations with members that socialize a great deal are said to rate high on the sociability dimension. Organizations with isolated members are low in sociability.

Solidarity reflects the degree to which the organization's members are on the same sheet of music, so to speak. That is, whether the members agree on the direction and objectives of the firm. When members agree and understand their goals, the organization measures high on solidarity. Those members of organizations having little understanding or interest in the goals of their firm measure low in solidarity.

When these two dimensions are combined, four organizational culture types result. These are networked, mercenary, fragmented, and communal cultures.

A networked culture measures high in sociability and low in solidarity. While friendly with open communication, the focus is more on social issues than the business at hand.

A mercenary culture is just the opposite. That is, this organizational culture measures high in solidarity and low in sociability. With low sociability, organizational members tend to communicate solely to get the job done and be rather formal in doing so. They are, however, very committed and focused on reaching their organizational goals.

A fragmented culture ranks low in both solidarity and sociability. These organizations are not very friendly and communication is at a minimum. There is little commitment to organizational goals.

The culture that measures high in both solidarity and sociability is referred to as the communal culture. These are friendly organizations with a high level of commitment and understanding to the organization.

PROCEED WITH CAUTION

While organizational culture and climate are somewhat similar and are often confused, they refer to very different concepts. Climate reflects an immediate situation and atmosphere within the organization. Culture deals with the deeply ingrained values in the organization.

YOUR ROLE IN BUILDING AND REINFORCING CULTURES

As a manager, you are responsible for supporting cultures, or in some cases, for building and creating cultures. Your responsibility is likely to be more managing an existing culture instead of creating cultures. Although, you may be responsible for creating a culture in a new unit.

Managing an organizational culture generally involves one of three major issues:

- Supporting current culture
- Teaching culture
- Changing culture

To support the current culture, you will use the existing culture and its value system to elicit the desired behavior from your employees. Some tips to consider which may assist you in supporting culture include the following:

- **Know your culture and values inside and out in order to skillfully manage the culture.** Know the lessons learned from the stories and the significance of the symbols. Be sure that the values are supported in the artifacts of the organization. Understand through experiencing the culture by working in it and living the values.

- **Use the culture's values to manage the behavior of others.** Use these values as the guides to reinforce appropriate, acceptable behavior. You must use these values to evaluate how employees perform.

- **Share your understanding of the culture with others.** As this understanding permeates the individuals in the organization, less direct control or management influence is needed.

- **As new employees are hired, they must be oriented to the company.**
  Referred to as the socialization process, teaching about the culture
  helps new employees to become acclimated to the organization and to
  understand what is valued.

Teaching the culture of your organization becomes critical. Employees must
know and understand their corporate culture. Only then can the culture
help internally integrate the workforce. Employees cannot be guided by values that they don't know about.

Relating as much about the culture as possible is a crucial component of the
orientation process of new hires. But new employees must also see this
appropriate behavior modeled. You yourself must be a role model to reinforce the values of the culture.

New employees learn by observing as well as doing what they are told.
Employees must see that others are walking the talk. This adherence to the
core values should be reinforced in both the formal and informal socialization processes of the organization.

Changing culture is hard to accomplish because culture is deeply ingrained
within an organization. But, with systematic attention to the cultivation of
core values, the culture can be changed.

When external environments change, it is often necessary to change the
culture of the organization as well. While processes within the organization
must be revised and a redesign of the organization itself may be in order, the
basic values must also be changed. These values are at the heart of the
changes needed. A change consultant may be used to help effect this
change.

GO TO ▶
Refer to Hour 7,
"The Basics of
Process Develop-
ment," concerning
the organizational
change process and
a more complete
discussion of ways
to overcome resis-
tance to change.

This may be especially important in an organization where the current values may not reinforce good performance. Many organizations today are
making the transition to high-performance organizational cultures and team-
based organizations.

Changing culture requires that you create new stories. You must reinforce
the new values being created. This means that you must replace the old stories supporting the old values. Sometimes the same story can be used with a
new "lesson" that supports a new value.

While changing culture is not an easy process, constant monitoring is necessary. You must be on guard to take advantage of opportunities to support the

new culture and continually shape the behavior of your employees. The new values can be institutionalized to become habit, but it does take time and hard work. This change took over a decade as Lee Iacocca revamped the culture of Chrysler. To implement a new strategy, a new culture was required to support the new direction of Chrysler.

The building of a corporate culture is just as critical to an entrepreneur as developing a strategy for that business. You may be required to assist in building a corporate culture in your organization, or you may find it necessary to build a subculture in your unit. Consider these suggestions when building a culture:

- Develop basic beliefs concerning the environment within which the organization (or your unit) operates.

- Create values to guide employee behavior to help the organization (or your unit) meet its goals. Do this by asking what it really takes to get the job done and get the job done well.

- Develop a strategic vision outlining the future state of the firm (or your unit). This requires combining the basic beliefs and values guiding employee behavior.

- Implement the steps to achieve the vision. A vision with no movement toward its achievement is useless.

- Use selection and recruitment to create the desired culture. Hire people with consistent values who will support the culture you are building.

- Provide support for the culture to maintain it long-term. That is, ensure that organizational reward systems and other processes are aligned with this culture to support its continuance in the organization. Ensure that you are supporting the behaviors you really want.

- You must walk the talk and actively support the new values to be successful in building a culture. That is, you must role model the expected behaviors.

- Revisit the values to ensure that they change with the times and remain useful and appropriate.

WHEN TWO CULTURES MERGE

With the number of mergers and acquisitions increasing, the role of culture in these transactions becomes critical. Because no two cultures are exactly alike, a merging of two cultures is more accurately called a culture clash.

PROCEED WITH CAUTION

 There is a big difference between a strategic fit of two firms and a fit of their cultures. Until recently, the impact of cultures in mergers and acquisitions was not a primary concern.

As two cultures come together, there is inevitable tension and friction created. When involved in the merging of two cultures, consider the following:

- Really get to know the culture. This takes time. Don't rush or jump to conclusions.
- Listen, but don't really believe everything that you hear. What you hear may not be accurate. Look for verification of your information.
- Explore the physical environment to get insight into the culture. For example, examine offices, common areas, and status differences.
- Watch for inconsistencies in the culture and clues of unhealthiness. A few of the warning signs are poor morale, negativity by organizational members, and poor organizational performance. Sometimes you may simply get a "bad feeling" that should cause you to start exploring for concrete signs.
- Prepare your resume and seek out another job if, after close examination, your values are not aligned with those of the surviving culture.

As a prospective employee of any firm, you want to find out as much about the organization's culture as possible to ensure that the culture fits with your personality and value system. The reverse of this is also true. No longer do you just try to match the applicant to the job, but you must also consider the match to the organization. This is where organizational culture plays a major role.

HOUR'S UP!

After learning the fundamentals of corporate culture, take a minute to assess how much you have internalized by answering these 10 questions.

1. Corporate culture …

    a. Does not play any role in organizational performance.

    b. Can be the source of an organization's competitive advantage.

    c. Has a singular, well-accepted definition.

    d. Reflects values understood only by top management.

2. Larger organizations may have …

    a. More than one culture.

    b. A dominant culture.

    c. Several subcultures in different functional areas.

    d. All of the above.

3. Corporate culture serves the function of internal integration to …

    a. Tell those outside the organization what you do.

    b. Ensure employees do not become too committed to the organization.

    c. Prescribe acceptable behavior.

    d. All of the above.

4. A characteristic not included in the cultures of "excellent" companies according to Peters and Waterman is …

    a. Encouraging innovation.

    b. Valuing stockholders.

    c. Believing people are your most important asset.

    d. Focusing on core competencies.

5. Sagas …

    a. Are always entertaining though not usually true.

    b. Are entertaining, but don't really teach anything important.

    c. Help socialize new employees to the company by communicating culture.

    d. Can't explain what is appropriate behavior.

6. Jargon …
   a. Can include gestures.
   b. Can extend to an industry.
   c. Is a special language understood by the organization's members.
   d. All of the above.

7. To build or reinforce culture …
   a. You must first know your culture and the values associated with it.
   b. You must keep what you know about the culture secret.
   c. Ensure that artifacts do not support the culture and its values.
   d. More direct control is necessary.

8. A merger or acquisition …
   a. Often results in a clash of two cultures.
   b. Seldom creates tension because one culture immediately becomes dominant.
   c. Only brings together two cultures exactly the same.
   d. Is never concerned with cultures.

9. You can use selection and recruitment …
   a. To alter the founding father's stories of the firm.
   b. To do many things except manage culture.
   c. To create the desired culture by hiring people with consistent values.
   d. All of the above.

10. When involved in the merging of two cultures …
    a. There is seldom any tension created.
    b. Listen and believe everything that you hear.
    c. Take the time to really get to know the new culture.
    d. Don't worry about any "bad feelings" you have; just get over them.

QUIZ

HOUR 18

Organizational Politics and Power

CHAPTER SUMMARY

LESSON PLAN:

In this hour you will learn about ...

- Power and influence in today's organization.
- The bases of power.
- How to build a power base.
- How to use upward influence.
- Organizational politics and political alliances.

Organizational politics is an organizational way of life. While you may want to be excluded from political life, it is not possible if you want to succeed. You must have a good grasp of how power is acquired and used—especially in your own organization.

Some people try to avoid organizational politics thinking that politics is inherently bad. As you will see from this hour's discussion, politics is neither inherently good nor bad. It is, instead, more of a double-edged sword—cutting both ways depending on the individual's use.

POWER AND INFLUENCE

Power is defined simplistically as the ability to get other people to do something that you want them to do. It may not necessarily be what they would have done. Power, then, is all about strong interpersonal skills. Power is essential to leadership.

Power enables you to be more effective. It also gives you more control over your career development. It is not just the power that you actually have that is important, but your potential for power that is critical.

Power is not etched in stone. The center of power in any organization can be thought of as a moving target. Power is actually a dynamic process. Power changes as the environment changes and the performance of the organization changes.

GO TO ▶
Refer to Hour 19, "The New Leadership," for a more complete discussion of leadership and the role of leadership in effective management.

Influence is said to be the result of using this power that you have. It is the net effect of using your power. You need to use influence outside of the formal chain of command. You rely on people and must get their cooperation.

JUST A MINUTE

Influence is not just used inside the organization. These tactics are used outside the organization as well—including suppliers, clients, and so on.

THE BASES OF POWER

Classic research conducted several decades ago still provides the foundation for a basic understanding of the concept of power today. While there is a difference in how power is acquired and used, the sources of power remain the same.

Basic to building power is an examination of the types of power to which you have access. You can only build your bases of power if you have a clear understanding of the sources and how they work.

There are five major bases of power on which you can build. These are grouped into two types: position power and personal power.

POSITION POWER

Position power is the power that you have as a result of the position that you occupy. When you leave the position, you also leave behind the power that is inherent in that position. The power then belongs to the new person who subsequently occupies that position.

The three types of position power are legitimate, reward, and coercive power. While the three are all related (in that they are related to the position that you occupy), they remain distinct bases of power on which you can build.

Legitimate power is the formal "right to command" or the authority that you are given by the organization as a result of the position that you occupy. As a manager, you have legitimate power over your subordinates. The organization has given you formal authority over these subordinates. Your superior, in turn, has legitimate power over you. This power, however, is very situational. That is, this legitimate power is relative. You do not have legitimate power over other individuals in another organization—or even in another unit of your own organization.

Often linked to legitimate power is reward power, though this connection is not automatic. *Reward power* is the power you have to dole out rewards that people may want. You can get people to do things that you want them to do by rewarding them with what they want—if you control the rewards that they value. Controlling the rewards that others value gives you power.

As a manager, you have reward power over your subordinates if you can grant them the promotion or the raise that they desire. These rewards can also include intangibles such as praise for a job well done. A manager who has no authority to reward employees is working from a weakened power base. The ability to provide rewards strengthens your power base.

Coercive power is the ability to withhold rewards or give punishment to people. If, as the manager, you can demote your subordinates or withhold a coveted promotion, you are said to have coercive power. Just the threat of punishment may be enough to control the behavior of others. These threats can be effective, even if not explicitly communicated.

With the move away from the command-and-control manager, the position power bases (legitimate, reward, and coercive) are not as important as they once were. Now, the personal power bases have become more critical with the move to teamwork and less emphasis on the formal structure of the organization.

PERSONAL POWER

Personal power is unrelated to the position that you occupy within the organization. These power bases reside within you as an individual and are derived from your personal characteristics. The two personal power bases are referent and expert power.

Expert power is the power you have as a result of the knowledge you acquire that someone else may need. It doesn't even matter if they need the knowledge now—if it is needed in the future, you are building your power base. Knowledge experts are generally those who wield considerable power within the organization.

JUST A MINUTE

The move to skill-based pay reflects the importance of acquiring additional skills in today's workplace. You can get double the pay-off now because acquiring these additional skills or knowledge can increase your power base.

As organizations change software packages, those individuals who quickly learn the new packages often acquire great power as resident experts until everyone else gets up to speed. You want to constantly be searching for knowledge areas where you can become the resident expert for your company. And you may very well have to change this base of knowledge as others become more knowledgeable in your area. Your expert power can be short-lived if you don't constantly update your skills.

Referent power could be said to be your "likeability" index. This is your level of personal attraction. The more likable you are, the more power you have. If people generally like you and respect you, they are more likely to do things that you want them to do.

When others want to be like you, you are said to have referent power over them. An old adage suggests that imitation is the sincerest form of flattery. This is at the heart of referent power. Others want to be like you and will imitate you and your behaviors. To be accepted, they will likely engage in the behaviors that you want them to engage in.

How to Build a Power Base

Now that you know what the power bases are, it is important to know how you can build power in each of them. Your ability to effectively manage is a product of both your position power and your personal power. You cannot rely solely on your position power to be effective as a manager in today's world.

It is important to remember that the perception of power is critical. You want to have power and you want to be perceived as having a lot of power. If you have power, but others don't see that you do, it is irrelevant to a large extent. Also important is your potential for power. It is not just the power that you actually have, but the potential for power that is important.

Because power helps you get things done, consider the following tips for building a better power base:

- Acquire very specialized knowledge few others have that is important to the organization's performance.
- Create a good, positive reputation for yourself.
- Increase your credibility in and outside the organization.
- Form political alliances. (Don't stretch yourself too thin with so many alliances that you are ineffective, but rather select critical relationships with peers and superiors.)
- Gain access of key resources to control what others need.
- Increase your visibility. Take on risky projects that get your name and face before top management.
- Develop charisma. This is especially important in dealing with your peers because you have no legitimate power over them and must rely upon your personal power.
- Build relevance for your unit. Ensure that the work of your unit is integral to the organizational mission and is central to the work of the overall organization.
- Share power when you acquire it. Giving power to subordinates actually will increase your power exponentially.
- Volunteer to work on committees or special projects. This helps you to gain access to information and increases your visibility.
- Take advantage of training opportunities in your organization. This will help to build your expert power.
- Constantly update your technical skills. You can easily lose your expert power if you don't continually update your skills.

To be more effective as a manager, you must build your own power base. Equally important, you must be able to read power in others. You want to know where the power is and who has the power. You also want to be able to recognize who lacks power.

It is also important to be able to recognize the warning signs of people who have little or no power. Some of the signs to indicate this powerlessness are as follows:

- **Little or no use of delegation.** Powerless managers are often insecure and keep what little power they have to themselves.
- **Very close supervision of subordinates.** These managers often engage in micromanagement as a result of their insecurity and lack of power.

- **Little confidence displayed.** These powerless individuals often feel insecure and threatened by their own employees. They lack self-confidence and communicate a lack of confidence in their subordinates as well.
- **Have little trust for others.** Their own lack of power and insecurity make them distrustful of others.
- **Protect their "turf."** They often try to make their job and their unit more important than it really is. This reflects the old "empire building" technique whereby people build an "empire" of people and jobs that they control in order to increase their power and importance.

A Paradigm Shift: Empowerment of the Workforce

Just a decade ago, most organizations reflected the traditional pyramid with the power concentrated at the top-most levels of the hierarchy. Today the reality is very different in many organizations. Now, power is distributed more evenly throughout most organizations. This is the result of the empowerment of the workforce.

PROCEED WITH CAUTION

While many organizations are following the trend toward a more empowered workforce, there are still plenty of organizations that continue to remain highly centralized. They can be expected to eventually follow suit, but that may still take considerable time. You must carefully diagnose the situation in your organization rather than just assume that a more even distribution of power exists.

This empowerment, however, has resulted in a major paradigm shift. It has required that everyone think very differently about the concept of power today.

Top managers in many organizations today actually are reporting that they have less power now than they had only a decade ago. This is a direct result of the empowerment of the workforce. Empowerment requires that you as a manager initially give up power. While this may be difficult at first, you must grant more power to your employees. You will benefit in the long run.

Part of effectively empowering the workforce is sharing information so that people can make better-informed decisions. An empowered workforce gives you as a manager fewer opportunities to use coercive power, thereby cutting in to another source of power. You are more effective developing your expert power base in an empowered organization.

In the past, most people thought about power as being a finite amount in the organization. Everyone sought to acquire a bigger piece of the power pie. Today, however, with empowerment, the idea is to think about how to make the power pie larger. With a larger pie, everyone automatically gets a larger slice. There is, in essence, a win-win situation with the new paradigm. No one's slice gets smaller for another's slice to get larger. Everyone gets a larger piece of power.

This new paradigm also suggests that the view of power itself is different. Power can no longer be acquired for the sake of having the power itself. Today, the key is to acquire power for what it can do for you—how it can lead to getting people to do more of what you want them to do.

Equally important in the concept of empowerment is the idea that middle management still may feel somewhat threatened.

JUST A MINUTE

Open-book management is a progressive management concept that is being used to further empower workers today. The financial books of the company are opened up to employees. This open sharing of financial information helps workers to better understand how their jobs contribute to the overall performance of the firm. This is just one example of novel approaches being implemented to empower America's workforce.

How to Manage Upward Influence

Three political relationships are important to you: upward, downward, and lateral relationships. Each of these relationships is managed somewhat differently. That is, the power bases used in each case may be altered to best meet the needs of the situation.

Contrary to the more traditional view of power, it flows in several directions (not just downward). It is important to understand all the political relationships, but it is critical that you know how to manage upward relationships.

Peer relationships require that you cooperate with your peers. You must coordinate work without going through formal channels of communication. The relationships require that you cover each other and provide support. The political system of favors (known as reciprocity) is instrumental in peer relationships.

The political relationship with your subordinates is more critical than many may think. These relationships must be carefully nurtured. These individuals have power that is often overlooked. Your subordinates can make you or break you. They can make you look good or bad.

In dealing with superiors, the legitimate power balance is tipped in favor of the superior. The astute use of organizational politics helps to even out this power. In using your upward influence, you may want to begin by adopting your superior's overall style. Minor adjustments are all that are usually needed. Because everyone likes people who are similar to himself or herself, you will get farther with your superior if you adopt a similar style.

You also must be loyal to your boss. Don't openly criticize your boss to others or be present when others are criticizing. Be careful to be honest with your boss as well. Don't try to hide bad information from him or her. They always find out anyway.

Know how your manager likes to receive communication—verbal or written. And then, deliver communications in the way they prefer. Also provide your boss with positive reinforcement. Because there is less positive feedback the higher up they move in the organizational pyramid, the feedback you provide will be important. Make sure, however, that your feedback is sincere. Insincerity will be quickly detected.

Upward relationships are important in building your power base. To be more effective in your upward relationships, you might consider the following suggestions when presenting ideas:

- Get your idea out to as many people as possible in as many different ways as possible.

- Buy as much face time as possible in presenting your idea. Try to increase your visibility and your connection with the issue—to own it, if you will.

- Ensure that the issues you are presenting are consistent with your area of expertise. You will lose some credibility if your idea is outside of your realm of expert knowledge.

- Be sure that your purpose is truly noble and is not being presented for your own self-interest. Also be sure that the issue is closely aligned with the overall mission and objectives of the firm. You will not find support in ideas that are not aligned with the organization's mission.

- Be sure to offer possible solutions when presenting a problem. Identify the members of the organization that will be instrumental in helping to solve the problem.

- Be clear about the organizational benefits to be gained. You must give your superiors a reason for buying in and help them see just what it is that they will gain.

JUST A MINUTE

Some organizational units are more powerful than others. Historically, the functional unit representing the founder's background or area of expertise tends to be among the most powerful in the organization.

ORGANIZATIONAL POLITICS

Politics is one of the mechanisms that enable you to get things done through other people. Politics even helps share the culture of your organization.

Organizational politics is concerned with the use of actions to meet individual goals through means that the organization doesn't necessarily sanction. Political behavior is generally outside the formal authority of the organization. You can use political behavior to achieve organizational or individual goals.

JUST A MINUTE

Organizational politics is more likely to be used in situations of uncertainty or ambiguity and where policies are not clear. Scarce resources also create a climate for the use of politics.

It is the misuse and abuse of power and politics that has given both bad names. *Politics* is defined as the process of gaining and using power in the organization. The negative connotation is founded in the highly visible cases of abuse. Politics, however, is simply the medium of exchange in organizations. In itself, politics is not inherently good or bad. It is how people play the game that makes it good or bad.

Political behavior can enhance your power base. Astute, politically savvy individuals have a strategy. They know what they want to achieve and how they are going to do it. They also know the tactics to be used. Everyone can devise these strategies—this is not just for management.

Common tactics in organizational politics include the following:

- Exercise control of information (the most popular of the political tactics). Several approaches can be taken to control information (because knowledge is power). You might be careful in choosing who has access to your information, or even consider not providing information to others that portray you in a less than favorable light.

PROCEED WITH CAUTION

Using information overload to your favor can also control information. Providing excessive amounts of information can overwhelm a colleague and ultimately help you control access to that information. Others won't want to wade through too much information. Care, however, should be exercised in using this tactic so that it does not backfire on you.

GO TO ▶
Refer to Hour 24, "Gaining an Edge: Business Etiquette," for a more detailed discussion of impression management and its importance to effective management.

- Engage in impression management. Ensure that you are projecting the appropriate corporate image. Managing your impression includes managing the perception of power others have of you. Ensure that you are optimistic. Use the power of positive thinking.

JUST A MINUTE

Those individuals who are particularly adept at changing their images are now referred to as organizational chameleons. The name reflects their ability to cultivate the image the organization values at the time.

- Gain support from others. The norm of reciprocity is especially important here. Creating obligations and alliances is instrumental in political behavior. You can gain support by giving support. When you grant a favor to someone, they then owe you one. And when someone does you a favor, you owe one back. Everyone keeps this mental tally and knows who to call upon for favors and support.

- Engage in networking. The development of relationships is critical. The astute manager recognizes the critical nature of networking to getting things done.

- Use political alliances. Coalitions are critical to political behavior. Coalitions are networks of alliances. You rely upon others to get things done, and these alliances enable you to be more effective.

- Control the agenda for decision-making. Decisions will then be made at the most advantageous time to get the desired result.

- Use co-optation, that is, influence people to adopt your way of thinking. This helps reduce blocks and resistance by getting them on your side early in the process.

POLITICAL ALLIANCES

The connections you have (that is, the relationships with important people in the organization) can build your power. Even if you don't necessarily have the power yourself, you're plugged into the people who do have the power. This leads to the perception of power. Others will perceive that you have power.

You also get more resources based on whom you know. The old adage still pertains, "It's not what you know, it's who you know." It is crucial that you network with influential people. Rubbing elbows with powerful people ultimately ensures that some of that power rubs off onto you.

Aligning yourself with the power in the organization is crucial. Being linked to power gives you power—or at the very least—it gives you the perception of having power.

JUST A MINUTE

The majority of top managers identify the support of others that they work with as the most commonly used source of power. Because management is all about getting things done through other people, intuitively, this makes good sense.

GENERAL TIPS TO POLITICS

Before you can actually begin to build your power base, you must understand the context within which you are operating. The following is a general list of tips to dealing with politics:

- Diagnose the political climate of your organization. Locate where the power resides and with whom. You may have to look inside and outside the organization. Also determine how the power is used.

PROCEED WITH CAUTION

You need more than an organization chart to identify power. Many of the powerful people are at lower levels in the organization or don't even appear on the chart. Don't be fooled by boxes on a chart.

- Learn to understand how the politics in your organization work to reduce uncertainty and function effectively in the organization.
- Know the dominant power bases of individuals and the goals they are trying to attain. This will provide you with an understanding of how the politics works, and will help you identify opportunities for building your own power bases.

You must learn what it takes to be successful in your organization's political realm. Following are parting general tips to navigate the waters of organizational politics:

- Make sure that you understand the culture of your organization.
- Promote yourself (only in an ethical way).
- Avoid surprises for your boss. Keep your boss informed.
- Be honest. Earn the trust and respect of others. You must be a team player and this means you must be cooperative.
- Use the grapevine to plug into informal information.
- Consider networks outside the organization (such as professional associations).
- Don't let conflicts go unresolved. Get to the bottom of conflict. Confront the issue (and the people involved) head-on.

HOUR'S UP!

After spending the last hour reviewing information on power and politics, take a few minutes to check if you are ready to play the political game in your organization.

1. Organizational politics …
   a. Should be avoided at all costs.
   b. Is an organizational way of life.
   c. Is inherently bad.
   d. Can never impact your effectiveness as a manager.

2. Power …
   a. Enables you to be more effective.
   b. That you actually have is more important than any potential for power that you may have.

    c. Is stable and never really changes.

    d. Has only one critical base—your position in the organization.

3. The two major types of power bases include ...

    a. Personal and position.

    b. Position and legitimate.

    c. Personal and legitimate.

    d. None of the above.

4. Personal power ...

    a. Is considered more important than position power in today's organizational structures.

    b. Is unrelated to the position that you occupy in the organization.

    c. Resides in the individual.

    d. All of the above.

5. When building a power base, you should do all of the following except ...

    a. Acquire specialized knowledge.

    b. Create a good, positive reputation for yourself.

    c. Avoid risky projects.

    d. Share the power that you acquire with your subordinates.

6. Organizational politics ...

    a. Uses only means that are sanctioned by the organization.

    b. Includes only behaviors that are within the formal authority of the organization.

    c. Is only used for individual goals.

    d. Is defined as the process of gaining and using power in the organization.

7. The empowerment of the workforce ...

    a. Has resulted in a paradigm shift.

    b. Reflects a more even distribution of power throughout the organizational ranks.

    c. Has resulted in thinking of ways to make the power pie larger rather than concentrating on making a single slice of the pie larger.

    d. All of the above.

QUIZ

8. Contrary to the more traditional view of power …

    a. It flows only downward in most organizations.

    b. It flows in several directions.

    c. You must manage only lateral relationships.

    d. Power over others is the critical issue.

9. According to the dark side of power …

    a. Few people ever abuse their power.

    b. Deception and lying are not used in the political realm.

    c. Once you obtain power, it is tempting to engage in behaviors to perpetuate that power.

    d. This is the only side of power seen in organizations today.

10. To navigate the waters of organizational politics …

    a. Diagnose the political climate of your organization.

    b. Understand how the politics work.

    c. Know the dominant power bases of individuals and their goals.

    d. All of the above.

HOUR 19

The New Leadership

CHAPTER SUMMARY

LESSON PLAN:

In this hour you will learn about ...

- Leadership and management roles.
- Leadership research that influences today's perspective.
- Transactional and transformational leadership.
- The characteristics of the charismatic leader.
- Followership, the flip side of leadership.

Effective management is all about getting things done through other people. The tools by which this is accomplished are changing. With the environmental changes outside the organization and the structural changes taking place within the organization, the very way in which you work is being altered.

Today you cannot rely solely upon your official position within the organization to get things done. The discussion of power and politics highlighted the fact that power is more evenly distributed throughout the organization. This requires that you build strong interpersonal skills and a personal power base to more effectively perform your job.

In addition, you must develop your leadership potential. Leadership is a critical component of both organizational and managerial effectiveness. Leadership is all about affecting the performance of others. This in turn, impacts your performance.

Leadership is defined as using influence to direct the activities and attitudes of other people. This implies that force is not used. Coercion is not a part of leadership. Any formal authority you may (or may not) have is also irrelevant to leadership.

Your subordinates accept your influence as a result of the respect that they have for you. Any formal authority that you may have over them is irrelevant (and unnecessary) with leadership.

JUST A MINUTE

Leadership is the most studied of all the management issues. American managers have a thirst to learn more about leadership and what it takes to be a more effective manager.

THE ROLES OF LEADERSHIP AND MANAGEMENT

Leadership and management both serve critical functions in organizations. Though these two terms are often used interchangeably, these functions are actually quite different. Management tends to support stability in the firm while leadership supports change.

A leader is said to determine the vision and strategy for the organization, outlining the actions required for reaching that future state. A manager is said to be responsible for operationalizing that vision; that is, implementing the strategy to get there. Management, then, promotes the smooth running of the organization.

The leadership role promotes change within the organization. Leadership, then, is more focused on energizing people in their performance while management is more focused on monitoring their performance levels. Managers rely more upon their formal authority in the organization in order to influence others.

GO TO ▶
Refer to Hour 1, "What Is Management?" for a discussion of the management functions as proposed by Fayol with an exploration of the control function and how em-ployee performance is monitored.

Granted, the line between the manager and the leader has become fuzzy. You might think from this perspective, then, that only top managers are leaders. This is certainly not true today, with strategic management responsibilities being delegated down the organizational hierarchy and throughout the organization. Leadership, then, is needed at all levels in every company.

Leadership and management may be thought of as two separate circles that intersect. This area of intersection represents the population of those who are both managers and leaders. Unfortunately, this is not a large area. It is still a rare breed of manager who is also a leader. In too many cases, a manager will take it for granted that the management role automatically includes the leader role. This, however, is not the case. The leadership role must be developed separately from the management role. This is the group that must be increased in today's organizations.

Companies need both managers and leaders to be successful. While more managers (if not all) should be leaders, all leaders don't have to necessarily be managers.

THE LEADERSHIP RESEARCH: HOW WE GOT TO THIS POINT

In examining what leadership is today, it is important to explore former theories and research directions. This helps to understand where we are today, what impact former research has had, and where we are going.

Most people agree that there is a difference between leaders and followers. There are numerous famous leaders of the past who helped shape history. These individuals certainly can be distinguished from their followers. While most can sense this difference, it has been hard to pinpoint the heart of these differences. Leadership, like beauty, has often been said to be in the eye of the beholder. Researchers have, however, attempted to shed more light on effective leadership through the decades.

THE GREAT PERSON TRAIT THEORY

The early leadership studies in the 1930s believed that there was a list of magical traits that leaders possessed. This list of traits was thought to be relatively stable over time and would be critical in determining leadership potential. If an individual possessed these traits, then they were likely to exhibit success in managerial positions. Conversely, if an individual did not possess these traits, then they were unlikely to be an effective leader.

With more research, the list got longer and longer. The problem, of course, was that there was no magical list of traits. While there may have been some common agreement about some general traits, there was no definitive list that exhibited a strong positive correlation with leadership success across all situations and across all leaders.

You can list out a dozen leaders—both past and present—to find that they don't share all the same characteristics. For example, Joan of Arc and Adolf Hitler are both considered leaders from history—though for very different reasons. Yet the traits that they possessed are not exactly matched. Researchers could not find a definitive list applicable to all leaders.

Some of the traits researchers tried to propose included such characteristics as height, strength, bravery, intelligence, and self-confidence. Unfortunately, there were known and proven leaders that could disprove nearly every trait. For example, Napoleon was known to be a leader and yet he was not tall.

FYI Extraordinary characteristics have been examined in the trait research. Even patterns in handwriting have been examined in an attempt to identify a correlation with leadership success. However, this line of examination certainly did not hold up to rigorous research.

While the research evolved through a number of different approaches, there has recently been a renewed interest in trait theories, and a list of leadership traits is once again being explored. This list, however, is somewhat different in nature and integrates the knowledge gained over the last century in the leadership studies conducted.

PROCEED WITH CAUTION

 While some may suggest that trait approaches are obsolete, they have been used to some extent unconsciously by many. Studies have shown that those individuals who are physically attractive are perceived more as leaders and generally given more opportunities in which they can increase their effectiveness.

Contemporary researchers have suggested that leaders are extraordinary individuals—certainly distinguished from others. This has led to a return to the great person trait theory, examining the characteristics that distinguish leaders from the other people.

It was finally determined that the researchers should turn their attention to the actual activities that leaders engaged in to more effectively determine the differences between successful and unsuccessful leaders.

Behavioral Theories

Because the trait theory did not prove successful in determining leadership potential, researchers during the 1940s began to examine behaviors that leaders engaged in. They saw leadership as an activity. The hope was that common behaviors would be identified to predict leadership success. The behavioral theories examined what leaders actually do (versus what characteristics they possess).

Classic studies were conducted at Ohio State and the University of Michigan. Both of these studies examined employee-centered and task-centered behaviors. They sought to determine which leadership style resulted in the best performance. The assumption was that behaviors of successful leaders were different from ineffective leaders, and that these leadership behaviors were the same from situation to situation.

The University of Michigan studies examined both task-centered and employee-centered leadership behaviors. The task-centered behaviors focused on the task at hand, how it was to be completed, and the actual performance. Employee-centered leadership behavior paid attention to the human element on the job. They found that employee-centered leadership styles resulted in the more effective performance of the group.

While initially researchers depicted leadership style as a continuum, with employee-centered behavior at one end and task-centered behavior at the other, this did not prove true. Researchers eventually thought that leaders needed both employee-centered and task-centered behavior.

The Ohio State researchers examined the same two dimensions, but referred to them with different names. Their terminology was consideration behavior and initiating-structure behavior. The consideration behavior was concerned with the feelings of subordinates (similar to the employee-centered behavior of Michigan). The initiating-structure style included behaviors focused on how the task was to be accomplished. (This was similar to the job-centered behavior.) The researchers concluded that leaders should be high on both consideration and initiating structure.

The University of Michigan researchers then concluded that the two behaviors were not opposite ends of one continuum, but rather two separate continua. A leader could then be high or low on both, independently. In addition, they saw a leader's behavior as relatively stable over time. They then suggested that the situation might impact which leadership style was actually best.

Robert Blake and Jane Mouton, authors of *The New Managerial Grid* in 1978, developed a leadership grid reflecting this idea that a leader might need both types of behavior. They concluded that the best leaders were actually high in both behaviors. That is, these leaders paid a great deal of attention to both the task and the employees.

Blake and Mouton used the terminology concern for production (which is task-oriented) and concern for people (which is human-relations-oriented). On a scale of one to nine, they proposed that the leader scoring a nine on both concern for people and concern for production was needed in many situations. Bottom line, however, they suggested that there was no one best way.

Grid training has been used to help improve the behaviors of leaders. "Impoverished managers" (those low in both concern for production and concern for people) can improve their scores on both dimensions with this process.

CONTINGENCY APPROACHES

Leadership is a complex process with a variety of factors that can influence it. At this point, researchers began to consider that perhaps the situation impacted leadership. And, with this decision to include the elements of the situation, was a conclusion that there was no one best management style. Instead, the most effective style of the leader depended on the situation.

This is still the approach that is most subscribed to today. This is why you need a mix of leadership styles that you can change from one situation to the next. Your effectiveness as a leader depends on your ability to match the requirements of the situation to the style that you use at that given time.

Fred Fiedler developed one of the early contingency approaches in the mid-1960s. Author of *The Leader Match Concept*, Fiedler proposed the least preferred co-worker theory of leadership. This theory helps to explain how a leader can be effective in one situation and yet ineffective in another situation.

Fiedler suggested that leaders were either relationship-motivated or task-motivated in their styles. That is, leaders emphasize either the relationship with their subordinates or the job at hand.

Because leadership is part of your basic personality, Fiedler suggests that if there is no match between the situation and your style, you need to change the situation. You can accomplish this in part by restructuring the tasks performed. The warning from Fiedler is that you should only change your leadership style as a last resort—because it is thought to be rather inflexible. This was a big departure from prior research conclusions.

This theory has been important when hiring managers. The interviewer can match the situation to the leadership style of the applicants in an attempt to increase the effectiveness of the potential applicants once hired.

Fiedler's least preferred co-worker (LPC) scale is the instrument used to identify the type of leadership style that you possess.

George Graen, author of *Instrumentality Theory of Work Motivation: Some Experimental Results and Suggested Modifications,* proposed the leader member exchange model (LMX). Developed in 1969, this theory explored the employee-superior relationship. The basic assumption is that the leader has a unique relationship with each subordinate. And, these relationships must be examined individually.

They characterized each of these relationships as in-group or out-group. It is possible to distinguish the behaviors of each. In-group members generally enjoy more personalized exchanges with their leaders. These are the individuals who are more satisfied with their jobs and tend to be more productive. They even enjoy higher salaries and are provided more opportunities for promotions.

In the school situation, you may have referred to these in-group members as the "teacher's pets." In social situations you may describe these in-group members as being "in the clique." While you may use a number of different terms to reflect these members, they all can be considered in-group members by the leader member exchange model.

Paul Hersey and Kenneth Blanchard proposed the situational contingency theory of leadership. In their 1988 book, *Management of Organizational Behavior,* they reinforced the idea that there is no one best leadership style for all situations. Their research focused on the readiness level of the followers. This is the maturity level of those who are being led.

Readiness is defined as ability and willingness. Those followers considered to be at high-readiness levels have the abilities and the willingness to perform their jobs. Once a leader diagnoses the readiness level of his or her followers, they must choose a leadership style that emphasizes either relationship behaviors or task behaviors.

There are four leadership styles that result from this diagnosis:

- **Telling.** This is used when employees are new and don't know how to perform a task. These followers demonstrate the lowest readiness level.

- **Selling.** This approach is most effective when followers are willing to learn, but have not quite fully mastered the job at hand. The readiness level of the followers is low, but not the lowest possible.

- **Participating.** As the maturity level of your followers increases, let employees have more involvement in what they are doing. Followers at this point are said to be at moderate levels of readiness.

- **Delegating.** This technique is used with very capable employees. The followers are at the highest levels of readiness. They are both able and willing to perform the job.

CONTEMPORARY VIEWS OF LEADERSHIP

Contemporary researchers have suggested (in returning to the great person trait theory) that there are some characteristics generally possessed by many who are perceived as leaders. Examine the following list to see how many of these characteristics you possess:

- **High energy level.** Leaders not only know what it takes to be successful, but they can physically go the distance. These are the individuals that can tirelessly work around the clock.

- **Take initiative.** Leaders don't wait to be told what to do. They step in and act when it is necessary.

- **Honest.** Leaders have a sense of integrity. They have high moral values that are recognized by others.

- **Possess a motivation to lead.** These true leaders don't control others, but work with them. They want to lead and make a difference—in their organizations and with others.

- **Self-confident.** Knowing their strengths and weaknesses is critical to leaders. They know just what their abilities are—and what they lack.

- **Intelligent.** The intelligence critical to leadership is not the genius level. Quite the contrary, leaders need relevant intelligence and should be able to adeptly integrate critical information.

- **Technical know-how.** Effective leaders possess an in-depth knowledge of relevant job information. Part of their self-confidence stems from the possession of this technical knowledge.

- **Creative.** Leaders must see old things in new ways and be prepared to create change. They must also think and act creatively.

- **Flexible.** Leaders adapt their behaviors to meet the needs of changing situations.

TRANSACTIONAL LEADERSHIP

Management is all about transactional leadership. The management role is said to focus on stability and the smooth running of the organization. Transactional leadership reflects the daily exchanges that occur between the leader and his or her subordinates. This tends to be more routine in nature—as the name transactional implies.

These daily exchanges include rewarding employees, monitoring their performance, and avoiding making decisions. The transactional leader is responsible for rewarding subordinates when they meet their goals. This leader also monitors the performance of subordinates in order to take corrective action when performance does not meet expectations. Avoiding decisions altogether is also an intended role of the transactional leader.

Organizations need more than just transactional leadership. The most effective leaders will actually combine different types of leadership. One of the best combinations of styles is transactional and transformational leadership.

TRANSFORMATIONAL LEADERSHIP

Transformational leadership is critical today. At the heart of this type of leadership role is the transforming of both individuals and organizations. The transformational leader truly excites subordinates. There is a greater reliance on his or her personal power, while the transactional leader relies more on his or her position power.

The transformational leader focuses more on the change aspects of leadership. This leader inspires change throughout the organization. They are said to transform their subordinates. A prime example of a transformational leader is Jack Welsh. As CEO, he transformed General Electric and its employees. This was an effort that began in the early 1980s and continued for almost two decades.

Transformational leaders are charismatic individuals, but these leaders need other characteristics as well. Transformational leaders need the following:

- An ability to stimulate their subordinates intellectually
- An ability to support each subordinate as a unique individual
- An ability to inspire subordinates to achieve organizational objectives

The most effective leadership style combines approaches. Transactional leadership is not enough in today's organizations. You also need transformational leadership. To become a transformational leader consider the following tips:

- **Create a vision and clearly communicate that vision.** Articulate the steps to achieve it also. Be confident about your vision, and others will be more likely to buy in.

- **Celebrate mini successes.** As progress is made in part toward achieving the larger vision, recognize these smaller successes. Make a big deal of them.

- **Reinforce core values.** Demonstrate actions to uphold these values.

- **Be an exemplary role model.** Set an example of the behaviors you expect from your employees.

CHARISMATIC LEADERSHIP

The charismatic leader inspires followers to go that extra mile. With personal charisma, you are more likely to be a more effective leader. Generally, the charismatic leaders will have more self-confidence and will have confidence in their subordinates as well.

Traits generally associated with the charismatic leader include the following:

- Vision of a future with knowledge of specific actions to get there. They clearly articulate this vision to their followers. The charismatic leaders are also able to model the appropriate behaviors.

- Good role model to motivate others' successes.

- Supports subordinates in their efforts.

- Tends to be zany; unconventional.

GO TO ▶
Refer to Hour 17, "Organizational Culture," for a more detailed discussion of the role of core values in organizational cultures and how these values impact the performance of organizations.

JUST A MINUTE

Herb Kelleher, CEO of Southwest Airlines, has been cited as being somewhat unconventional and an example of a charismatic leader.

- Challenges the status quo; actually enjoys change.

- Is aware of his or her limitations—in both the organizational and personal realms.

Charismatic leaders inspire their followers. They propel their followers to higher levels of performance that far exceed what is minimally acceptable. Their followers are truly enthusiastic—often "catching" this enthusiasm from the charismatic leader. In addition, the charismatic leader develops followers who are incredibly loyal.

THE FLIP SIDE OF LEADERSHIP: FOLLOWERSHIP

While organizations spend billions of dollars each year to develop leaders, little attention is paid to the flip side of the leadership issue: followership. Organizations should be equally concerned with the development of good followers.

Everyone is not a leader in every situation. After all, leadership is situational. While you may be a leader in one situation, you may be a follower in another situation. Leaders are only half of the leadership equation. Followers are the other half of this equation.

Organizations need good followers as much as good leaders to meet their objectives. While leaders may work more in the limelight, the followers who work behind the scenes are equally important. The significance of followers has been reinforced by research. The follower and the situation have been examined in the more recent studies. That is, more attention is paid to those who are being led and the specific circumstances in which leadership is being performed. There is a recognition that these factors will impact what type of leadership will be most effective.

PROCEED WITH CAUTION

Many times the finger is pointed to a leader when attributing the success or failure of an organization. The leaders, however, may only symbolize the romance of leadership. In many cases, leadership is said to be irrelevant or have exaggerated importance.

Research has suggested that effective followers will be critical thinkers and will be active. Those followers who are not critical in their thinking blindly accept directives. Organizations need those who tactfully challenge the status quo and critically assess directives.

Effective followers will also be active in their roles. Passive followers contribute little to the organization's performance. Active followers present suggestions for improvement. Followers, then, must know how to voice challenges to the status quo. This requires rethinking the traditional view of followers in which they blindly obey authority figures.

It is essential to your career success that you know how to be an effective follower. You must be able to move back and forth between the two roles. While you may be the manager in one situation, you will be a follower in another situation.

Followership also becomes critical with the move toward teamwork. With distributed leadership, team members rotate in and out of the follower and leader roles.

How to Lead Self-Managed Teams

To be effective, leaders overseeing self-managed teams cannot direct and control the team's efforts. Instead, they must empower the team members so they can manage their own jobs.

Tips for leading self-managed teams include the following:

- Encourage teamwork. Provide opportunities for employees to interact and work together.
- Encourage continuous development.
- Develop team members. Provide them with the skills and resources to get the job done.
- Instill confidence that they can do the job. (This comes from giving them the training and the resources they need to do their jobs.)
- Develop the identity of the team. Celebrate team successes. Develop and communicate the mission and goals of the team. Completing these initiatives will provide direction for the team members.
- Use conflict in a positive way. Disagreement and conflict can lead to the best ideas—those that are creative and innovative.
- Create change. It is not enough to just manage change or cope with it. You must create change by reading the trends and monitoring the external environment for the signals of needed change.

GO TO ▶
Refer to Hour 15, "Teamwork," for a discussion of self-managed teams in organizations today.

HOUR'S UP!

The critical nature of leadership has been explored in combination with your role as a manager. Because research has concluded that leaders can be made (and not just born), review these questions to test your leadership IQ.

1. Leadership …
   a. Is essentially the same thing as management.
   b. Uses coercion.
   c. Is using influence to direct the activities and attitudes of others.
   d. Requires that you have formal authority.

2. Much of the leadership research has sought to …
   a. Identify what makes a leader effective.
   b. Determine a magical list of traits that the successful leader possesses.
   c. Determine the specific behaviors that a leader engages in.
   d. All of the above.

3. It was finally concluded that employee-centered and task-centered behaviors …
   a. Were opposite ends of one continuum.
   b. Were both important to effective leadership.
   c. Were not independent.
   d. Were irrelevant to leadership effectiveness across all situations.

4. The contingency approach to leadership …
   a. Still is an integral part of understanding leadership today.
   b. Considers situational variables that impact leadership effectiveness.
   c. Concluded that there is no one best way to lead.
   d. All of the above.

5. In-group members …
   a. Are a juvenile approach to the workplace.
   b. Are more satisfied and productive in their work.
   c. Are just pets of the leader that don't really impact performance.
   d. Don't really exist.

6. The transformational leader …

    a. Is the same as the transactional leader.

    b. Is all about transforming individuals and organizations.

    c. Is all that is needed for effective leadership today.

    d. Is irrelevant if the organization has a written mission statement.

7. To become the most effective leader …

    a. Forget any past successes and concentrate on the future.

    b. Avoid the reinforcement of core values.

    c. Combine transactional and transformational leadership.

    d. Create a vision and keep it to yourself to protect it.

8. Charismatic leaders …

    a. Articulate a vision to their followers.

    b. Are good role models to their followers.

    c. Support their subordinates.

    d. All of the above.

9. Followership …

    a. Is as important as leadership—just a different role.

    b. Is not that important because companies spend money only on leadership training.

    c. Develops on its own.

    d. Gets plenty of attention in organizations today.

10. In leading self-managed teams …

    a. Develop the team members.

    b. Develop the identity of the team.

    c. Use conflict positively.

    d. All of the above.

QUIZ

HOUR 20
Organizational Communication

CHAPTER SUMMARY

LESSON PLAN:
In this hour you will learn about ...

- The components of the communication process.
- Miscommunication as the norm.
- Barriers to effective communication.
- The role of nonverbal communication.
- How to be an active listener.
- Communication flow: upward, downward, and lateral.
- Technology's role in organizational communication.
- Tips to effective communication.

Communication is absolutely essential to management. The only way to get things done through others is to be able to communicate. Communication is key in building relationships with others. While communication is crucial to your career development, it is one of the most poorly developed skills for most managers. Communication skills continue to rank among the first on the list of skills that top managers believe business students should learn.

Unfortunately, miscommunication is the norm—not effective communication. This occurs as people think they don't have to put much effort into the process. Many think it just comes naturally. The problem, however, is that everyone thinks they are good communicators.

As a result, two errors are committed. The first is that you assume others know what you are saying. The second is that others assume they know what you are saying. And these are two dangerous assumptions.

Organizational communication has been referred to as the nervous system of the organization. The exchange of information is critical to organizational performance. The communication process has even been described as the lifeblood of organizations—thereby conveying its critical nature. Improved communication often results in improved performance levels.

So as a manager, you must understand interpersonal communication and organizational communication in order to increase your effectiveness as a manager.

PROCEED WITH CAUTION

Considering that there are over 4,000 different definitions for the 500 words that are most used in the English language, there can be little doubt that miscommunication is the norm. How often do you think you are picking the "right" definition that the sender intended you to pick when decoding the message?

THE COMMUNICATION PROCESS

Communication is used to convey both thoughts and feelings. The communication process is utilized to influence others, inform others, and express feelings. The primary components of the communication process are as follows:

- The sender
- The message
- The receiver
- Feedback

On the surface this may seem like an extremely simple process. In actuality, this is an extraordinarily complex one. It is fraught with pitfalls and barriers. Seldom are people effective in their communication. Instead, they make the two false assumptions and pay little attention to the complexities of the process.

PROCEED WITH CAUTION

Seventy-five percent of the communications heard are actually incorrectly received. And, of the 25 percent that are heard correctly, more than 75 percent of them are forgotten within one month's time.

The sender is the person who encodes the message and "sends" it to the receiver. This person is also referred to as the source of the communication, or simply as the communicator. This is the person who originates the message. In some cases this may be more than one person.

The message is the communication that is intended. The message is encoded in symbols and transmitted to the receiver. The symbols are generally thought of as words, which can be either written or verbal. What you might not always realize is that these symbols can also be nonverbal, like body language, gestures, or facial cues.

JUST A MINUTE

Seventy-five percent of the manager's time is spent communicating. Part of this time is spent listening and part of it is spent talking—but all of it is considered communicating.

The message is communicated through a channel to the receiver. This channel is the mechanism by which the message is transmitted. The most commonly used channel is face-to-face communication. Voice mail, e-mail, billboards, magazines, and television are just a few of the various channels of communication available to you today.

The receiver is the person responsible for decoding the message on the receiving side. Decoding is the process whereby the symbols are interpreted. This tends to be an extremely critical phase of the communication process. Seldom are people as effective here as they think they are. The receiver does have to accept responsibility in the communication process because listening is active, rather than passive.

Feedback is a return to you of the message that you sent. This is an opportunity to check to see if the intended message is actually the message that was received. While a powerful tool in the communication process, it is underutilized. Too often, one-way communication is engaged in, and feedback is never sought to confirm the intended message was actually the one received.

Noise can negatively impact the effectiveness of the communication process. *Noise* is any factor that hinders the receipt of the intended message. Noise, then, can include physical barriers, static, or actual noise during the communication.

BARRIERS TO COMMUNICATION

Physical separation creates barriers to effective communication. Even with the use of phones and computers, the richness of face-to-face communication is lost. This reduces the effectiveness of the communication, as many of the nonverbal and emotional elements of the process are lost.

Gender differences really reflect stylistic differences, which nonetheless impact the process. The differences in perspective and attitude are primarily due to the socialization process from birth. Women like to sit in circles, in close proximity to one another, and like to be seated across from one another. They are able to pick up on more nonverbal cues. Men prefer to sit side by side and prefer to have more space between them.

On average, women hear more of the emotional content of messages than men do. Men and women also communicate differently nonverbally. Women tend to use more eye contact and smile more. Men tend to speak with a more relaxed body position that communicates higher status.

It is more likely that miscommunication will occur when people come from different cultures. Care must be taken to be especially clear and to solicit feedback to overcome this barrier.

JUST A MINUTE

A greater awareness of your own culture helps you to learn more about others. The American culture tends to be more direct and relies very heavily on verbal communications. Asian cultures appear to be less direct and rely heavily on nonverbal cues in the communication process.

A lack of trust or credibility also serves as a barrier to effective communication. When trust is not present, both the sender and the receiver tend to be more defensive. Time and energy are spent on defending themselves rather than concentrating on sending or interpreting the message. Getting to know your employees helps develop this trust. It is also important to develop a climate for open discussions.

While language is a critical component of the communication process itself, it also poses a barrier. Many of the words and phrases are vague. With so many different definitions of words, you must look to nonverbal cues to help you pick the "right" definition. Language is further complicated by jargon. *Jargon* is language specific to an industry or a company. Initially, jargon may be used to avoid miscommunication, but in the long run it can create a complication if everyone does not understand the jargon.

Acronyms are widely used in various industries today. Care must be taken, though, because these acronyms often have one meaning in one industry, and another meaning in a different industry. For example, in business curriculum in higher education, the OB is used extensively. It is also regularly used in the medical community. However, the two meanings are quite different. In higher education it refers to Organizational Behavior, and in the medical community it means obstetrician. Same term—very different meanings.

Information overload serves as a tremendous barrier to effective communication. Everyone today is bombarded with large amounts of information. The key is to know the "right" information, not all the information. Being selective in the information that you process will help you to combat information overload.

 FYI The number of e-mails sent has increased astronomically in the recent past. The number has increased from 764 billion in the mid-1990s to more than 4 trillion in 2000. This has also increased the pace of business.

NONVERBAL COMMUNICATION

The communication process is comprised of more than just the words spoken. The old "Actions speak louder than words" adage is so true. The gestures you use, your body language, your gender, your dress, and the tone of your voice all add to the communication. Sometimes these are the only components of the communication process. Nonverbal communication includes all communication that is conveyed without words. The key is to use the nonverbal component to complement the verbal component.

Much of this nonverbal communication is unique to your culture and will vary from one culture to another. This, then, presents an additional barrier to an already difficult communication process. Even generally accepted American gestures such as the "A-OK" sign carry different (and sometimes offensive) meanings around the world in other cultures (such as Japan).

JUST A MINUTE

 The communication process is said to be comprised using the following breakdown: 60 percent by body language, 30 percent by tone of voice, and only 10 percent by the actual words. This certainly conveys the importance of the nonverbal elements.

Proxemics is the study of how space is used. This includes the comfort zones surrounding each individual's personal space and even the dynamics of seating in a business setting.

GO TO ▶
Refer to Hour 22, "Facilitating Meetings," for a further discussion of seating at meetings.

Kinesics is the study of body language. Body language can communicate everything from anxiety to primping. Your posture also communicates a great deal about you.

Facial cues are critical to the communication process. Your face often gives your real message away. Direct eye contact communicates honesty. (This is culturally specific; for example, this is not true in the Japanese culture.) Raised eyebrows communicate surprise. Smiles communicate happiness, while frowns communicate unhappiness.

Sitting on the edge of your seat communicates interest and an attentive demeanor. Slouching while seated communicates a lack of interest.

PROCEED WITH CAUTION

Care must be taken when using gestures in the international arena or with people from other cultures. Simple gestures communicate very different meanings across different cultures. Some cultures consider the "A-OK" sign (made with the thumb and forefinger) to be an insult.

Your personal appearance and your clothing also communicate something about you. This is why dressing for success has been studied by many, and for many years. The way you look when you walk through the door says something about you. To be perceived as having more power, men have been advised to wear long sleeve shirts. Physical appearance has been particularly important in the courtroom. Jurors respond to the credibility of the testimony of witnesses based in part on whether they "look the part."

Unfortunately, people are not very skilled at reading nonverbal communication. Many times cues are missed or they are misinterpreted. Nonverbal communication is part of the total communications package. You must be skilled at reading this nonverbal communication.

Consider the meanings of some nonverbal communication messages:

- Glaring at someone communicates anger.
- The rolling of eyes usually means superiority and a failure to take the speaker seriously.
- Looking away communicates a clear lack of interest.
- Sighing while someone is speaking often means disgust.
- Crossing one's arms signals a closed mind.
- Staring too much at someone can be a form of intimidation.

Because the communication process is so critical to your effectiveness as a manager, it is a good practice to periodically videotape yourself when speaking. This gives you an opportunity to objectively evaluate your communication style and your nonverbal communication. This can give you valuable insight into how others perceive you.

ACTIVE LISTENING

Contrary to what many may think, listening is an active skill. This is not a passive process—if it is to be effective. Good listeners are at a premium.

Listening is a critical skill in the communication process. It greatly impacts your ability to be more effective as a manager. Empathetic listeners understand the message and the feelings being communicated.

Cicero, a Roman statesman and orator from the first century B.C.E., once said that it is a blessing that human beings were given one mouth and two ears—in light of the way that they are used.

It is no wonder that listening has been called an art—and in some cases, a lost art. Use these tips to become a better listener:

- Be cognizant of the fact that you cannot listen and speak at the same time.

- Understand that when you stop talking, you are communicating that you want to hear what the other person has to say.

- Help the speaker feel more at ease. Part of this includes giving them your undivided attention. Don't engage in other activities while you are supposed to be listening.

- Be sure to empathize with the communicator. Let them know that you can put yourself in their place.

- Don't focus on delivery errors. Too often listeners get caught up in how the message is delivered and miss the message being sent.

- Use questions to get clarification. If you are unsure of what is being said, don't guess. Ask for a clarification.

- Avoid making quick judgments. Hear the speaker out prior to making decisions.

- Take notes when appropriate. Generally, people retain only about half of what they hear—even immediately afterwards. Any notes you take will increase the probability that you will remember the communication and remember it more accurately.

- Use nods and verbal recognition that you are listening. Encourage the speaker. This support will help the speaker to be more effective in communicating.

- Don't be distracted. Keep your attention focused on the speaker and the message being conveyed.

DIRECTIONS OF ORGANIZATIONAL COMMUNICATION FLOW

The direction of organizational communication flow focuses on who communicates with whom. The three directions of communication flow in organizations are upward, downward, and lateral. Each has a very different focus and a personality of its own.

UPWARD

Upward communication flows from lower levels in the organization to higher levels. The primary purpose of upward communication is to inform superiors about organizational performance. Meetings, memos, and reports are some of the common channels used for upward communication.

There have been significant concerns with the information being communicated upwardly. It is understood that this information is definitely biased. People who are lower in the organization tend to filter out negative information so that they will be seen in a more favorable light.

The other concern with upward communication is with the initiation of this communication type. Rather than actually soliciting information, superiors just wait to hear what they are told. Lower-level employees then may not initiate enough communication. Superiors must open up the lines to encourage communication. Informal discussions and suggestion systems can be used. The old "open-door" policy is still effective. More organizations are also using employee surveys to solicit information.

Of all the time devoted to communication, it has been estimated that only about 15 percent is spent on upward communication. And yet information from subordinates is critical to the organization. It is important that you tap into this information. As the manager you are responsible for soliciting this information, rather than just waiting for it to happen.

DOWNWARD

Downward communication flows from higher levels in the organization to lower levels. It generally follows the chain of command as outlined by the organization chart. This downward communication commonly includes directives about work to be performed, an explanation of company goals, and feedback concerning employee performance.

Those lower-level employees often view this communication as very narrow and very lean. It is also not very accurate—perhaps attributed to the fact that downward communication uses the face-to-face communication channel less. The simple passing of information from one hierarchical level to another negatively impacts the actual message being communicated.

PROCEED WITH CAUTION

A recent study of organizational communication concluded that 80 percent of the message is lost once the communication passes through just five different levels in the hierarchy. This should provide food for thought before handing critical communications down through several organizational levels.

A link has been found between turnover and effective downward communication. Those companies with more effective downward communication have lower turnover rates. Job satisfaction is also greater, and productivity is higher.

LATERAL

Lateral communication has also been referred to as horizontal. This is communication that occurs between peers. The primary purpose of lateral communication in the organizational context is that of coordinating work. Without this horizontal communication, work could not be coordinated.

If your company does not effectively utilize lateral communication, you might not be able to get a product to market before your competition. Communication must flow laterally from all the units involved, such as engineering, production, marketing, and accounting. Without the necessary lateral communication to coordinate the efforts of the product development, a competitor could easily beat your firm to market and capture the first mover advantage in the marketplace.

It also serves to fill the need for friendship and affiliation. The social needs of people are often fulfilled in the organization with the use of lateral communication.

 FYI The grapevine is alive and well in every organization. The *grapevine* is informal communication that does not follow any of the organizational lines. It has been estimated that approximately three quarters of the communication in organizations flows through the grapevine.

THE ROLE OF TECHNOLOGY IN COMMUNICATION TODAY

Advanced technology is changing the very way that people communicate with one another today. Some of the technological advances include computer mediation, voice mail, e-mail, facsimile machines, and cellular phones.

GO TO ▶
Refer to Hour 24, "Gaining an Edge: Business Etiquette," for a discussion of netiquette, which focuses on the new technology.

With the new technology available today, information is available to everyone more quickly and in greater amounts than ever before. Even more important, more people can access this information. This means that the formal channels of communication do not have to be followed because information is more readily available to larger numbers of people. In the past, organizational members had to follow the formal chain of command to get information. Today this is not necessary.

More participation is also encouraged with information being disseminated faster and more broadly than ever. More people can participate in the decision-making process intelligently because information is not as limited as it once was.

Unfortunately, with the advantages, there also come disadvantages. The technological advances have created communications that are less personal. There is also a loss of the nonverbal aspects of the process.

For example, e-mails are not as rich as face-to-face communication because the communicators cannot see one another. All of the nonverbal signals are missing from these new communications. Even the telephone is not as rich because body language and facial cues cannot be read over the phone.

Hour's Up!

Recognizing that it is impossible not to communicate, check these questions to see how much you learned about the communication process in this hour.

1. Communication …
   a. Is irrelevant to effective management.
   b. Is essential to effective management.
   c. Is a simple process.
   d. Includes only messages of words.

2. The message is …
   a. The intended communication.
   b. Is encoded in symbols.
   c. Is transmitted to the receiver.
   d. All of the above.

3. The receiver in the communication process …
   a. Is responsible for decoding the message transmitted.
   b. Is not a critical component of the communication process.
   c. Is usually very effective.
   d. Has a passive role.

4. Information overload …
   a. Is a barrier to communication that continues to increase.
   b. Prohibits barriers to communication.
   c. Is improving with modern technology.
   d. Helps us filter information.

5. The old adage, "Actions speak louder than words" …
   a. Reflects the importance of choosing your words carefully.
   b. Reflects the importance of nonverbal communication.
   c. Overstates the importance of nonverbal communication.
   d. Reflects the 50-50 relationship of words and actions in the communication process.

6. Active listening ...

  a. Is not a passive process.

  b. Requires that you stop talking.

  c. Requires that you give the speaker your undivided attention.

  d. All of the above.

7. Upward communication ...

  a. Is more negative in nature.

  b. On average is very free.

  c. Is generally biased and filtered.

  d. Is quickly initiated by subordinates.

8. Informal communication ...

  a. Is not very important in the organization.

  b. Is captured in the grapevine outside of formal communication channels.

  c. Can be controlled by management at all times.

  d. Serves no real purpose in the organization.

9. Technological advances today ...

  a. Have done little to actually change the communication process.

  b. Have eliminated the need to choose words carefully.

  c. Have eliminated much of the emotional and nonverbal content of the communication process.

  d. Have provided richer communication channels in most cases.

10. To communicate more effectively ...

  a. Remember the importance of the nonverbal component.

  b. Use feedback to verify that your intended message was actually the one received.

  c. Remember that listening is a key component of communicating.

  d. All of the above.

QUIZ

PART V

Special Management Challenges

HOUR 21
Stress

Everybody talks about being stressed out today. And there is certainly enough stress to go around. Some stress is actually good for people and good for organizations. The key is to manage appropriate stress levels such that too much is not experienced. Stress negatively impacts employees' physical and psychological health while also reducing organizational effectiveness.

Organizations are concerned with stress for a number of reasons. Organizations do take some responsibility for the very fact that they do create some of this stress. They are concerned that insurance claims for stress-related illness have become a significant expense for most firms. And, the number of these claims is increasing. Stress also directly impacts the performance of its employees and the performance of the organization overall.

Stress is described to be at epidemic levels—and it is not just an American phenomena. Seven percent of the workforce in Finland has been estimated to be experiencing burnout. The high costs of stress are increasing globally.

Potential stressors are everywhere. While stress is said to be unavoidable, it is not unmanageable. This hour provides insight into stress and the tools to better manage stress.

Nearly 50 percent of American workers perceive their jobs to have high levels of stress.

What Is Stress?

Stress is simply defined as the emotional and physical wear and tear of life. Stress may be thought of as your body's response to life itself.

FYI The cost of problems that are stress-related has been estimated to be as much as $150 billion annually in American businesses. The cost of lost productivity alone is estimated to cost organizations more than $20 million a year.

Hans Selye, an endocrinologist, researched the cycle of stress in 1936. Known as GAS (General Adaptation Syndrome), Selye identified three stages that comprise this cycle of biological events:

- Alarm
- Resistance
- Exhaustion

The first stage is alarm. This is characterized by panic and helplessness when a stressor is observed. Hormones are secreted and the alarm is sounded throughout the body. The alarm is the "fight-or-flight" response. Changing the stressor is the fight response while avoiding it is the flight response.

Resistance is the second stage. At this point people try to overcome the negativity of the stressor and return to normal. If a ball is going to hit you in the head, the adaptation is to step aside to avoid being hit.

If the stressor continues, exhaustion occurs. The person is tired of resisting the stressor. Over time, stress-related illnesses may result.

STRICTLY DEFINED

Hot reactors is the term coined in the 1980s to describe those who react very negatively to stress. These individuals are not resilient.

The body goes through physiological changes during stress. During the alarm stage, the physiological responses may include the following conditions:

- Rapid breathing
- Rapid heart beat

- Increased hormone production
- Increased perspiration
- Interrupted digestion
- Tense muscles
- Dilated pupils

With stress, the body is prepared physiologically to fight or run. The adrenaline flow during stress enables individuals to better handle any dangers that are present.

STRESSORS

Stressors are the conditions that trigger stress in people. There are both work and nonwork stressors. And, there are several different categories of stress within each type.

Different people perceive stressors very differently. And, the person's interpretation of the stressor is the key. It is the way that you perceive your world that determines how you react to stress. What is stressful for one individual is not necessarily stressful for another individual.

WORK STRESSORS

Work stressors include the following categories:

GO TO ▶
Refer to Hour 8, "Relationship Management," for a discussion of the role of personality in the perceptual process.

- Task demands
- Role demands
- Interpersonal demands
- Physical demands

Task demands focus on the job itself. They include change and uncertainty for employees. When people feel they have no control over what they do, they experience stress. Having too many demands, fewer future job opportunities, and new technology introduced can create stress. Examples of task demands can be the need for quick or serious decisions with big consequences.

FYI   Employees with little control over their work and heavy workloads have more heart attacks.

Role demands include role conflict and role ambiguity. Roles involve the expectations that others have of people. Employees may experience conflicting roles—that is, conflicting expectations that cannot both be met. Organizations may expect something of an employee that is not consistent with his or her own values. These ethical dilemmas can create stress. A stressor is experienced when people are not sure what is expected (which is known as role ambiguity).

Interpersonal demands reflect stressors related to relationships in the organization. These include dealing with abrasive people (or any conflicting personality type), sexual harassment, and difficult, conflicting leadership styles. Pressures to conform to group norms may also cause stress. If the management style of the supervisor doesn't match the direct subordinate's, stress is also likely to occur.

Physical demands create stress; and, when there are unpleasant conditions on the job (such as unsafe conditions or extreme temperatures), stress can result. Physical stressors include strenuous activities such as physically demanding work as well as unsatisfactory office conditions, including poor design, poor lighting, no privacy, noise, or even the use of computers.

Noise is a big stressor. The sound of human voices has been found to be very distracting. The move to open office plans has increased the noise and distraction levels while decreasing privacy for employees.

NONWORK STRESSORS

Nonwork demands can impact the job and result in lower work performance levels. Employees do not leave their home lives at the door when they come to work. Today's demands are placing even greater stress on employees.

Two of the biggest nonwork stressors include daycare issues and aging parents. The term "sandwich generation" has been used to refer to the working generation today that is wedged between their parents and their children's care needs.

Integrating work and nonwork demands are important to reduce stress levels, and are important to the performance of individuals on the job. This compatibility is critical. More organizations are recognizing that they have a responsibility to help their employees balance these issues—because it directly impacts the organization.

INDIVIDUAL CONSEQUENCES OF STRESS

There are two types of stress: eustress and distress. *Eustress* is positive stress that results in increases in physical strength. Getting a promotion is an example of eustress. *Distress* is negative stress that may result in behavioral problems, psychological issues, and medical sickness. This distress is dysfunctional.

People need some stress in their lives. Too much or too little stress results in less-than-enthusiastic, lethargic attitudes with poor performance levels. Everyone needs some stress to work at optimal performance levels. There is an energy boost with optimal levels of stress.

STRICTLY DEFINED

Karoshi is the Japanese term translated to mean death by overwork. This is the classic workaholic distress.

Psychological illness as a result of work ranks at the top of health issues today. Depression and burnout can result in reduced efficiency, a loss of interest in work, and exhaustion. Sleep disturbances have become critical issues that have direct and indirect costs for the organization.

Depression ranks second among the illnesses that disable workers. Ten percent of American workers suffer clinical depression, and these numbers are expected to increase.

Stress is estimated to play a role in 70 percent of physical illnesses. Stress-related illnesses include the following:

- Heart disease
- Stroke
- Ulcers
- Headaches
- Backaches

Behavioral problems such as violence, substance abuse, and accidents hurt the individual and hurt the organization and its performance. Violence can be physical or interpersonal conflict. Substance abuse can target alcohol, tobacco, prescription drugs, or illegal drugs. If people are preoccupied or distracted, accidents can also occur.

People respond very differently to stressors. What is a stressor for one person is not a stressor for another. Individual differences impact our response to stressors. One of the biggest differences is personality.

PERSONALITY: TYPE A AND TYPE B

The type A personality tends to display "coronary-prone behavior" (because they are predisposed to coronary heart disease). They are twice as likely to have coronary heart disease as type B personality types. Type A individuals also display a sense of urgency, a focus on achievements, insecurity about status, and are competitive, impatient, work-oriented, and driven.

The type B personality is just the opposite. These individuals have a weaker sense of time urgency, are less confident, have a more balanced life, and are more relaxed. The type B personality is more contemplative and works at a steady pace. They don't feel as pressured by deadlines as the type A personality. Interestingly enough, type B people are also more creative because they are more contemplative.

Those individuals that are type A personalities need to consider changing. The first step in changing is to recognize that you are a type A. If you hang out with more type B personalities, you will observe their behaviors and begin to engage in more of their type of behaviors. You also need to use more humor, become a better time manager, and learn not to overextend yourself with too many commitments.

ORGANIZATIONAL CONSEQUENCES OF STRESS

If you and your organization fail to manage stress, you may experience the following conditions:

- Low morale
- High levels of employee dissatisfaction
- Poor communication
- Flawed decision-making
- Poor productivity
- Poor quality work
- Increased downtime of equipment
- Poor relationships with colleagues

- Work stoppages
- High accident rates
- High levels of turnover
- High levels of tardiness
- High levels of absenteeism

PROCEED WITH CAUTION

 Stress-related claims made by employees against their employers are on the rise. Judgments as high as $1.5 million have been awarded.

STRESS MANAGEMENT

Preventive stress management is the joint responsibility of the organization and the individual. This can be thought of as preventive medicine. The three stages of preventive stress management on both the organizational and individual levels are …

Stage 1: Primary prevention

Stage 2: Secondary prevention

Stage 3: Tertiary prevention

PRIMARY PREVENTION

Primary prevention by the organization focuses on the elimination or reduction of the source of the stress. This can include job redesign and career management. Both of these improve the individual's control over his or her job and reduce uncertainty.

Individual prevention focuses on how you can manage stress. Primary prevention includes optimism, time management, and leisure activities. You learn optimistic or pessimistic thinking over time. You need to learn optimistic thinking and view bad experiences as temporary in order to have hope. When you keep a positive outlook, you generally use more humor and laugh more. These behaviors are both critical in dealing with stress.

Learning to use your time more efficiently will reduce stress. Part of time management includes learning to write a to-do list each day. This list must be prioritized with critical, important, and optimal items. And, spending time enjoying leisure activities gives you rest and pleasure from your work.

JUST A MINUTE

People with a high sense of self-esteem have a better response to stressors. Those with more self-confidence tend to take stress more in stride and have the confidence to deal with set-backs more easily.

SECONDARY PREVENTION

Secondary prevention involves the modification of the response to the stressor. Team-building is a good example of secondary prevention.

Secondary prevention includes physical exercise, relaxation training, and diet. Physical exercise should include both aerobic exercise (to help you recover better after stressful events) and flexibility training (to stretch muscles to reduce muscular tension). Exercise also tends to make people feel more self-confident and improves their mental outlook. Those who exercise also are less likely to get sick with common illnesses and even miss less work. Exercise lowers blood pressure and cholesterol while improving the elasticity of arteries.

Relaxation training is the opposite of the stress response. Relaxation makes people better able to adapt to stress. Relaxation runs the gamut from regular vacations to rest periods at work. Muscle massage and abdominal breathing are common relaxation techniques. Abdominal breathing involves taking long, deep breaths. This can be done anywhere at any time to get a calming effect. The key to relaxation is to find a quiet setting and a comfortable setting.

Transcendental meditation (known also as TM) uses a mantra to reduce the anxiety. People are then conditioned to calm themselves when they use the mantra. Biofeedback is a more advanced technique of relaxation. People use advanced equipment to monitor and report on your body's responses. You then learn to control the responses to stress and make adjustments.

A good diet provides you with better overall health. You should minimize your sugar and high cholesterol foods. You should eat wisely because the old adage still holds true: "You are what you eat." It is best to eat a variety of foods, eat regularly, and avoid too much caffeine.

TERTIARY PREVENTION

Therapy to heal the symptoms is the focus of tertiary prevention. The organization can provide help through employee assistance programs. Counseling may help to heal the effects of stress.

Opening up and getting professional help are part of tertiary prevention. Opening up is the sharing of stressful events with others. It can even be helpful to share your thoughts and feelings in a diary or a journal.

Professional help is therapeutic assistance. This can include seeing a professional counselor, a psychiatrist, or even joining a professional self-help group.

JUST A MINUTE

Employee assistance programs (EAPs) are available in most organizations to refer employees to professionals who can help. Your human resource department can provide you with details of the program.

STRESS PREVENTION PROGRAMS

Stress prevention programs are designed to decrease distress. The objective is to keep people happy and healthy. The hope is that this will result in more productive organizations.

Some of the more common stress prevention programs include the following:

- **Goal-setting.** This program reduces ambiguity and provides employees with some control when joint goal-setting is used.
- **Role negotiation.** Expectations are clarified and modified during role negotiation.
- **Social support system.** This program focuses on emotional caring and feedback from others.

Goal-setting can reduce stress levels by identifying clear objectives. Particularly when the manager and employee jointly set goals, there is agreement and a clear vision of what is to be accomplished. And generally, these goals also include time frames for achievement.

Negotiating roles helps reduce stress by removing some ambiguity. Role negotiation involves clearly identifying expectations. There is less stress when you know what others expect of you (as well as what to expect of others).

Social support can be gained from others such as colleagues, supervisors, subordinates, spouses, children, parents, friends, support groups, social clubs, business associations, and doctors.

Support systems are crucial in helping people feel connected to others. If people feel alone, the stress is experienced at a higher level. Support systems provide individuals with empathy, direct help, information, or evaluations. The family unit has been found to be the most important of all support systems.

There are some quick fixes available. These are simply temporary techniques to calm you when under stress:

- **Muscle relaxation.** Relax the muscles in your body one by one. Tighten then relax the muscles starting with your feet and moving up the body to your head.

- **Use of imagery.** Picture your fantasy vacation or a favorite quiet place and see yourself there. Focus on any pleasant place or event.

- **Deep breathing.** Take slow, deep breaths. Pay attention to the breathing itself. This technique can be used almost anywhere, anytime to temporarily calm you.

How to Recognize Stress in Others

It is important that you be able to recognize stress in others. With the rise in workplace violence, it is especially critical that you recognize stress in others. As a general rule of thumb, you look for changes from whatever is normal for an individual.

There is actually less stress reported by top management levels in organizations than at lower levels—contrary to what people may initially think. This may be the result of more control being given to those higher in the organization. Lack of control adds to stress.

While individuals may exhibit stress in a number of different ways, some of the signs of stress include the following:

- Fatigue and low energy level
- Inability to concentrate
- Low resistance to sickness
- Anxiety
- Compulsive eating disorders
- Different work habits
- Moodiness

- Emotional outbursts
- Aggression
- Violence
- Depression
- Depression
- Heart problems
- Chronic worrying

Remember, however, that there are many signs of stress that you cannot see. You cannot observe high blood pressure, heart palpitations, and stomach disorders.

TIPS FOR EFFECTIVE MANAGERS

As a manager, you can make a difference for yourself and others. The key is to recognize that you can't eliminate stress in its entirety, so you must learn to manage it. Consider these general tips to managing stress for yourself and others:

- **Review workloads.** Requiring too much of employees will create stress and ultimately reduce performance levels.
- **Eliminate ethical dilemmas where possible.** When employees' values and ethics are aligned more closely with yours, the possibility for stress will be minimized.
- **Create interesting jobs for employees.** Boring, routine jobs often create stress.
- **Recognize stress is different for everyone.** Just because a certain condition would not create stress for you, doesn't mean that it is not a major stressor for one of your employees. Watch for signs of stress and be open-minded.
- **Recognize there is life (and stressors) outside the job.** Part of your responsibility is to help your employees balance work and nonwork issues (including stressors). Nonwork stressors can impact your employees' performance on the job. Policies that support families (like flexible scheduling) increase control for individuals. As a result, less conflict is experienced between work and family.

- **Involve employees in change.** Uncertainty and the unknown create stress. Involving people in the changes that will affect them will help to minimize some of this stress.
- **Encourage employees to create healthier lifestyles.** Some organizations now provide incentives to employees to lose weight or stop smoking. More on-site fitness centers also exist to encourage healthier employees.
- **Set a good example.** Be a good role model for stress prevention.
- **Determine the optimal stress level for each employee.** Everyone needs some stress, but that optimal level of stress will be unique to each individual.
- **Learn where stressors are.** You can only help with those stressors that you are aware of. Change the environment where possible to eliminate unnecessary stressors.
- **Develop a supportive environment.** Less formal environments are more supportive. Formal, rigid bureaucracies tend to create more stress.
- **Use career planning.** Career action plans allow employees to know their next move and thereby reduce some uncertainty about the future that leads to stress.

JUST A MINUTE

Power napping is a new technique used in many organizations today. While helping to combat a lack of sleep in more employees, it also serves as a relaxation technique. Employees return to their offices more refreshed and thinking more clearly.

HOUR'S UP!

Review these questions to see how much you've learned about helping yourself, your employees, and others in dealing with stress.

1. Stress is …
    a. Manufactured in the minds of many.
    b. The emotional and physical wear and tear of life.
    c. Cannot cause physical illness.
    d. Never good for organizations in any amount.

2. Alarm is …
   a. The first stage of Seyle's General Adaptation Syndrome.
   b. Characterized by panic and helplessness when a stressor is observed.
   c. The fight-or-flight response.
   d. All of the above.

3. Work stressors include all of the following except …
   a. Task demands.
   b. Interpersonal demands.
   c. Family demands.
   d. Physical demands.

4. Eustress …
   a. Is positive stress.
   b. Results in decreases in physical strength.
   c. Is negative stress.
   d. Is also known as distress.

5. If there is too little stress in people's lives …
   a. They are happy and extremely productive.
   b. They are lethargic and work at poor performance levels.
   c. There will be an energy boost.
   d. They are lethargic, but very productive.

6. The type A personality …
   a. Is twice as likely to have coronary heart disease as a type B personality.
   b. Displays a sense of time urgency.
   c. Is impatient.
   d. All of the above.

7. Preventive stress management …
   a. Is geared toward eliminating all stress.
   b. Removes people from stressful situations.
   c. Is really preventive medicine for stress.
   d. Is focused only on healing.

8. Physical exercise …

   a. Makes people feel less self-confident.

   b. Should include aerobic exercise and flexibility training.

   c. Makes people more susceptible to sickness.

   d. Increases muscular tension.

9. When trying to recognize stress in others …

   a. Look for changes from what is normal for the individual.

   b. Wait until violence is displayed.

   c. Recognize that you can always observe signs of stress.

   d. Look first for drug abuse.

10. You can make a difference in managing stress for yourself and others by …

    a. Reviewing workloads.

    b. Recognizing that stress is different for everyone.

    c. Involving employees in change.

    d. All of the above.

HOUR 22
Facilitating Meetings

LESSON PLAN:

In this hour you will learn about ...

- Understanding why managers dislike meetings.
- Identifying how the type of meeting impacts the meeting itself.
- Premeeting planning and setting an agenda.
- Facilitating a meeting effectively.
- Taking minutes and postmeeting responsibilities.
- Determining meeting participant roles.
- Overcoming special challenges in meetings.

A *meeting* is defined as a structured discussion led by a facilitator that has been scheduled to bring people together. The facilitator or chairperson conducts the meeting. They guide the members in their discussion.

Facilitating meetings is a major responsibility of effective managers. Meetings are a critical component in getting things done in your organization. If effective, they can save a great deal of time and resources for the organization.

While you spend a great deal of time in meetings each day, most managers come to dislike meetings tremendously. There are good reasons for this phobia of meetings. Some of the more common reasons are as follows:

- The meeting wasn't necessary and was actually a waste of time.
- No agenda existed or if it existed, it was ignored.
- The reason for the meeting was never made clear.
- The facilitation was poor.
- The meeting became too political and resulted in conformity with ineffective solutions.
- There was insufficient preparation time or notification time.
- The right people were not present, so the work could not be effectively completed.

This hour provides you with the tools and techniques to avoid these meeting mistakes.

 FYI The price tag for unproductive meetings (which is the majority of meetings) is estimated at $37 billion annually.

DIFFERENT TYPES OF MEETINGS

All meetings are not the same. Meetings are held for different reasons. Meetings may be held to find out information, to brainstorm, to plan other meetings, or for system maintenance (ongoing business).

Two of the most common reasons for holding meetings are to share information and to make decisions. It is important to determine the type of meeting because it impacts the planning and how the meeting should be conducted.

 FYI Each day it is estimated that over 12 million meetings are held in America businesses.

You will be able to better plan the meeting if you have identified the purpose of the meeting. If the meeting is to share information, the number of attendees is not a crucial issue. Generally, one-way communication is expected in an information-sharing meeting. Attendees are not expected to participate. Even the configuration of the room is different when you are just sharing information.

GO TO ▶
Refer to Hour 14, "Groups," for a discussion of the problem of social loafing (also known as the Ringlemann effect). The problem of social loafing increases as the group gets larger.

When the meeting's purpose is to make a decision, the scenario is very different. To allow for participation, only a small number of people should attend. Generally, it is recommended that the number of participants be held to no more than 12.

A round configuration of chairs or a square table is recommended to enhance two-way communication. This gives participants the opportunity to see each other as they speak. Rows encourage one-way communication where participants do not interact with one another. This is generally the configuration used in lectures—which encourages one-way communication with the speaker doing all the talking.

PREMEETING PLANNING

Planning is the key to an effective meeting. While meetings can be formally structured or informally structured, planning is still necessary. Several issues should be examined in advance of the meeting to ensure the success of the meeting.

The purpose of the meeting must be determined and clearly communicated to those who will attend. The *purpose* is a statement of what you want to achieve. Written objectives help to organize the meeting. The purpose should be included in the agenda.

Premeeting planning includes a determination of who should attend the meeting. A time and location for the meeting must also be planned, and an agenda must be written.

DETERMINING WHO SHOULD ATTEND

Determining the right people to attend is at the heart of an effective meeting. You need to identify those who can contribute. This saves time by having those who are needed at the meeting. Equally important is to include only those people who are necessary. You don't want to clutter your meeting with people who can't contribute to the purpose of the meeting.

Those who will be impacted by the work of the meeting should be invited. Those who have the knowledge necessary to achieve the objective must be invited. Not only are participants needed who have the knowledge, but also those who have experience with the topic. It is important to invite those with differing viewpoints. Diversity is critical to a successful meeting. And finally, you want to invite those who can effectively communicate.

When inviting people, it is important to consider the size of the group. The meeting cannot have too many members participating. A small group is defined as up to 12 people. The ideal group size is between five and seven members.

SETTING A MEETING TIME AND PLACE

You must also identify a good meeting time. This is more important than most people think. The date and time of the meeting can impact the effectiveness of the meeting itself. Part of identifying meeting times is determining start and end times of the meeting.

Scheduling meeting times around any holidays is not recommended. People tend to lose focus at this time. Instead of exceptionally long meetings, consider multiple meetings. Most importantly, ask members what is convenient for them.

Consideration must be given to the location of the meeting. The room must be of appropriate size to accommodate the meeting participants. It should be clean, have good lighting, and an appropriate temperature. A meeting, no matter how well planned, is doomed to failure if the room is too small and too hot.

JUST A MINUTE

A meeting can be designed so that the participants have fun. The more effective meetings will ensure that attendees actually enjoy themselves during the meeting.

Generally, the environment of the meeting sets the stage for the meeting effectiveness. The room should be comfortable, have no distractions, have clean air (that is, not be smoky), and have a comfortable temperature. It is better to be too cool than too warm. If the room is too warm, participants are likely to become drowsy.

DEVELOPING THE AGENDA

The agenda lists what has to be done in the meeting; that is, it outlines the discussion items. The order that the topics will be covered is also denoted. The agenda is a requirement for every meeting. Meetings without an agenda have a significantly higher failure rate.

The agenda organizes the meeting. As a preparation tool, it helps you to manage the time you need for the meeting and for each of the items. It is also used as an evaluation tool—afterward assessing if the objectives were met during the meeting.

The agenda is a road map—telling participants where they are going and what to expect from the meeting. An agenda minimizes straying from the topics at hand. While a little bit of flexibility is needed, the agenda provides direction for the meeting. Formal rules may tend to diminish creativity, so the flexibility is important.

In designing the agenda, the generally accepted procedure is to address the simpler items first. Place the more complex topics in the middle of the agenda and place simpler agenda items once again at the end of the meeting.

As a rule of thumb, the agenda will include the following information:

- Name of participants
- Meeting time, date, and location
- Approval of minutes
- Any reports to be presented by individual participants of subcommittees
- Unfinished business from prior meetings
- New business
- Adjournment

Some agendas may include the time allotted for each item. This is left to the discretion of the facilitator. The names and/or titles of the people presenting any reports may also be included.

It is also your responsibility when facilitating a meeting, to determine what materials are needed. Any relevant reports and preliminary information must be distributed to the participants in sufficient time for them to prepare.

As the facilitator, you also want to ensure that any equipment needed is available. This includes computers, overhead projectors, flip charts, televisions, and VCRs to name just a few. Pencil and paper is often recommended for the participants when heavy work is anticipated. If the participants do not know each other and don't work together regularly, name badges are appropriate.

Prior to the meeting, then, the facilitator should perform the following tasks:

- Notify participants of the meeting in writing with a copy of the agenda.
- Distribute preliminary materials in sufficient time for preparation.
- Send a reminder of the meeting at the last minute.

THE MEETING ITSELF

You want to ensure that you have additional copies of the agenda and any preliminary information that was distributed. Any members that forgot their materials can then get copies.

As the facilitator or chairperson, your most important role is to maintain order and facilitate discussion at the meeting. The agenda that you distributed prior to the meeting is one of the tools that you use to accomplish this.

FYI Nearly two and one-quarter hours each day are spent in meetings. Considering an 8-hour day as the norm for managers, this means over 25 percent of the manager's day is spent in meetings.

Always begin the meeting at the predetermined time. Consistency in starting on time will quickly gain you a good reputation in your organization. Participants in your meetings will also learn to come on time.

Make sure that you take attendance. This information will be included in the minutes of the meeting as well. Introductions may be in order if people don't know each other well or don't regularly work together.

Your primary task is to keep the group on track. You need to encourage debate on the topic at hand and ensure that no one individual dominates—including yourself. It is important to keep the group moving through the agenda items.

As the facilitator, you must ask questions to get the discussion started. You want to address people by name and really listen to what they are saying. You are also responsible for monitoring destructive participants and providing the necessary interventions. You should repeat questions posed by participants so that everyone gets a chance to hear them. In addition, you need to provide periodic summaries of the group's activities.

At the end of the meeting, it is your responsibility to bring closure. This usually entails recapping the progress made and summarizing the work assignments. You also want to set the time for the next meeting and end this meeting on time. Once again, consistency in promptly ending will gain you a reputation that people appreciate.

THE MINUTES

Minutes provide a written documentation of the activities of the group. Participants can assess the long-term progress of the group by reviewing the group's minutes over a period of time. The minutes, then, provide a history of the group's activities.

JUST A MINUTE

Handing over the notebook of minutes is almost a ritual in some organizations. As the position of chairperson changes, the importance of the minutes is highlighted as the history of the group is passed from the old chairperson to the new.

The minutes provide a number of functions for the group. They can provide an update to members that were unable to attend a meeting. Recognition is also given to people as they see their name mentioned in the minutes. When there is confusion over what has occurred, the minutes can prevent arguments over what was decided—because the minutes are the formal record of what actually happened.

A recorder or a secretary takes notes during the meeting for the minutes. As the chairperson, you must assign someone this role. You, however, are responsible for reviewing the minutes as submitted and then distributing these minutes to all the participants.

The minutes should include the following items:

- The name of the group
- The date of the meeting
- A list of the members in attendance
- The name of the facilitator or chairperson
- The time the meeting was called to order
- A summary of the topics of discussion (following the agenda)
- The name of the recorder
- The time the meeting was adjourned

Some minutes may also highlight the tasks specifically assigned to meeting participants.

Good minutes don't have to be lengthy. The key is to be accurate, yet concise. The minutes must be objective and factual. The recorder must also be careful to determine what comments should be considered off the record (and excluded from the minutes). Because the minutes are a formal documentation of the group, some comments may be better considered off the record.

It is best for the recorder to prepare the minutes as soon as possible—while the information is easier to recall. The minutes should include attachments of the agenda and any reports presented during the meeting (or any handouts provided). Members are given an opportunity to revise minutes at the next meeting.

FYI Parliamentary procedures date back to the British Parliament's House of Commons. Thomas Jefferson adapted these procedures for the U.S. Senate.

POSTMEETING PLANNING

Even though the meeting has ended, your job is not complete. You still have responsibilities to fulfill. You must distribute the minutes of the meeting to the members. These will be approved (or revised) at the next meeting of the group.

You must also follow-up on any assignments made during the meeting. If reports are to be presented at the next meeting, you need to ensure that work is progressing satisfactorily.

JUST A MINUTE

 A Postmeeting Reaction Form (PMR) may be used to evaluate the effectiveness of meetings. Members are generally asked to fill it out before they leave the meeting. The facilitator can then use the feedback to assess the meeting afterward.

Most important, you must assess the overall effectiveness of the meeting. You will be able to use this information to improve upon the next meeting. You may use questionnaires or just speak informally with people to get feedback. This input can help you improve your ability to facilitate meetings, address your own weaknesses, and decide if the objectives were met.

YOUR ROLE AS FACILITATOR

As a facilitator, you must first ensure that a meeting is really necessary. Ask yourself if a memo or perhaps a telephone call could handle the situation. If the answer is yes, the meeting is unnecessary. Using meetings unnecessarily wastes time and resources. Keep the following in mind when determining if a meeting is necessary:

- Use a meeting only when you need a fast response and need input from group members, or if you must notify them quickly of some critical information.
- Ensure that the meeting participants want to meet. If they don't want to meet, the meeting will not be effective.

- Begin and end at the predetermined times. Time is a precious resource for everyone. If a meeting is found to be necessary, keep within the predetermined times.

PROCEED WITH CAUTION

 When you are not the facilitator, but are a meeting participant, you have an equally crucial role to fill. It is an active role—contrary to what many may think. You have a responsibility to be active in the meeting and to prepare. You must contribute to the achievement of the objective and support the facilitator.

As the facilitator, during the meeting ensure that you pay attention to the following:

- Make sure you did your homework and you are prepared for the meeting.
- Arrive early for your meeting. This gives you an opportunity to check that everything is in order. You are also present to greet your attendees as they arrive.
- Start on time. You will quickly acquire a good reputation for starting on time and valuing other people's time.
- Assign a participant the responsibility for recording the minutes.
- Stick to the agenda—including honoring the times allotted for each topic. Also be sure to cover the entire agenda. The agenda announced what you were going to discuss and you have to be sure to follow through.
- Move the group along and facilitate the discussion.
- End on time. This timeliness will be greatly appreciated by all the participants.

SPECIAL CHALLENGES: MANAGING INDIVIDUALS WHO INHIBIT MEETING SUCCESS

Because meetings are comprised of people, there are bound to be problems with different types of personalities coming together. Some of the more common issues are explored in this section.

The people who don't participate may not seem to be a problem at first glance, but they are. They have been included as participants because they have something important to contribute. If they don't contribute, you are missing the knowledge that they have and you need. You may consider making more eye contact with the individual and drawing him or her into the discussion. You may also have to direct questions toward nonparticipants.

The opposite of the nonparticipant is the person who talks too much and tends to monopolize the discussion. Once you call them out, you need to then ask others for their input. You may have to publicly stress the need to hear everyone's viewpoint. If this still is not successful in curbing this individual, then the role of recorder can be assigned to this individual. In all likelihood, some of their attention will be turned from talking to taking the minutes—and listening.

There is another problem with the individual who constantly interrupts other speakers. While the person may not intend to be rude, his or her excitement and desire to share ideas may cause him or her to be less than courteous. This situation requires that you take control. You must ask the speaker to finish what he or she was saying and ask the interrupter to wait.

If you fail to address these personnel issues, members will lose interest. You may find that people will not attend your meetings, and your ability to be successful will be threatened. Remember, however, when trying to address one of these issues to focus on the behavior—not the individual's personality.

HOUR'S UP!

Recognizing that you will spend a significant amount of your time in meetings, check out these questions to see how much you have learned about more effectively facilitating meetings.

1. Managers tend to dislike meetings for all of the following reasons except …

    a. The meeting wasn't even necessary.

    b. There was no agenda.

    c. The right people were present to actually get the work done.

    d. The facilitation was poor.

2. An information-sharing meeting …

    a. Can be planned for in the same way that a decision-making meeting can be planned.

    b. Requires more two-way communication than a decision-making meeting.

    c. Can utilize rows for seating where a decision-making meeting would better be served with a circle configuration.

    d. Generally expects a great deal of participation from attendees versus a decision-making meeting.

3. Planning is the key to ...

    a. Only formally structured meetings.

    b. Every meeting—regardless of structure.

    c. Only informally structured meetings.

    d. Writing a good agenda.

4. Planning includes ...

    a. Deciding who should attend the meeting.

    b. Writing the agenda.

    c. Deciding the time and location of the meeting.

    d. All of the above.

5. The agenda ...

    a. Organizes the meeting.

    b. Just tells people where the meeting is to be held.

    c. Is distributed as you walk in the door of the meeting.

    d. Is optional for facilitating effective meetings.

6. During the meeting, as a facilitator you should ...

    a. Start on time.

    b. Stick to the agenda.

    c. Move the group along.

    d. All of the above.

7. Meeting minutes ...

    a. Are optional in effective meetings.

    b. Are used to let everyone see his or her name in print.

    c. Provide a written documentation of the activities of the group.

    d. Give the recorder something to do during the meeting.

8. After the meeting ...

    a. The facilitator's job is finished.

    b. You must assess the effectiveness of the meeting.

c. You are not concerned with assignments given during the meeting because the participants are trustworthy adults.

d. You should avoid any discussion of the minutes.

9. As the facilitator (or chairperson) of the meeting, your most important role is ...

a. To distribute an agenda.

b. To maintain order and facilitate discussion at the meeting.

c. To hand out materials that participants may have forgotten.

d. To end the meeting on time.

10. People who talk too much in meetings ...

a. Are never a problem.

b. May have to be reminded of the need to hear everyone's input.

c. Always ask others for their input.

d. Should never be assigned the role of recorder.

HOUR 23

Interviewing

Your success in the staffing function directly impacts your success as a manager. You have a responsibility for hiring people for your organization. With the costs of recruitment so high today, the importance of your role is further heightened.

Strategic human resource planning is getting the right people into the right jobs so the organization can meet its goals.

The two main components of staffing are recruitment and selection. Both are critical in assuring that your organization attracts and hires the best qualified applicants for the position—and ultimately, for the organization.

Recruitment is the process whereby you get the right people notified of the job so they can apply for the position. Selection is actually choosing among these potential applicants.

THE RECRUITMENT PROCESS

Human resource staffing is determining how many employees are needed and the type of skills that are needed in these employees. This begins with job analysis, which entails analyzing the tasks to be completed in the organization. This analysis generates two documents: the job description and the job specification.

The job description lists the actual tasks that are to be performed in each specific position. The job specification

LESSON PLAN:

In this hour you will learn about …

- Strategic human resource planning.
- How to recruit and attract the best candidates.
- Internal versus external recruitment options.
- Steps in the selection process to choose the best applicant.
- Different types of interviews.
- Questions to avoid during an interview.
- How to plan and conduct the interview.

identifies the worker characteristics necessary to successfully perform the job. Both of these documents are critical to the selection and recruitment process. The job specification helps to ensure the person with the appropriate skills is hired and the job description enables you to communicate exactly what the person will be doing on the job. After completing these documents, you must then decide how and where to find these employees.

In attracting the best candidates, each organization must determine how to best announce its openings. That is, organizations must decide if positions are to be filled by advertising internally or externally. Announcing the position may also be accomplished by using a combination of the two.

INTERNAL RECRUITMENT

There are a number of options available when recruiting internally. You can choose from job posting, company newsletters, bulletin boards, employee referrals, and skills banks. Each comes with its own advantages and disadvantages.

Job posting is one of the most commonly used methods of recruiting internally. Openings for positions are announced to employees within the organization. This can be accomplished in a variety of ways. Print bulletin boards can be used to simply post a notification of the opening. Intranets may carry electronic bulletin boards announcing openings as well. Employees within the organization are aware of the openings prior to recruiting externally. Any interested employees are then given an opportunity to apply for the job or bid on it in some instances.

PROCEED WITH CAUTION

Internal posting is sometimes used for political reasons and can demoralize workers. A recent survey found that nearly three fourths of the internal postings already had identified likely internal applicants when the job was posted.

Employee referrals are often successful in finding internal applicants for a position. Employees refer other workers from other departments for the position. (When these referrals are individuals outside the organization, the technique is considered external recruiting.)

Significant bonuses are being paid (in times of tight labor markets) to employees who can refer applicants for an opening.

Skills banks (also known as skills inventories) have been established to help track the skills of employees within the organization. While these banks are instrumental in determining the training and development needs of the organization, they are also critical in identifying the skills of the current workforce. Then as openings occur, you can refer to the skills bank to identify the employees within the organization that possess the required skills.

EXTERNAL RECRUITMENT

There are numerous alternatives for externally recruiting. Some represent more traditional alternatives while others reflect the use of current technology.

Advertising for openings is one of the most commonly used alternatives for recruiting individuals outside the organization. Over 97 percent of American firms use advertising.

Announcing positions by advertising includes using general and local newspapers and trade journals or magazines. Many times a better response for the best matches is found by using trade journals. For example, colleges and universities advertise positions for professors and administrators in the Chronicle for Higher Education—a trade publication for colleges and universities. Placement agencies are of a wide variety. These agencies can be public, private, or management consultants. Public agencies are government agencies that can provide you with applicants. Private agencies are the traditional placement organizations. Management consultants are those organizations commonly referred to as headhunters or executive search firms. They generally specialize in certain fields and in higher-level executives.

Employee referrals or recommendations can include applicants outside the organization. Just as employees may refer people within the organization (an internal recruiting technique), they may also recommend those outside the organization.

Professional organizations are a good source of applicants for specific fields. Most professional associations have placement divisions that can be contacted when your organization has an opening. They can then help you match your opening with the qualifications of their members that may be seeking opportunities. The Institute of Management Accountants is well known for its placement division for accountants.

School job fairs are good sources of entry-level employees or specialized employees. Most college campuses host job or career fairs at least annually. Employers are invited in to interview students on campus who will graduate shortly. High schools and vocational schools often offer prospective employers the opportunity to interview on their campus.

The Internet has changed the way that many organizations recruit today. Posting on electronic bulletin boards and specialized employment sites are regularly used by large numbers of organizations. More large companies are also choosing to list their openings on their own Web sites.

The Internet has rapidly become an important choice in recruiting externally. One of the most recognized Internet sites for job posting is www. monster.com. Companies can post job openings and job seekers can post their resumes. This Internet recruiting is expected to continue to grow in the next few years.

Internships have been very successful in recruiting employees. High school or college students are given the opportunity to obtain work experience while continuing their education. Employers have the opportunity to track the intern's performance.

ADVANTAGES AND DISADVANTAGES OF INTERNAL AND EXTERNAL RECRUITING OPTIONS

Recruiting internally provides several advantages. Applicants are already familiar with the culture of the organization and the manner of conducting business. Therefore, the training and development costs are lower for internal hires.

Internal recruitment is generally less expensive than external recruitment. It is a boost to employee morale to know that the organization is committed to hiring from within. And, recruiting internally enables you to have knowledge of the applicants' track record—that is, you know their past performance on the job. This makes their performance more predictable. Internal applicants are familiar with the culture of the organization. Promoting from within also helps the organization to develop its management talent.

There are, however, drawbacks to internal recruitment. When there are positions available, there are a limited number of positions for which many employees tend to compete. This sets the stage for political infighting and for disappointed employees who don't get the positions.

Committing to hiring from within can shortchange the organization if the best candidate is not found internally. If the organization settles for a less than ideal candidate just to promote from within, everyone loses. There is also a danger of inbreeding when promoting from within fills too many positions. New perspectives are not gained.

Internal recruitment creates a ripple effect. As an opening in one area is filled, there is another opening in the area from which that employee came. This can be especially detrimental and disruptive in smaller organizations.

PROCEED WITH CAUTION

You must be careful when you use internal recruiting methods too much. You may be found guilty of discrimination. Hiring from within (especially with employee referrals) may result in continuing to hire the same groups of people and adversely impacting other minority groups.

There is also a lack of new blood with hiring from within. New talent is not available with internal applicants. A balance must be struck between the fresh perspectives gained with external recruiting and the stability gained with internal recruiting.

External recruitment promotes creativity with new blood. These external hires are not wed to the past or biased by the way that the organization does things. They may also bring with them new skills that have not been developed in-house, thereby avoiding the risk of high levels of employee inbreeding. With external recruiting, you also avoid pirating employees from other departments.

Unfortunately, however, recruiting externally may be more expensive than internal recruiting. External recruitment may also result in a poor fit with the organizational culture because these new employees don't already know the culture. It takes longer to get an outside hire up to speed because they have no history with the organization or with the culture. In addition, you have no firsthand knowledge of their track records. Other employees may also be demoralized when there is a need to go outside the organization to hire.

THE SELECTION PROCESS

Selection is the process used to choose the best person for the job. The selection process generally involves the following steps:

1. Complete application
2. Perform screening in the Human Resource department
3. Administer employment tests
4. Perform background checks
5. Conduct interview
6. Administer physical examination and drug tests
7. Finalize decision to hire

THE APPLICATION

The application today can be a hard copy or it can be in electronic form. The application is a form developed by each organization to obtain background information, education, and work experience. It summarizes the applicant's skills. Some organizations recognize that specific items on their applications are good predictors of success on the job and pay particular attention to these items.

Candidates are usually asked to complete an application even when they submit a resumé. The application generally requires the signature of the applicant attesting to the integrity of the information. Should any information later be deemed untruthful, even after hiring, the applicant can be terminated.

PROCEED WITH CAUTION

There are greater levels of exaggeration on resumés today than ever before. The area most frequently lied about on resumés is the level of education achieved by applicants. Interestingly enough, when people lie about their education, they tend to select the best colleges and universities as the ones they've attended.

PRELIMINARY SCREENING

In larger organizations, the human resource department generally performs the preliminary screening. This screening is intended to weed out the obvious, unqualified applicants.

This screening stage is also used to ensure that the applicants possess the necessary job skills. The job description and the job specification are used to determine the most qualified applicants. The applicants are also informed of the salary range at this stage to ensure only those interested applicants continue in the process.

EMPLOYMENT TESTS

Employment tests enable the organization to make more effective selections. Any tests that are administered must be job relevant. Employment tests include cognitive, aptitude, ability, and personality tests. Because the interview is not reliable, employment tests have become more critical.

Testing can be conducted by professional firms (or consultants outside the organization) or by in-house, human resource personnel. Knowledge, skills, and abilities can be tested. Aptitude testing determines the applicant's capacity to learn. Achievement tests measure what the applicant can do now. The cognitive ability tests measure mental capabilities. More organizations are choosing to administer IQ tests to measure the applicant's capacity to learn.

Personality tests are on the rise as organizations pay more attention to the person-job-organization fit. Insights into personal characteristics provide some indicators of this fit with the organization, the culture, and the other people within the organization.

Job knowledge tests are good predictors of success on the job. Job sample tests enable the applicant to perform the actual job. In-basket exercises have become especially popular with management applicants.

FYI Over 70 percent of organizations administer some type of employment testing. The objective is to predict the success of applicants on the job.

Some of the more common tests given to applicants today include work sampling, assessment centers, graphology, and honesty tests.

Work sampling is used to test applicants' ability to perform the actual job. A sampling of the actual work is presented to the candidate for completion. Work sampling has been proven to better predict on-the-job performance. Unfortunately, work sampling is not available for every job—especially in the managerial ranks.

Assessment centers are used for management applicants. A series of exercises that simulate managerial work are presented to managerial candidates. These assessment centers can include in-basket exercises that require the applicant to prioritize work, case studies, and business games and simulations.

While somewhat controversial, graphology is being used in more organizations. Several thousand U.S. companies are analyzing the handwriting of their applicants to gain better insight into their personality characteristics.

Honesty tests are being administered in the hopes of combating the $40 billion price tag for employee theft in American businesses each year. These honesty tests predict the integrity of applicants. They are used especially in the retail industry.

PROCEED WITH CAUTION

 While pencil and paper honesty tests may be administered in the pre-employment setting if they are job-related, polygraphs cannot be administered. Lie detector tests cannot be used in pre-employment screening (with the exception of pharmaceutical companies and companies hiring security personnel related to health and safety) according to the Employee Polygraph Protection Act of 1988.

BACKGROUND CHECKS

The purpose of background investigations is to verify the information on the application. Background checks are also commonly referred to as "reference checks" because part of this process is contacting personal references provided by the applicant. Employee privacy issues must be carefully considered when performing background checks.

Firms walk a thin line with regard to background checks. It is best to obtain a signed waiver from the applicant when conducting reference checks. You should solicit only job-related information and request this in writing.

Internal or external investigations can be conducted. An internal investigation is performed as the human resource department solicits information on former employees and personal references. It should be remembered that these references are biased as a result of being selected by the applicant. External investigation agencies can obtain more detailed (and perhaps more valuable) information.

THE INTERVIEW

The interview is used to solicit additional information and obtain clarification of information from the application and his or her resumé.

During the interview, a realistic job preview (RJP) should be used. This is the presentation of an objective overview of the job during the interview—including negatives as well as positives. Both the positive and negative aspects of the job are clearly related to the applicant. An RJP will likely result in more realistic expectations by the applicant. Research has also indicated that use of RJPs do not lower the acceptance rate—they only lower the turnover rate. Those applicants accepting the job have more realistic expectations and are better satisfied with the job because they had a realistic picture of the job presented.

THE PHYSICAL EXAMINATION AND DRUG TEST

The physical examination comes late in the selection process. In most cases, the physical should be conducted after the conditional offer has been made. The physical exam must be a job-related requirement. It must be kept completely confidential. Drug tests are more commonly administered today. The urine test is the most common.

GO TO ▶
Refer to Hour 8, "Relationship Management," for a discussion of the perceptual errors that can bias the interview.

JUST A MINUTE

A measure of general intelligence (IQ) has become one of the most popular employment tests administered today.

THE DECISION TO HIRE

While the tendency to make the decision to hire is often early in the process, you should wait until all the information has been gathered and analyzed before making the final decision. The decision to hire is often made with input from the human resource department.

The decision to hire is critical. If you don't hire the right people, your organization cannot function effectively. There are two hiring errors. One is not hiring those that you should have. The second is hiring those that you should not have. Both errors come with significant costs for the organization—and, perhaps for you as well.

This decision to hire is followed by the socialization of the employee, which is actually the last step in the staffing function.

The Effective Interview

GO TO ▶
Refer to Hour 17, "Organizational Culture," for a discussion of socializing new employees and Hour 13, "Career Development: Your Responsibility," for a discussion of career development after employment.

Even though the reliability and the validity of interviews have been questioned, they continue to play a major role in the selection process. There are a number of steps that you can take to ensure that you use the interview technique more effectively to successfully perform the staffing function.

Planning the Interview

For a more effective interview, the key is to develop a plan. As a starting point, you must know the job requirements for the position to be filled. This serves as the foundation for all the questions to be posed in the interview. You must also have the candidate's completed application form and a list of standardized questions (to compare applicants).

JUST A MINUTE

Ironically, interviewers are better able to verbalize why an applicant would be a poor choice rather than why an applicant would be a good selection for the organization. Selecting structured interviews and making notes on both positive and negative responses helps interviewers overcome this.

Selecting the Appropriate Type of Interview

The amount of structure differentiates two types of interviews. These are the nondirective interview and the structured interview.

The nondirective interview is the least structured of interviews. The applicant provides the direction of the interview. Open-ended questions are asked to give freedom to the applicant.

The advantage of the nondirective interview is obtaining information not normally received during the more structured interview. Applicants may provide information that the interviewer would not normally think about asking. The lack of structure, however, results in inconsistencies across interviews. The interviewer, then, cannot compare applicants because different information is obtained in each of the interviews. This type of interview is best used for interviews at executive levels.

Structured interviews provide consistency across all applicants because the same standardized questions are asked of each applicant. These structured interviews are also more effective in avoiding charges of discrimination because the questions can be planned and evaluated for discriminatory potential.

There are a number of specialized interviews that may be conducted when appropriate. These include the situational interview, the behavioral description interview, the panel interview, and the computer interview. While not used extensively today, each has its merits for specific situations.

The situational interview poses a hypothetical incident to the applicant. The interviewer than evaluates how the applicant responds to the situation.

The behavioral description interview poses an actual situation likely to have been encountered by the applicant. The applicant then describes what they actually did when he or she encountered the situation. This interview is similar to the situational interview, but the event is a real one instead of hypothetical. The interviewer still evaluates the applicant's response to the situation.

The panel interview is generally used in the academic arena to hire professors. A panel of interviewers takes turns posing questions to a single candidate. The panel then must reach a consensus. The value is in the multiple perspectives of the panelists.

Computer interviews are growing in popularity. A computer program assesses the candidate's responses in terms of an ideal profile developed by the organization for the position in question. These computer interviews are sometimes used to screen applicants in the early stages of the selection process.

POTENTIALLY DANGEROUS QUESTIONS

The interview today is fraught with legal pitfalls. You must be exceptionally careful about the questions that you pose to applicants. While some may seem innocent, they open the door for litigation—against you and your organization.

PROCEED WITH CAUTION

While substance abuse testing is conducted in over 80 percent of American businesses, the legal issues are still being determined. The privacy issues of employees are under close scrutiny. Companies must be careful in how these tests are administered.

Any questions that solicit information concerning the major discriminatory categories (race, color, age, religion, sexual orientation, or national origin) are treading on very dangerous ground and should be avoided. Potentially discriminatory questions include the following:

- What is your race?
- What is your ancestry?
- How old are you?
- Are you married?
- How much do you weigh?
- What are your hobbies?
- Do you have any children?
- What is your religion?

TIPS FOR CONDUCTING THE EFFECTIVE INTERVIEW

To conduct a more effective interview, consider the following general advice:

- Start the interview on a positive note. Always rise to greet the applicant and try to put them at ease. If they are more relaxed, you are likely to obtain more information from them.
- Actively listen. You must pay attention to what is said as well as what is not said. The nonverbal cues are critical in the communication process.
- Use realistic job previews when interviewing. An objective portrayal of the job results in lower turnover.
- Be aware of your personal biases when conducting interviews.
- Maintain control of the interview (unless you are using the nondirective interview).
- Ask for training on how to interview. Consider using role-playing and videotaping to improve your interviewing techniques.
- Always prepare for interviews. Ensure that you have detailed information about the job being filled (with a copy of the job description and the job specification).
- Use standardized evaluation forms. While they will help ensure that you are consistent in evaluating each applicant, they can be helpful if legal issues arise.
- Take notes during the interview and immediately afterward. Don't rely on your memory. Too much is at stake.

GO TO ▶
Refer to Hour 20, "Organizational Communication," for a detailed discussion of the roles of active listening and nonverbal cues in the communication process.

GO TO ▶
Refer to Hour 8 for a discussion of the perceptual errors that can bias the interview.

Hour's Up!

The recruitment and selection processes directly impact your effectiveness on the job. Check out these questions to see how much you learned about these key functions.

1. The recruitment process …
   a. Is the same as strategic human resource planning.
   b. Is getting the right people notified of the job so they can apply for the position.
   c. Is actually choosing among the potential applicants.
   d. Is only the responsibility of the human resource department.

2. The selection process …
   a. Is the same as strategic human resource planning.
   b. Is getting the right people notified of the job so they can apply for the position.
   c. Is actually choosing among the potential applicants.
   d. Is only the responsibility of the human resource department.

3. Internal recruitment methods …
   a. Yield applicants already familiar with the culture of the organization.
   b. Will be less expensive than external methods.
   c. Allow your organization to develop management talent.
   d. All of the above.

4. External recruitment options include all of the following except …
   a. A sign in the window announcing an opening.
   b. Placement agencies.
   c. Internships.
   d. Skills banks.

5. Employment tests …
   a. Must be job-related.
   b. Include polygraphs.
   c. Never include handwriting analysis.
   d. Cannot include work sampling.

6. Background investigations …

    a. Do not consider employee privacy issues.

    b. Are only conducted internally.

    c. Are used to verify the information on the applicant.

    d. Are only conducted externally.

7. The interview …

    a. Is fraught with legal pitfalls.

    b. Is of questionable reliability.

    c. May be structured or nondirective.

    d. All of the above.

8. Realistic job previews (RJPs) …

    a. Increase turnover.

    b. Increase job expectations.

    c. Decrease turnover.

    d. Decrease acceptance rates.

9. Potentially dangerous (illegal) questions to be avoided during the interview include …

    a. How old are you?

    b. Do you have children?

    c. Are you married?

    d. All of the above.

10. When conducting an interview, you should …

    a. Put the applicant on their guard immediately.

    b. Listen to verbal cues and ignore nonverbal cues.

    c. Use active listening.

    d. Let the applicant take control of the interview.

QUIZ

HOUR 24

Gaining an Edge: Business Etiquette

It should be noted that business etiquette varies by culture. The discussion in this Hour focuses on American business etiquette. For more information on business etiquette in other cultures, a good resource is *International Business Etiquette: What You Need to Know to Conduct Business Abroad with Charm and Savvy*, by Ann Marie Sabath.

There has been a renewed interest in the last decade in business etiquette. In a highly competitive business environment, everyone is finding that the fine details are making a big difference. Deals can fall through with a misstep on the part of an unsuspecting individual. The sloppy table manners of a sales person can offend a client to the point of taking business to a competitor. Job offers can often be lost when there's no awareness of etiquette —including how to shake hands or how to dress for the interview.

WHY BUSINESS ETIQUETTE IS ONCE AGAIN IMPORTANT

The cost of faux pas can be exceptionally high. These mistakes can cost you your career or your organization an important relationship. You are judged every day on how you conduct yourself. Good manners provide you with your personal competitive advantage in the workplace and can enhance your effectiveness.

CHAPTER SUMMARY

LESSON PLAN:
In this hour you will learn about ...

- Knowing the benefits of good manners.
- Handling introductions properly.
- Understanding the dining experience.
- Handling yourself at cocktail parties.
- Using etiquette in meetings.
- Using good manners in business correspondence.
- Giving and receiving business gifts.
- Using netiquette to correspond properly via e-mail and other forms of electronic communication.
- Creating a positive image.

When you use good manners, you will …

- Get better results.
- Gain more cooperation from people.
- Gain commitment from others.
- Enhance your probability of success.

It is now recognized that paying attention to business etiquette is actually good business and pays off on the bottom line. You represent your company. A manners mistake on your part can reflect negatively on your organization.

PROCEED WITH CAUTION

Lack of etiquette may cost your company more than you think. The overwhelming majority of dissatisfied customers that were offended don't tell you of their experience. They just never do business with your firm again. However, they will tell between 10 to 20 other people about their bad experience—thereby influencing even more of your business.

BUSINESS BASICS

While business etiquette involves using a lot of common sense, it is much more as well. It's about knowing the rules of behavior in today's workplace, and about social rules and business rules and how the two are blended today.

Most of all, business etiquette is all about packaging all the little things. It's knowing what to do, when to do it, and how to do it. It's also just as much about knowing what not to do. And, it is certainly not just about the big things. As any business knows, to be successful, a lot of little things must go well. The same applies to you in business etiquette. It's the small things that can seal you and your company's fate—either positively or negatively.

Some of the business basics to consider include how introductions are made, dining etiquette, conduct at cocktail parties, meeting etiquette, and how to handle business gifts.

INTRODUCTIONS

First impressions are critical to business relationships. And, the way that introductions are handled contribute to this all-important first impression.

When you are being introduced to someone, be sure to stop any activity that you are engaged in. Walk toward the person being introduced and offer your hand. If you are seated behind a desk, rise and walk around the desk to greet the individual.

GO TO ▶
Refer to Hour 8, "Relationship Management," for a detailed discussion of first impressions and the role they play in the perceptual process.

PROCEED WITH CAUTION

The handshake is no longer a gender issue where the man offers the hand first. All of business etiquette is founded more on status than on gender by today's standards.

When saying, "Hello," be sure to repeat the new person's name. This not only makes him or her feel good to know that you paid attention, but it serves as a memory aid. You will be more likely able to recall his or her name at a later time.

The handshake remains a critical element in introductions and ongoing relationships. Your handshake must be firm with a palm-to-palm grasp of the other person's hand. It should not be overdone or underdone. One or two shakes is sufficient; continuous pumping and back slapping are inappropriate. Make direct eye contact while shaking hands and repeating the person's name.

In the business setting, kissing should be avoided. It can be misunderstood and is generally inappropriate. It opens the door for too many faux pas, so the advice is to always avoid kissing in a business context.

When you are conducting the introductions, be sure to present the older person to the younger, people outside the organization to those inside the organization, and senior company people to junior company people. The host should extend his or her hand for the handshake.

Never use informal or pet names during business introductions; formal names should always be used. Cute stories are also not appropriate, and all introductions should be concise.

THE DINING EXPERIENCE

More business is being conducted over meals than ever before. This can be both good and bad for you. If you are up-to-speed on your dining P's and Q's, you can shine in these situations. If, however, you are less than prepared to exhibit your finest manners, you may seal your fate in a negative way.

The "test" begins before you ever sit down to the table. As the host of the business meal, you have many responsibilities. The biggest of which is to confirm the date, time, and place of the meal. You want to ensure that you arrive early to make sure your reservation is in order. This will also give you the opportunity to greet your guest upon arrival. Once your guest arrives, all cell phones and pagers should be turned off. Your guest should have your undivided attention and you should not allow any interruptions.

As you are seated at your table, allow your guest to be seated first. Your napkin should be placed in your lap within the first 10 seconds of sitting. Your napkin then remains in your lap for the duration of the meal. Should it be necessary to leave the table anytime before the end of the meal, place your napkin in your chair—not on the table. Your napkin is only replaced on the table when the meal is over.

PROCEED WITH CAUTION

It's not just the napkin that is not placed on the table. You should refrain from placing any papers, books, or folders on the table as well. Even keys and purses should be placed on the floor next to your chair. Because the conversation should not turn to business until after the meal is finished, any papers should remain off the table until this time.

There is often confusion over the use of utensils at the table. The general rule of thumb is to work your way in from the outside toward your plate when you are in doubt.

Forks are found to the left of the plate and the knives to the right. Should you find utensils horizontally positioned across the top of the place setting, these are to be used for the dessert.

Care should be taken to use the right glasses. Your glasses are found to the right of your plate. When multiple glasses are used, it is generally for water and wine. The bread plate is placed to the left of your place setting. This is one of biggest mistakes made in dining. Once one person uses the wrong bread plate, the error is compounded as all the place settings are corrupted.

Your guest should be allowed to order first. If the guest orders an appetizer, you should do likewise to make them comfortable. You take your cue from them. You should also let your guest begin eating first.

No one at the table should begin eating until everyone at the table is served. Even if others tell you to start, you should still wait until everyone is served.

When passing condiments, bread, sugar, cream, or any other food item, always pass to the right. Make sure that you pass any dishes with handles so that the handle is offered to the person to whom you are passing.

Eating requires special attention as well. When preparing bread for consumption, it should be broken into bite-size sections and buttered by these sections. Butter should be taken from a butter dish and placed on your plate.

When you have completed your meal, your knife and fork should be placed at the 4:20 position. That is, mirroring the hands of a clock, the knife and fork should be placed across the plate in this position to signal to the server that you have finished with your meal.

COCKTAIL PARTIES

A distinction is usually made between a cocktail party and a cocktail reception. Most invitations will stipulate which occasion it is. A cocktail party is less formal with standing. A cocktail reception is more formal with dressy attire expected. More food is usually served at the cocktail reception as well.

When you are invited to a cocktail party, special etiquette should be observed. While it is still a dining experience, it is one of a different nature with a different set of rules of conduct.

Because cocktail parties generally require that you stand, you want to ensure that you leave your left hand free to greet other people. Hold your plate in your right hand so that you are not awkwardly juggling when someone approaches.

 If you happen to be a smoker, recognize that there are caveats for you. Only smoke in areas designated as smoking in the building. Smoking at meals should wait until after the meal has been completed. It is best to avoid smoking in all business situations if at all possible.

A cocktail party is not meant to be a full meal, so don't arrive hungry and make a beeline for the buffet table. As soon as you arrive, size up the room and the people in attendance. Then, begin to make your rounds greeting people; this is an opportunity to become visible.

Extreme caution should be used in regards to alcohol. Any alcohol that is consumed at a cocktail party should only be in moderation. If you do not drink, do not voice disapproval over those who do. Alcohol should never, however, be consumed in any amount during business hours.

Following are some tips to consider when consuming cocktail party food items:

- When served from a tray, use a napkin or a toothpick (when provided) to remove the food item from the tray. Either eat the food immediately from the tray or place it on your plate.
- When raw vegetables are served on a tray with a dip, you should dip the vegetable one time. Double dipping is strictly prohibited.
- Red and white wine glasses are held differently. Red wine glasses are held by the bowl, while white wine glasses are held by the stem of the glass.
- When beer is served in a bottle or a can, ask for a glass and only drink from the glass.

MEETING ETIQUETTE

To be effective and create the right image, the etiquette of meetings should be followed. It helps to have a working knowledge of Robert's Rules of Order. Even if the rules are not strictly adhered to, they provide a good guideline for appropriate behavior.

It is proper to provide a minimum of two days' notice to anyone who is to attend a meeting. Any people from out of town should be given at least two weeks' notice so that they may make appropriate arrangements.

Out-of-town meeting participants should be provided some general information about the area if they are not familiar with it. This information might include the following:

- Area hotels
- Airports servicing the area
- Transportation available
- Restaurants
- Meeting location

Some tips to good meeting manners include the following:

- Smile and greet everyone. Make the introductions and be sure that you get everyone's name correct.

- Use nametags when meeting participants don't know each other.

- Always ask where you should sit if it is not your meeting. Do not assume that seating doesn't matter.

- Buy a good pen to take to meetings. This is part of the positive image that you should be projecting.

- Don't play with papers or pens during the meeting. If you have nervous hands, clasp them together on the table to avoid fidgeting with items.

- Be prepared with your remarks and be concise. Avoid any negative or confrontational remarks. And, never interrupt others; hear them out.

- Give breaks when facilitating a long meeting.

- Be sure to contribute and participate—even when the meeting is not yours.

GO TO ▶
Refer to Hour 22, "Facilitating Meetings," for a detailed discussion of meeting facilitation.

BUSINESS GIFTS

Gifts should be sent on a timely basis. Holiday and special occasion gifts should be sent one to two weeks before the event occurs (such as weddings). Remember that when you are invited to a special event, you are expected to send a gift (whether or not you attend).

When invited to someone's home (such as an open house) take an appropriate "house" gift. Food items are most appropriate in these situations.

Gifts to your supervisor should be modest, but somewhat personal. They should not be expensive. This makes others feel uncomfortable. The best course of action is to determine what the person likes and choose a gift accordingly. These are gifts that are generally well received and appreciated because you took his or her likes into consideration. Be sure to also take the recipient's culture into account.

If you would like to give a gift and don't know the hobbies or preferences of the person, you might consider more professional gifts. These would include such items as a professional pen, a calendar, a fruit basket, or an appointment book.

When accepting gifts, a handwritten note of appreciation is most appropriate. Sending an e-mail or making a phone call are not as appropriate. A proper, conservative thank you note should be a staple among your stationary supplies.

If you must refuse to accept a gift (due to a violation of your company's ethics code or a feeling that it may represent a conflict of interest) be prompt. The gift should be returned within 24 hours with a handwritten note thanking the person. You must be clear that you cannot accept the gift.

PROCEED WITH CAUTION

In most cases when you have returned a gift for legitimate reasons, you want to retain a copy of the note for your personal records. This serves as protection for you if any questions should arise in the future concerning your ethical behavior.

BUSINESS CORRESPONDENCE

In formal business correspondence an inside address is required. This should include the full name and title of the person with whom you are corresponding, his or her department name, company name, and the address of the company. No abbreviations should be used. This inside address is left justified about four to five lines from the top of the page.

PROCEED WITH CAUTION

If you are not sure how to spell someone's name you are corresponding with, call and ask prior to sending the letter.

The salutation in a formal business letter should include a colon. (Commas can be used in informal handwritten correspondence.) If you don't know the person's name, but know their position, you may address them by title in the salutation. For example, you may write "Dear Human Resource Manager."

The closing is placed two lines after the end of the body of the letter. This is also left justified, matching the salutation. "Sincerely" is still the most appropriate closing. Four to five lines should be left after the closing before your name is typed (for your signature).

JUST A MINUTE

Courtesy is extended to all the new advances in technology. When leaving a voice mail message, always include a phone number where you can be reached. When faxing to a shared fax machine, call to warn the person the document is on the way.

NETIQUETTE

Reflecting the proliferation of electronic communication, a new term has been coined—netiquette. This outlines the appropriate ways of using these new advanced technologies. Contrary to what many may think, courtesy is still important. New technology is not an excuse to be rude. The best rule is to use common courtesy. You should always remember to use please and thank you in your communications.

E-mail has grown tremendously in popularity. It is used as a regular form of communication in most businesses today. You should, however, remember that it is not the only means of communication. It is one method from which to choose. When selected as the appropriate channel to use, it has to be used properly. There are rules of conduct to govern its use.

The use of e-mail should be restricted to informal communications. And, these messages should be kept concise. Sensitive information (such as a warning or a termination) should not be transmitted via e-mail. For personal communications (such as a thank you) a handwritten note is still recommended.

Even though it is used for informal communications, spelling and grammar should still be considered important. Proof your message and use the spelling check. Review your message for neatness as well. And, be sure to divide your message into appropriate paragraphs.

All e-mails should be concise. The subject line should be used to let the recipient know what the message is about. This too, should be brief. In addition, a greeting and a closing should be used regularly. A reply should be sent immediately. Generally, a reply is expected within 24 to 48 hours—reflecting the "instant" nature of the communication technology.

PROCEED WITH CAUTION

Capitalizing an entire message should be avoided in e-mail communications. This is the equivalent of shouting when using the spoken word. Using lower case exclusively should also be avoided. The proper use of both upper and lower cases is recommended.

Many people use e-mails today in a more informal way to communicate as if they were talking to the other person. Cute language and jokes don't usually translate well on e-mail. Most importantly, any inappropriate remarks that you make can be recovered even after you have deleted them. These recovered e-mails may also be used in a court of law. They are not your private property. Your company owns your e-mail communications.

A few parting e-mail tips may help you to navigate the new rules of netiquette:

- Don't forward spam (that is, junk mail such as advertisements).
- Don't send graphic and distasteful jokes.
- Don't send chain letters.
- Don't share your password under any circumstances.
- Don't try to see other people's passwords.
- Remember that nothing is ever really deleted.
- Don't give out anyone's e-mail address without obtaining his or her permission in advance. (This address is just like a phone number.)

GENERAL ETIQUETTE DO'S AND DON'TS

A general list of do's is helpful when trying to gain an edge in the competitive workplace today.

Consider these tips:

- Be a good listener. The person who constantly interrupts is not well respected and projects the wrong image.
- Do accept compliments gracefully by saying thank you. Don't try to minimize (or maximize) what you've done.
- Respect other people's personal space. And, remember that their cubicle is their office. Uninvited intrusion is a violation of their personal space.
- Watch your personal appearance. Take care in how you present yourself. Adhere to your company's dress code.
- Follow through when you say you will do something. Your word is everything, and your reputation hinges on it.

GO TO ▶
Refer to Hour 20, "Organizational Communication," for a detailed discussion of active listening.

Equally important is to know what behaviors to avoid when trying to engage in appropriate behavior. Consider these don'ts:

- Don't discuss religion, politics, diets, cost of personal items, or personal tragedies in a business setting.

- Don't assume it is the responsibility of a man to open doors. The first person to arrive at the door is expected to hold the door—regardless of gender.

- Don't openly criticize people in front of others. Share your comments in private.

- Don't gush insincere compliments. Save compliments for those that are genuinely meant.

- Don't remind others when they are not using good manners. Just be a role model for appropriate behaviors.

- Don't visit colleagues without an appointment. You are an interruption to their day and are not being courteous.

CREATING A POSITIVE IMAGE

Projecting a positive image is not about the possession of just one characteristic. It is a package of qualities that create this unique image. It may be considered part of your style. These ingredients include your dress, posture, smile, handshake, and general mindset—to name a few.

With the move to business casual dress codes, many managers have fallen into the trap of thinking that dress does not count. On the contrary, dress still counts. The way that you dress communicates volumes about you nonverbally.

To gain a competitive advantage in the marketplace, you need to manage the impression you create. Dress is a big part of impression management. You can control to some extent the impression others have of you by using dress to create a favorable first impression.

Both men and women should build a business wardrobe around neutral and conservative colors such as black, gray, navy, camel, and white. Your accessories can pick up the popular accent colors. These accessories will update your wardrobe and can reflect some of the current fashion trends—without being too fashion forward. You can be trendy after work hours.

The key is to choose classic styles. And, even on a budget, try to buy good quality items. These will last longer and will be an investment. Once you invest in your wardrobe, you also have to maintain it. Professional dry cleaning will prolong the life of your clothes.

GO TO ▶
Refer to Hour 20 for a more detailed discussion of the importance of nonverbal components in the communication process. The nonverbal component actually comprises the vast majority of the communication process.

Special attention should be paid to shoes. Scuffed and unpolished shoes do not make a good impression. Worn down heels should be avoided at all times. Others do look at your shoes and draw conclusions about you as a result of what they see.

JUST A MINUTE

Take your cue from what others on your organizational level wear. (Also observe what others wear on the level to which you aspire.) Dress to fit in—not make a statement. This is part of group membership.

Posture is critical. Slouching can send the wrong message. Slouching may be interpreted as being uncertain or not energetic. Stand up straight. This communicates that you are confident and relays a sense of "can do." You must also walk decisively.

A smile communicates that you are approachable. People are more comfortable approaching you when you smile. A smile also encourages people—especially when conversing. And, a smile completes the package of a positive image.

A good sense of humor also makes you more approachable. A good sense of humor (that is positive and directed toward yourself) is like a magnet drawing others to you.

A PARTING TIP TO BETTER MANNERS: GOSSIP

You must be skilled in navigating the waters of organizational politics. Part of this is an understanding of the role of gossip in the organization.

GO TO ▶
Refer to Hour 18, "Organizational Politics and Power," for a detailed discussion of how to play the political game in your organization.

The best course of action when confronted with gossip is to follow the old adage: "If you don't have anything good to say, don't say anything at all." Be sure to avoid those who are gossiping. Simply associating with those who gossip can taint your reputation as well. Be sure to filter what you say so that negative or unfavorable comment cannot be attributed to you. Avoiding gossiping about others is a critical component in creating this positive image.

HOUR'S UP!

With the renewed interest in business etiquette, review these questions to see how much you have learned about good manners in business situations.

1. The cost of making manners missteps ...
   a. Is really low in the grand scheme of business.
   b. Can impede your career and harm your company's business relationships.
   c. Doesn't affect the commitment you can gain from others.
   d. Cannot jeopardize your career success.

2. When you are being introduced to someone ...
   a. Stop what you are doing and offer your hand.
   b. If you are seated, remain so and offer your hand.
   c. Wait until they extend their hand to be sure that they want to shake hands.
   d. Don't repeat their name.

3. When attending a business meal ...
   a. Turn off your cell phone and pager.
   b. Place your napkin in your lap as soon as you are seated.
   c. Don't start eating until everyone at the table has been served.
   d. All of the above.

4. The first person to order at a business meal is ...
   a. The first to arrive.
   b. The first to decide what they want.
   c. The guest.
   d. The host.

5. When passing dishes with handles ...
   a. Always use the handle yourself.
   b. Pass to the left.
   c. Pass to the right.
   d. Avoid passing at all costs.

6. During meetings …

   a. Always be prepared with remarks and be concise.

   b. Only prepare remarks when it is your meeting.

   c. Take the seat closest to the facilitator.

   d. Be sure to interrupt if someone is giving inaccurate information.

7. Business gifts …

   a. Are never needed.

   b. Should be sent on a timely basis.

   c. Don't require a thank-you note to acknowledge them.

   d. Should not be modest when presented to your boss.

8. Netiquette …

   a. Refers to the good manners associated with new technology (such as e-mail).

   b. Refers to the good manners associated with the World Wide Web.

   c. Refers to the lack of etiquette in new technology.

   d. None of the above.

9. General guidelines for proper etiquette include …

   a. Not visiting colleagues without an appointment.

   b. Not reminding others when they are using bad manners.

   c. Follow through when you say you will do something.

   d. All of the above.

10. When projecting a positive image …

   a. One characteristic can make the difference.

   b. Dress is not important.

   c. It's a package of qualities that creates this image.

   d. A mindset is not part of the package.

QUIZ

APPENDIX A
Twenty-Minute Recap

Hour 1: What Is Management?

In this hour, you begin your journey to an understanding of management. The roles performed by managers are discussed. An opportunity is also presented to analyze whether you have the skills that are necessary for effective management in today's world. The hour concludes with a discussion of the transition to management.

Hour 2: Management in the New Workplace

This hour provides a review of the context within which managers operate in the twenty-first century. The trends impacting management are reviewed. The importance of ensuring that your business becomes a learning organization is discussed with a focus on the skills for change in today's dynamic environment.

Hour 3: The Global Environment

In this hour, the discussion started in Hour 2 of the context of management is continued with an examination of the impact of the global environment. A presentation of the dimensions of culture offers insight into understanding cultural differences. The importance of learning in a global environment is explored. Tips for conducting business internationally are also presented.

Hour 4: Managerial Decision-Making

The rational decision-making model is presented with a discussion of bounded rationality. In addition, the types of decisions are explored along with the need for creative problem solving in appropriate situations. Tips to encouraging creativity and characteristics of creative organizations are also presented.

Hour 5: Financials

This hour will provide an understanding of financial statements. The basics of balance sheets, income statements, cash flow statements, and statements of changes in stockholders' equity are explored. An examination of financial ratios helps you to see how the organization is performing as a whole. The budgeting process is also discussed. Open-book management is presented as one tool used today.

Hour 6: Project Management

Because most managers today are responsible for multiple projects, the basics of project management have been included in this hour. You can learn how to better plan, schedule, and control your projects. A discussion of why plans fail is also included. The various people involved in the project are explored. These roles include the project manager, the project sponsor, and the project team members. The hour concludes with an examination of closure for the project.

Hour 7: The Basics of Process Development

Organizations focus on total quality management and continuous improvement to better meet the needs of their customers and to improve efficiency. This hour addresses the basics of process development to provide an understanding of reengineering and job design choices. Job simplification, job enlargement, job rotation, and job enrichment are described and examined. The change process is explored in depth and includes a discussion of resistance to change and suggestions as to how overcome that resistance.

HOUR 8: RELATIONSHIP MANAGEMENT

Because management is all about getting things done through others, this hour focuses on how to more effectively manage the many relationships that a manager must cultivate. The perceptual process is presented as the foundation within which relationships are explored. The element of trust is also discussed. Relationships with customers, independent contractors, your boss, and your subordinates are examined specifically. The hour concludes with tips for all your relationships.

HOUR 9: MANAGING CONFLICT

Negotiation skills are addressed in this hour. It is critical while working with others for managers to be successful in managing conflict. The distinction between functional and dysfunctional conflict is explored. Recommendations for getting to a win-win resolution are presented. Tips to successful conflict management are examined with a focus on how to discuss the issue and how to control the conflict. Finally, methods for stimulating conflict are presented.

HOUR 10: MANAGING PEOPLE

This hour emphasizes the diverse nature of the workforce today. One-size-fits-all solutions no longer work. Managing diversity includes people with disabilities and an understanding of sexual harassment. The benefits of a diverse workforce are explored. Tips to manage diversity are presented. Ineffective management techniques of micromanaging, laziness, and power-happy management are examined with tips to avoid these traps. The hour concludes with a discussion of typical, ineffective management styles and how they can be avoided.

HOUR 11: MOTIVATION

A discussion of fundamental motivation theories is presented in this hour. Each theory is examined in the context of today's workforce with appropriate examples of how these theories can be used to more effectively manage. Techniques to increase individual performance are discussed. The role of money is examined and tips for building a motivated environment are presented.

Hour 12: Managing Performance

This hour focuses on the management of performance. The performance appraisal is discussed including the types of appraisal systems, how the appraisal is conducted, and the errors to avoid. Also included is a discussion of how performance is reinforced and rewarded, and how to effectively use discipline.

Hour 13: Career Development: Your Responsibility

Career development is instrumental in managing people today. This hour presents a view of careers in today's environment. A discussion of the benefits to the organization when assisting in career development is included. Contemporary approaches and alternative career tracks are examined. The use of a personal SWOT analysis is discussed in career management. The hour concludes with tips to spot trouble in your career and how to effectively manage your career.

Hour 14: Groups

More work is being accomplished in teams today. This hour begins the discussion of groups and teamwork. In this hour, the advantages and disadvantages of groups are examined. The primary methods of group decision-making are discussed. These include brainstorming, the Delphi technique, and the nominal group technique. The role of technology in groups is explored, and a caution concerning groupthink concludes the hour.

Hour 15: Teamwork

A distinction between groups and teams is made in this hour. The characteristics of high-performance teams are discussed followed by an examination of how to effectively build teams. A discussion of self-managed teams in organizations is presented. Special human resource problems found in teams are explored.

Hour 16: Organizational and Structural Design

An examination of organization-wide issues begins in this hour. The concepts presented in the prior hours are used as the fundamentals to discuss these organization-wide issues. An understanding of these organizational processes is critical to effective management. This hour focuses on the design and structure of organizations today. The factors influencing design are discussed. Structure decisions such as span of control, centralization, division of labor, and departmentation are examined. The boundaryless organization is discussed as a more creative organizational type.

HOUR 17: ORGANIZATIONAL CULTURE

Organizational culture is defined and emphasized in this hour. Subcultures and countercultures are also explored. The functions of culture are discussed with the different aspects of culture—including sagas, symbols, rites and rituals, jargon, and values. Your role in building and reinforcing culture is examined. The hour concludes with the impact of merging two cultures.

HOUR 18: ORGANIZATIONAL POLITICS AND POWER

This hour addresses organizational politics and power. The bases of power are discussed with a focus on the role of personal power in today's changing environment. The means for building a power base are examined. Power is discussed in terms of the empowerment of today's workforce. The importance of managing upward influence is explored. The hour concludes with general tips to navigating the waters of organizational politics.

HOUR 19: THE NEW LEADERSHIP

The new leadership is examined in this hour. The different roles of management and leadership are discussed. Traditional leadership theories help to explain how leadership has evolved to this point. Contemporary views of leadership, transactional leadership, and transformational leadership are examined. No discussion of leadership would be complete without a mention of the flip side: followership. The hour closes with tips to leading self-managed teams.

HOUR 20: ORGANIZATIONAL COMMUNICATION

This hour presents a review of organizational communication. Only by effectively communicating are people able to be successful in their performance. The role of nonverbal communication and active listening are presented. The different flows of communication are addressed (upward, downward, and lateral). The grapevine as the organization's informal communication system is explored. A discussion of technological advances (including e-mail) and how these advances have affected communication is presented. Finally, tips to more effectively communicating are listed.

HOUR 21: STRESS

This hour begins with a definition of stress and then reviews the three stags of stress: alarm, resistance, and exhaustion. The issue of both work and non-work stressors are examined. The organizational and individual consequences of stress are discussed. Stress management and stress prevention programs are highlighted. A discussion of how to recognize stress in others is included to round out the hour.

HOUR 22: FACILITATING MEETINGS

With an inordinate amount of time spent in meetings, this hour addresses meeting facilitation. The planning of meetings, location, time, and the role of the agenda are examined. Your role as the facilitator is discussed with an emphasis on the importance of generating minutes for the meeting. The hour concludes with an examination of the special challenges in meetings—those individuals who inhibit the success of meetings.

HOUR 23: INTERVIEWING

This hour focuses on the role of interviews in the recruitment and selection process. Both internal and external methods of recruitment are discussed. The selection process is examined step by step with an emphasis on the effective interview—including how to plan it and avoid potentially dangerous questions. This hour concludes with a list of general tips on how to conduct an effective interview.

HOUR 24: GAINING AN EDGE: BUSINESS ETIQUETTE

The journey to teach yourself management skills concludes in this hour with a discussion on business etiquette and how to gain an edge in the workplace. Business basics (including introductions, dining, and gifts) are discussed. Correspondence with a focus on netiquette is examined. The hour concludes with a warning about gossip in the workplace.

APPENDIX B

Glossary and Recommended Readings

GLOSSARY OF TERMS

agenda An outline of items to be discussed during a meeting.

assets Accounts that list what is owned by the business.

awareness training Provides employees with an awareness of diversity.

balance sheet Provides information concerning a company's assets, liabilities, and owner's equity.

capital stock The face value of the number of shares of company stock the company has outstanding multiplied times the par or stated value of the stock.

cash flow statement Details the sources and uses of cash within the company.

centralization Refers to the place in the organization where the decisions are made.

conceptual skills The ability to see the big picture and understand the interrelated nature of your organization.

content plateau When job responsibilities have been mastered and boredom sets in.

continuous process improvement (CPI) Making incremental improvements on the current process over a long period of time that will cause fewer disruptions to the work.

corporation   A legal entity in which the company is separate from its owners. The owners hold stock and are known as shareholders.

cosmopolitan   Belonging to the world, another term for global manager.

decision-making   Choosing among alternative courses of action.

departmentation   The way in which jobs are grouped together.

distress   Negative stress that may result in behavioral problems, psychological issues, or medical illness.

diversity   All the differences, demographically and personality-related, that make people unique.

effective   Doing the right job.

efficient   Doing the job right.

equity theory   People will correct inequities.

eustress   Positive stress that results in increases in physical strength.

expatriates   Managers for a multinational company who are from the parent company's country.

expectancy theory   Behavior is based upon the expectation that a behavior will lead to a specific reward and that reward is valued.

Fiedler's least preferred coworker (LPC) scale   The instrument used to identify the type of leadership style that you possess: relationship-motivated or task-motivated.

financial statements   A way to monitor financial resources.

Gantt chart   Developed by Henry Gantt, it is a graphical depiction of the progress of your projects.

global economy   An economy where international competitors are as much a threat to your business as the store down the street.

groupthink   An agreement (whether conscious or not) by the group not to disagree.

Herzberg's Two-Factor Theory   Dissatisfaction and satisfaction are not opposite ends of a single continuum; the opposite of dissatisfaction is no dissatisfaction and the opposite of satisfaction is no satisfaction.

human relations skills   Strong people skills and the ability to get along with others.

income statement   Depicts the income generated and the expenses incurred by a company over a specified period of time.

liabilities   Obligations to creditors that the company has acquired throughout the normal course of business.

life plateau   Lack of success threatens self-identity because who a person is, is tied to the job he or she holds.

long-term assets   Assets that have an expected life greater than one year.

management   The stabilizing factor that enables the work of the organization to be completed.

Maslow's Hierarchy of Needs   People are motivated by a hierarchy of needs. Each lower level need must be satisfied before moving onto the next higher level need.

McClelland's Learned Needs Theory   People are motivated by the need for achievement, the need for affiliation, or the need for power. The dominant need will vary by individual.

McGregor's Theory X and Theory Y   Theory X and Theory Y assumptions influence the behavior of managers. The Theory Y view of people holds that people will look for responsibility while the Theory X manager believes that people are lazy.

minutes   Written documentation of the activities of a meeting.

multinational corporations   Companies that conduct business outside of their home borders.

net income (or profit)   Occurs when revenue exceeds expenses.

open-book management   The process of opening up the operating numbers to the employees of the company.

owner's equity   Accounts that deal with the net worth of a business.

partnership   A company with two or more owners.

payables turn   The speed at which the business is paying its bills.

perceptual process   The way you process information by deciding which information to gather, how to organize it, and how to make sense of it.

productivity   A measure of how efficient your organization (or your process) is by comparing the outputs to inputs by generating a ratio.

project managers   Individuals who manage the projects that make significant contributions to the organization.

receivables turn   The speed at which receivables are collected.

reengineering   Radical widespread changes that have a ripple effect felt throughout the organization.

resource provider   Obtains financial and human resources that are needed for the projects of the organization.

retained earnings   Prior earnings the company has generated that it decides to retain in the business in order to help it grow.

self-actualization   The need to reach your full potential.

short-term assets   Assets that can be converted to cash in less than one years time.

skills-based training   Provides employees with the skills needed to manage a diverse workforce and work effectively in that workforce.

sole proprietorship   A company with one owner.

structural plateau   No more promotions are available in the current organization.

talent pool   Employees that actually perform the work of the organization.

team   A highly committed group with a specifically defined task.

technical skills   The ability to understand the technology available to perform the job.

technophobia   Fear of trying new technology.

10-K report   Financial statement.

10-Q report   Quarterly financial statements.

Thorndike's law of effect   Behavior that is followed by positive consequences is more likely to be repeated.

upward mobility   Upward movement through the ranks to the executive management levels.

RECOMMENDED READINGS

Reading is a critical component of becoming a life long learner. All business people should read at least one publication from the popular business press (for example, *Fortune, Forbes,* or *Business Week*) to stay abreast of changes. The business section of your local paper (or The *Wall Street Journal*) should also be scanned daily. It is important to regularly read at least one trade publication for your industry to stay informed of industry trends likely to impact your business (and perhaps your job).

In addition, the following books are highly recommended for management reading. Some are classics and offer time-worn lessons for businesses while others are more recent titles that present new perspectives for today's environment. Several business publications generate annual lists of recommended readings. You should always check out the books on these lists to update your readings and open your mind.

- *The 7 Habits of Highly Effective People* by Stephen R. Covey (Simon & Schuster, 1989)
- *Competing for the Future* by Gary Hamel and C. K. Prahalad (Harvard Business School Press, 1994)
- *The Fifth Discipline: The Art and Practice of the Learning Organization* by Peter Senge (Doubleday, 1990)
- *Gung Ho* by Kenneth H. Blanchard and Sheldon Bowles (William Morrow and Company, Inc., 1998)
- *The Horizontal Organization: What the Organization of the Future Actually Looks Like and How It Delivers Value to Customers* by Frank Ostroff (Oxford University Press, 1999)
- *Jack Welsh and The G.E. Way: Management Insights and Leadership Secrets of the Legendary CEO* by Robert Slater (The McGraw-Hill Companies, 1998)
- *Leading Change* by John P. Kotter (Harvard Business School Press, 1996)
- *Leading the Revolution* by Gary Hamel (Harvard Business School Press, 2000)
- *Personal Magnetism* by Andrew DuBrin (American Management Association, 1997)

- *Strategic Renewal: Becoming a High-Performance Organization* by Michael A. Mische (Prentice Hall, 2001)
- *Who Moved My Cheese?* by Spencer Johnson (G.P. Putnam's Sons, 1998)
- *Working with Emotional Intelligence* by Daniel Goleman (Bantam Books, 1998)

It is also recommended that you read humor. An important part of success in today's world (in any position) is maintaining a healthy attitude. This includes having a good sense of humor. The Scott Adams books help business people to laugh at themselves and to take a second look (from a new perspective) at what they do. The *Dilbert* comic strip provides a good dose of daily humor and any Scott Adams book assists in achieving this levity to ensure that you don't take yourself too seriously. My personal favorite is *The Dilbert Principle* (HarperCollins, 1996).

APPENDIX C

Answers to
Hour's Up Quizzes

HOUR 1

1. b
2. a
3. d
4. d
5. a
6. d
7. b
8. a
9. a
10. d

HOUR 2

1. a
2. b
3. d
4. b
5. d
6. c
7. c
8. b
9. c
10. d

HOUR 3

1. d
2. b
3. b
4. b
5. c
6. b
7. d
8. b
9. d
10. a

HOUR 4

1. b
2. b
3. d
4. c
5. b
6. d
7. c
8. c
9. d
10. c

Hour 5

1. b
2. a
3. c
4. b
5. d
6. a
7. c
8. d
9. c
10. a

Hour 6

1. a
2. b
3. a
4. d
5. c
6. b
7. a
8. d
9. b
10. b

Hour 7

1. b
2. d
3. c
4. d
5. a

6. b
7. c
8. a
9. d
10. d

Hour 8

1. b
2. a
3. d
4. c
5. c
6. a
7. c
8. a
9. b
10. d

Hour 9

1. b
2. a
3. d
4. b
5. b
6. a
7. b
8. d
9. b
10. c

Hour 10

1. a
2. d
3. d
4. b
5. d
6. a
7. d
8. a
9. a
10. b

Hour 11

1. d
2. c
3. a
4. a
5. d
6. b
7. d
8. a
9. c
10. d

Hour 12

1. b
2. a
3. a
4. d
5. c

6. d
7. d
8. b
9. a
10. d

Hour 13

1. b
2. a
3. d
4. c
5. a
6. d
7. b
8. d
9. a
10. a

Hour 14

1. c
2. a
3. d
4. a
5. d
6. b
7. a
8. b
9. d
10. b

Hour 15

1. b
2. d
3. c
4. c
5. a
6. d
7. d
8. d
9. d
10. c

Hour 16

1. d
2. b
3. a
4. d
5. b
6. c
7. d
8. a
9. b
10. d

Hour 17

1. b
2. d
3. c
4. b
5. c

6. d
7. a
8. a
9. c
10. d

Hour 18

1. b
2. a
3. a
4. d
5. c
6. d
7. d
8. b
9. c
10. d

Hour 19

1. c
2. d
3. b
4. d
5. b
6. b
7. c
8. d
9. a
10. d

Hour 20

1. b
2. d
3. a
4. a
5. b
6. d
7. c
8. b
9. c
10. d

Hour 21

1. b
2. d
3. c
4. a
5. b
6. d
7. c
8. b
9. a
10. d

Hour 22

1. c
2. c
3. b
4. d
5. a

6. c
7. d
8. b
9. b
10. b

Hour 23

1. b
2. c
3. d
4. d
5. a
6. c
7. d
8. c
9. d
10. c

Hour 24

1. b
2. a
3. d
4. c
5. c
6. a
7. b
8. a
9. d
10. c

Index